Maui

A Paradise Guide

By Greg and Christie
Stilson

Cover design by Sharon Carter
Illustrations by Janora Bayot

Published by
Paradise Publications
Portland, Oregon

In affiliation with
Prima Publishing and Communications

Distributed by
St. Martin's Press

"Maui No Ka Oi"
(Maui is the best!!)

Dedicated to Maren and Jeffrey, two terrific travelers.

Paradise Publications
8110 SW Wareham Circle
Portland, OR 97223 U.S.A.

Copyright © 1988 Paradise Publication, Portland, Oregon

First Edition: December 1984
Second Edition: May 1986
Third Edition: May 1988

ISSN # 0895-9609
Printed in U.S.A.

COVER DESIGN: Sharon Carter
Sharon Carter received her BA in fine arts in 1972 from the University of Texas. Currently a resident on the Big Island of Hawaii, she is involved in a variety of freelance multi-media activities including cartooning and weaving and has been featured in a number of exhibitions.

PEN & INK SKETCHES: Janora Bayot
Janora Bayot is a freelance artist who especially enjoys cartooning. In addition to having her work appear in numerous publications, she spent six years with the Columbian newspaper in Vancouver, Washington. In her spare time she volunteers on behalf of animal agencies. Janora's keen sense of humor and vivacity are personified in her artwork.

Additional pictures by William Ballard.

TABLE OF CONTENTS

V. BEACHES AND BEACH ACTIVITIES

VI. RECREATION AND TOURS

OCEAN ACTIVITIES

LAND ACTIVITIES

AIR TOURS

VII. RECOMMENDED READING

VIII. INDEX

IX. READER RESPONSE – ORDERING INFORMATION

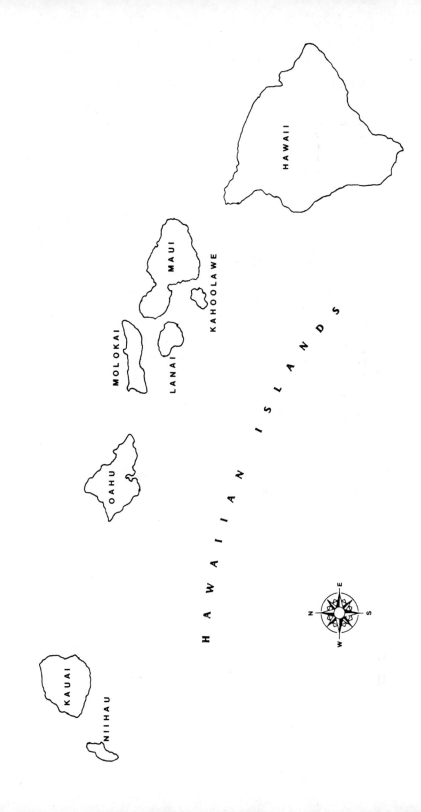

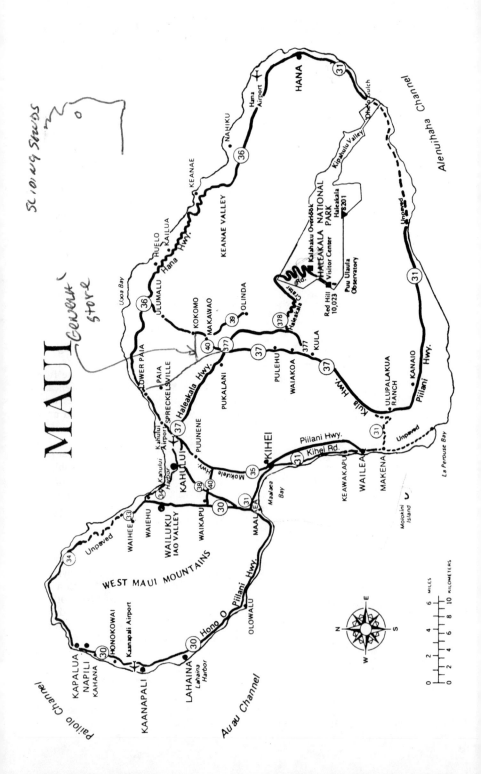

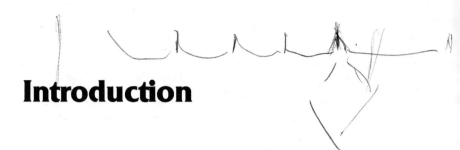

Introduction

Congratulations on choosing Maui as the site of your vacation. You will soon see why it has the deserved slogan, Maui No Ka Oi (Maui is the Best). The sun and lush tropicalness, and some of the finest accommodations, blend sublimely together to create a perfect holiday paradise – a place both magical and beautiful.

Our personal perspective is that of the visitor. We travel frequently to the island to update our information, discover new things, rediscover old things, make wonderful new friends, and to thoroughly enjoy the tropical energy and seductive charm of Maui. While first-time visitors will delight in the diversity of activities that Maui has to offer, even those making a return visit can enjoy discovering new sights and adventures on this magnificent island.

Maui can be relatively inexpensive, or extravagantly expensive, depending on your preference in lodgings, activities, and eating arrangements. Therefore, we have endeavored to give complete and detailed information covering the full range of budgets. The opinions expressed are based on our personal experiences, and while the positive is emphasized, it is your right to know, in certain cases, our bad experiences. To aid in your selections, *BEST BET* lists are included and *STAR*'s identify special recommendations.

Our guide is as accurate as possible at the time of publication, however, changes seem extremely rapid for an island operating on "Maui Time." Ownerships, managements, names, and menus change quite frequently and prices, of course, are always on the rise. For the latest breaking information on the island, Paradise Publications has available *THE MAUI UPDATE*, a quarterly newsletter. To order a complimentary issue or a yearly subscription see ORDERING INFORMATION.

The chapters on accommodations and sights, restaurants, and beaches are conveniently divided into areas with similar characteristics and indexes are provided for each chapter. This allows a better feel for, and access to, the information on the area in which you are staying, and greater confidence in exploring other areas. Remember that except for Hana, most of the areas are only a short drive and worth a day of sight seeing, beach exploring, or a meal at a fine restaurant.

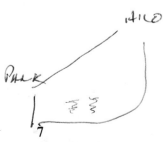

As this guide features pen and ink sketches, a couple of recommendations for picture books might be helpful. An inexpensive, 48-page, full-color photographic book *Maui The Romantic Island*, highlights the most memorable sights and gives you a good feel for the island. It is available through Paradise Publications; see ORDERING INFORMATION. A magnificent coffee table size publication, *Maui, On My Mind*, by Rita Ariyoshi contains outstanding photographs that depict the island at its best. The book is available at local island gift and book stores and at mainland travel bookstores.

If your itinerary includes a stay in Kauai, *Kauai, A Paradise Guide* by Don and Bea Donohugh is a must. This is another in the Paradise Guide Series; see ORDERING INFORMATION. Not only does the guide contain information on all the condos and hotels, restaurant reviews, specific recreational activity information, but also features an in-depth, around the island tour that tells how to find the many hidden beaches, historical sites, waterfalls and points of interest that most visitors never see.

As you explore the magical island of Maui, keep in mind the expressive words used by Mark Twain nearly 100 years ago when he visited and fell in love with Hawaii.

"No alien land in all the world has any deep strong charm for me but that one, no other land could so longingly and so beseechingly haunt me, sleeping and waking, through half a lifetime, as that one has done. Other things leave me, but it abides; other things change, but it remains the same. For me its balmy airs are always blowing, its summer seas flashing in the sun; the pulsing of its surfbeat is in my ear; I can see its garlanded crags, its leaping cascades, its plumy palms drowsing by the shore, its remote summits floating like islands above the cloud wrack; I can feel the spirit of its woodland solitudes, I can hear the splash of its brooks; in my nostrils still lives the breath of flowers..."

Although the islands have changed greatly during the century since his visits, there remains much to fall in love with. The physical beauty and seductiveness of the land remains despite what may seem rampant commercialism, and the true aloha spirit does survive.

Enjoy the book, enjoy Maui to the fullest, and make your friends buy their own copy.

Aloha,

Greg + Christie

Greg and Christie Stilson

General Information

OUR PERSONAL BESTS

BEST SPLURGE: Champagne sunday brunch at Raffles' (Stouffer Wailea Beach Resort), champagne sunday brunch at the Prince Court (Maui Prince Resort in Makena), or champagne sunday brunch at the Sound of the Falls (Westin Maui at Kaanapali).

BEST SUNSET, AND COCKTAILS: West Maui – Kapalua Bay Lounge East Maui – Maui Prince Resort, Molokini Lounge

BEST DAILY BREAKFAST BUFFET: Swan Court at the Hyatt and Sound of the Falls at the Westin Maui

BEST SALAD BAR: Royal Ocean Terrace

BEST DINNER VALUES: Early bird specials are offered at a number of the island restaurants. There are generally more specials offered during the summer months and the price may also reflect the time of year. Some of the better early bird offerings are at the Marriott's Moana Terrace at Kaanapali, and Idini's, Chuck's or Island Fish House in Kihei.

BEST RESTAURANT ATMOSPHERE: Swan Court at the Hyatt Regency Hotel, The Sounds of the Falls or The Villas at the Westin Maui

MOST OUTRAGEOUS DESSERT: The Lahaina Provision Company's Chocoholic Bar at the Hyatt Regency Hotel

BEST ICE CREAM & FUDGE: Maui Fudge & Ice Cream Kitchen in Kihei

BEST SHOPPING: Touristy – Lahaina waterfront; Practical – Kaahumanu Shopping Center in Kahului; Extravagant – Hyatt Regency and Westin Maui

BEST HOTEL VALUE: The Stouffer Wailea Beach Resort with a 50% off coupon from the Entertainment Book

MOST SPECTACULAR GROUNDS: Hyatt Regency and the Westin Maui at Kaanapali – Runners up: Kapalua Bay and Stouffer Wailea Beach Resorts

ALOHA WEAR: The traditional tourist garb is available in greatest supply at the Hilo Hattie's factory in the industrial area of Lahaina. A free shuttle provides transportation from the wharf shopping area in downtown Lahaina. The mumu factory at the Maui Mall in Kahului has a good selection as do the stores in the Kaahumanu Shopping Center, also in Kahului. Gentlemen might be especially interested in Kula Bay. On Lahainaluna just off Front St. in Lahaina, this new shop has taken the classic aloha shirt styles of the 1930's, 40's and 50's, updated the colors, and used an all cotton fabric for easy care and comfort.

EXCURSIONS: Most spectacular – a helicopter tour. Most unusual – a bike trip down Haleakala. Best adventure on foot – a personalized hike with guide Ken Schmitt. Best sailing – a day-long snorkel and picnic to Lanai with the congenial crew of the Trilogy

BEST BEACHES: Beautiful and safe – Kapalua Bay. Unspoiled – Oneloa (Makena Beach)

BEST BODY SURFING: Slaughterhouse in winter

BEST SURFING: Honolua Bay in winter

BEST WINDSURFING: Hookipa Beach Park

BEST SNORKELING: North end – Honolua Bay in summer. Kapalua area – Kapalua Bay and Namalu Bay. Kaanapali – Black Rock at the Sheraton. Lahaina – Olowalu. Wailea – Ulua/Mokapu Beach. Makena – Ahihi Kinau Natural Reserve. Island of Lanai – Hulopoe Beach Park. And Molokini Crater

BEST MAUI GET AWAY FROM IT ALL RESORT: Hotel Hana Ranch

BEST POSTCARD HOME: Stop in at Da Nut House on Front St. (near the Banyan Tree) and pick out an unhusked coconut. A felt pen transforms it into a personalized post card, which they mail. Total cost varies, $5 – $8, with size of coconut. Wait until your friends at home open their mailbox and find this!

BEST TOURS & TRIPS: Biking Haleakala, hiking with naturalist Ken Schmitt, Trilogy sailing trip, van trip to Hana.

UNUSUAL GIFT IDEAS: For the greenthumb, be sure to try Dan's Green House, on Prison Street in Lahaina for a Fuku-Bonsai planted on a lava rock. They are specially sprayed and sealed for either shipping or carrying home. Prices begin at $13 for a single. Perfumes made from all island products are a "scent-sational" gift from the original Waikiki Fragrance Factory at the Cannery in Lahaina. Chocolate Chips of Maui, "the ultimate munchie" is a combination of rich dark chocolate or milk chocolate and the original Maui potato chip. Try them frozen or use them as a scoop for ice cream.

BEST FREE STUFF: Free introductory scuba instruction offered poolside at the major resorts. A self-guided tour of the Hyatt Regency Maui or Westin Maui Resorts. The Maui Zoo in Wailuku. All the public beaches with their free parking. Canoe races held at Honokaoo Park. Halloween Parade in Lahaina. Sand Castle Contest in Kihei (November). The Makawao Parade held Fourth of July weekend. Fourth of July festivities at Kaanapali Beach. Free bus tour of Lahaina sponsored by the area merchants – pick it up behind the Wharf Shopping Center. Classic movies "under the stars" at the Wailea Village Shopping Center each Wednesday. Hula show at the Kapalua Shops (currently Thursday mornings), Aloha night each Friday at the Wharf Shopping Center.

BEST T–SHIRTS: A huge selection is available at the T-shirt Factory near the Kahului Airport. Sizes range from infants to XL adults and, with plenty to choose from, it is easy to mix and match styles and sizes. Crazy Shirts are more expensive, but of excellent quality and beautiful designs.

BEST FLORIST: A Special Touch in Lahaina has a magical way with floral arrangements.

BEST GIFT FOR FRIENDS TRAVELING TO MAUI: A copy of *MAUI, A PARADISE GUIDE.*

BEST NIGHT SPOTS: Banana Moon at the Marriott Hotel or Spatts at the Hyatt. For Hawaiian melodies at their best, visit the Molokini Lounge evenings at the Maui Prince Resort for the mellow strains of George Paoa.

BEST TAKE-HOME FOOD PRODUCTS: Paradise Fruit in Kihei

King Kamehameha I

HISTORY

Maui's beginnings were violent. Explosions of hot lava from two volcanos created the island. Puu Kukui (Poo'ookoo-KOO-ee) created the westerly section and the great Haleakala (HAH-leh-AH-kuh-LAH), now the world's largest dormant volcano, created the eastern portion of the island. A valley connects the two, hence the source of Maui's nick-name, The Valley Isle.

The first Hawaiians came from the Marquesa and Society Islands in the central Pacific. (Findings suggest that their ancestors came from the western Pacific, perhaps as far as Madagascar). The Polynesians left the Marquesas about the 8th century and were followed by natives from the Society Islands sometime between the 11th and 14th centuries.

The Hawaiian population may well have been as high as 300,000 by the 1700's, spread throughout the chain of islands. Fish and poi were diet basics, supplemented by various fruits and occasionally meat from chickens, pigs and even dogs.

Four principal gods formed the basis of their religion until the missionaries arrived. The stone foundations of Heiaus, the ancient religous temples, can still be visited on Maui.

The islands were left undisturbed by western influence until the 1778 arrival of James Cook. He first spotted and visited Kauai and Oahu and is believed to have arrived at Maui on November 25 or 26, 1778. He was later killed in a brawl on the Big Island of Hawaii.

The major islands had a history of independent rule, with open warfare at times. On Maui, Kahului and Hana were both sites of combat between the Maui islanders and the warriors from neighboring islands.

Kamehameha the First was born on the big island of Hawaii about 1758. He was the nephew of Kalaiopi, who ruled the Big Island. Following the King's death, Kalaiopi's son came to power, only to be subsequently defeated by Kamehameha in 1794. The great chieftain Kahekili was Kamehameha's greatest rival. He ruled not only Maui, but Lanai and Molokai, and also had kinship with the governing royalty of Oahu and Kauai. King Kahekili died in 1794 leaving control of the island to his son. It was a bloody battle (more like a massacre since Kamehameha used western technology, strategy, and two English advisors) in the Iao Valley which resulted in the defeat of Kahekili's son, Kalanikupule, in 1795.

Kamehameha united all the islands and made Lahaina the capital of Hawaii in 1802. It remained the capitol until the 1840's when Honolulu became the center for government affairs. Lahaina was a popular resort for Hawaiian royalty who favored the beaches in the area. Kaahumanu, the favorite wife of Kamehameha was born in Hana, Maui, and spent much of her time there. (Quiet Hana was another popular spot for vacationing royalty.)

13

Liholiho, the heir of Kamehameha the Great, ruled as Kamehameha II from 1797 to 1824. Liholiho was not a strong ruler so Kaahumanu proclaimed herself prime minister during his reign. She ended many of the Kapus of the old religion thus creating a fortuitous vacuum which the soon to arrive missionaries would fill. These New England missionaries and their families arrived in Lahaina in the spring of 1823 at the invitation of Queen Keopuolani. They brought drastic changes to the island with the education of the natives both spiritually and scholastically.

The first high school and printing press west of the Rockies was established at Lahainaluna. Built just outside of Lahaina, it now houses a museum, and is open to the public.

Liholiho and his wife were the first Hawaiian royalty to visit the United States. When their travels continued to Europe, they caught and succumbed to the measles while in London. Liholiho was succeeded by Kauikeaouli (the youngest son of Kamehameha the Great), who ruled under the title of Kamehameha the III from 1824 to 1854.

Beginning in 1819 and continuing for nearly 40 years, whaling ships became a frequent sight in the Lahaina Harbor. The whalers hunted their prey north and south of the islands, off the Japanese coast and in the arctic. Fifty ships were generally anchored off Lahaina, but at the peak of whaling days over 400 ships were once counted at Lahaina and an additional 167 in Honolulu's harbor. Allowing 25 to 30 seamen per ship you can quickly see the enormous number of sailors who flooded the area. While missionaries brought their Christian beliefs, the whaling men lived under their own belief that there was "No God West of the Horn". This presented a tremendous conflict between the sailors and missionaries, with the islanders caught right in the middle.

After months at sea, sailors arrived in Lahaina anxious for the grog shops and native women. It was the missionaries who put the island girls in muu-muus and set up guidelines that forbid them to visit the ships in the harbor. In 1832, a coral fort was erected near the Lahaina harbor following an incident with the unhappy crew of one vessel. The story goes that a captain, disgruntled when he was detained in Lahaina for enticing "base women", ordered his crew to fire shots at the homes of some Lahaina area missionaries. Although the fort was demolished in 1854, remnants of the coral were re-excavated and a corner of the old fort reconstructed. It is located harborside by the Banyan Tree.

An interesting fact is that in 1846 a Lahaina census reported 3,445 Hawaiians, 112 foreigners, 600 seamen, 155 adobe houses, 822 grass houses, 59 stone and wooden houses, as well as 528 dogs!

A combination of things brought the downfall of the whaling industry. The onset of the Civil War depleted men and ships, (one Confederate warship reportedly set 24 whaling vessels ablaze) and the growth of the petroleum industry lessened the need for whale oil. Lastly, the arctic freezes of 1871 and 1876 resulted in many ships being crushed by the ice. Lahaina, however, continues to maintain the charm and history of those bygone whaling days.

15

The whaling era strengthened Hawaii's ties with the United States economically and the presence of the missionaries further strengthened this bond. The United States supported the islands in their desire to maintain their independence against other nations who tried to dominate. The last monarch was Liliuokalani, who ruled from 1891 to 1893. Hawaii became a territory of the United States in 1900 and achieved statehood in 1959.

Sugar cane brought by the first Hawaiians was developed into a major industry on Maui. Two sons of missionaries, Henry P. Baldwin and Samuel T. Alexander played notable roles, and their construction of a water pipeline secured the future of the sugar industry and other agricultural development on the island. Coffee and cocoa beans are currently being tested for commercial feasibility on Maui.

Pineapple, another major agricultural industry, had its origins in 1813 when Don Marin planted the first pineapples. Later, in 1885 the smooth Cayenne variety of pineapple, which is now the major crop, was introduced.

It was about 100 years ago that the first Macadamia Nut trees arrived from Australia. They were intended to be an ornamental tree, since they had nuts that were extremely difficult to crack. It was not until the 1950's that the development of the trees began to take a commercial course. Today, some sugar cane fields are being converted to Macadamia. It takes seven years for the grafted root (they do not grow from seed) to become a producing tree. A slow process, but it is much less polluting than the sugar cane industry. However, beware of their hazards, 1/2 ounce of nuts contains 100 calories!

The Kula area of Maui has become the center for many delicious fruits and vegetables as well as the unusual Protea flower. Wineries are also making a comeback with the opening of the Tedeschi Winery a few years ago. They first began producing an unusual pineapple wine. In 1984, they introduced a champagne, and in 1985, a red table wine. Be sure to also sample the very sweet Kula onions (these are not the same as "Maui onions") which are grown in this area and are available for shipping home.

MAUI'S NAMES AND PLACES

Haiku   (HAH-ee-KOO)   abrupt break

Haleakala   (HAH-leh-AH-kuh-LAH)   house of the sun

Hana   (HAH-nuh)   rainy land

Honoapiilani   (HOH-noh-AH-PEE-'ee-LAH-nee) bays of Pi'ilani

Honolua   (HOH-noh-LOO-uh)   double bay

Iao   (EE-AH-oh)   cloud supreme

Kaanapali   (KAH-AH-nuh-PAH-lee)   land divided by cliffs

Kahana   (Kuh-HAH-nuh)   meaning unknown, of Tahitian origin

Kahului   (Kah-hoo-LOO-ee)   winning

Kapalua   (KAH-puh-LOO-uh)   two borders

Keawakapu   (Keh-AH-vuh-KAH-poo)   sacred harbor

Kihei   (KEE-HEH-ee)   shoulder cape

Lahaina   (LAH-HAH-ee-NAH)   unmerciful sun

Maalaea   (MAH-'uh-LAHeh-uh)   area of red dirt

Makawao   (mah-kah-wah-oh)   forest beginning

Makena   (Mah-KEH-nuh)   abundance

Napili   (NAH-PEE-lee)   pili grass

Olowalu   (oh-loh-wah-loo)   many hills

Paia   (PAH-EE-uh)   noisy

Pukalani   (poo-kah-lah-nee)   sky opening

Ulupalakua   (OO-loo-PAH-luh-KOO-uh)   ripe breadfruit

Waianapanapa   (WAH-ee-AH-NAH-puh-NAH-puh)   glistening water

Wailea   (WAH-ee-LEH-uh)   water Lea (Lea was the canoe makers goddess)

Wailuku   (WAHee-LOO-KOO)   water of slaughter

HAWAIIAN WORDS/MEANINGS

alii (ah-lee-ee) chief

aloha (ah-loh-hah) greetings

hale (Hah-lay) house

hana (HAHA-nah) work

Heiau (heh-ee-ah-oo) temple

kai (kye) ocean

Kamaaina (Kah-mah-ai-nuh) native born

kane (kah-nay) man

kapu (kah-poo) keep out

keiki (kayee-kee) child

lanai (lah-nah-ee) porch or patio

luau (loo-ah-oo) feast

makai (mah-kah-ee) toward the ocean

mauka (mah-oo-kah) toward the mountain

menehune (may-nay-hoo-nee) Hawaiian dwarf or elf

moana (moh-ah-nah) ocean

nani (NAH-nee) beautiful

ono (oh-no) delicious

paniolo (pah-nee-ou-loh) Hawaiian cowboy

pau (pow) finished

puka (POO-ka) a hole

pupus (poo-poos) appetizers

wahine (wah-hee-nay) woman

wiki (wee-kee wee-kee) hurry

WHAT TO PACK

When traveling to paradise, you won't need too much. Comfortable shoes are important for all the sightseeing. Sandals are the norm for footwear. Dress is casual for dining. Many restaurants require men to wear sports shirts with collars, but only one or two require a tie. Clothes should be lightweight and easy care. Cotton and cotton blends are more comfortable for the tropical climate than polyesters. Shorts and bathing suits are the dress code here! A lightweight jacket with a hood or sweater is advisable for evenings and the occasional rain showers. The only need for warmer clothes is if your plans should include hiking or camping in Haleakala Crater. While it may start out warm and sunny, the weather can change very quickly. Even during the daytime, a sweater or light jacket is a good idea when touring upcountry. (The cooler weather here is evidenced on the roofs of the homes where chimney stacks can be spotted.) Tennis shoes or hiking shoes are a good idea for the rougher volcanic terrain of Haleakala or hiking elsewhere as well. Sunscreens are a must. A camera, of course, needs to be tucked in. Many visitors are taking their memories home on video tape, and VHS rental units are available around the island. Binoculars are an option and may be well used if you are traveling between December and April when the whales arrive for their winter vacation. Special needs for traveling with children are discussed in the next section. Anything that you need can probably be purchased once you arrive. Don't forget to leave some extra space in those suitcases for goodies that you will want to take back home!

TRAVELING WITH CHILDREN

Traveling with children can be an exhausting experience for parents and children alike, especially when the trip is as long as the one to Maui. There are an increasing number of direct flights to Maui out of Seattle, San Francisco, Los Angeles, Chicago and Dallas, which saves stopping over in Honolulu. These flights are very popular and fill up well in advance. Packing a child's goody bag for the long flight is a must. A few new activity books or special toys that can be pulled out enroute can be sanity saving. Snacks (boxes of juice are a favorite with our children) can tide over the little ones at the airport or on the plane while awaiting your food/drink service. A thermos with a drinking spout works well and is handy for use during vacations. A change of clothes and a swim suit for the little ones can be tucked in your carry-on bag. (Suitcases have been known to be lost or delayed.) Another handy addition is a small nightlight as unfamiliar accommodations can be somewhat confusing for little ones during the bedtime hours.

Young children may have difficulty clearing their ears when landing. Many don't realize that cabins are pressurized to approximately the 6,000 foot level during flight. To help relieve the pressure of descent, have infants nurse or drink from a bottle, and older children may benefit from chewing gum. If this is a concern of yours, consult with your pediatrician about the use of a decongestant prior to descent.

19

CAR SEATS: By law, children under 3 must travel in child safety seats. While most rental agencies do have car seats for rent, you need to request them well in advance as they have a limited number. The one, and only, car seat we have rented had seen better days, and its design was only marginal for child safety. Prices run about $20 per week or $4 per day. You may wish to bring your own with you. Several styles are permitted by the airlines for use in flight, or it may be checked as a piece of baggage.

BABYSITTING: Most hotels have some form of babysitting service which runs $6 to $7 an hour. There is also an independent babysitting service which will send a person to your hotel or condominium. They charge $6 an hour with a three hour minimum for one to two children, and an additional 50 cents an hour for each additional child. They also have persons capable of working with handicapped children or adults. A 24-hour notice is appreciated. For more information contact Lisa at *Babysitting Services of Maui* (669-4839). We have used several of their people and found them all to be efficient and caring. Check with your condo office as they sometimes have numbers of local sitters. You might also consider the feasiblity of bringing your own sitter. We have tried contacting the Maui high schools, and even advertised in the local papers, with only marginal success.

CRIBS: Most condos and hotels offer cribs for a rental fee that may vary from $2 to $10 per night. Companies such as Maui Rent, charge $6 a day, $25 a week, and $35 for two weeks. For an extended stay you might consider purchasing one of the wonderful new folding cribs that pack up conveniently. We tried the new Fisher-Price version that weighs 20 pounds and fits into a small duffle bag. It checked easily as luggage and is very portable for car travel as well. We have heard recommendations about other types including the Snugli's carrier bed and diaper bag combo that zips easily to form a compact shoulder carryall, and the Houdini full-size playpen by Kantwent which weighs only 16 pounds and folds into a 8x8x42 inch space. Each of the units may be purchased for less than the cost of a ten-day rental fee. If you don't want to pack along a stroller, Fun Rentals (661-3053) in Lahaina rents them for $5 a day.

EMERGENCIES: There are several clinics around the island which take emergencies or walk-in patients. Your condominium or hotel desk can provide you with suggestions or check the phone book. Kaiser Permanente Medical Care Facilities are located in Wailuku (242-7311) and in Lahaina (661-0081). See the section on Helpful Information for additional numbers.

BEACHES: Among the best beaches for young children are the Lahaina and Puunoa beaches in Lahaina, where the water is shallow and calm. Kapalua Bay is also well protected and has fairly gentle wave action. Remember to have children well supervised and wearing floatation devices, for even the calmest beaches can have a surprise wave. Several of the island's beaches offer life guards, among these are the Kamaole I, II, and III beaches in Kihei. Kamaole III Park also has large open areas and playground equipment. Another precaution on the beach that is easily neglected is the application of a good sunscreen. (Remember to reapply after swimming.) If the beautiful sandy beaches and resort pools are not enough diversion, we offer some additional suggestions.

POOLS: A number of complexes have small shallow pools designed with the young ones in mind. These include the Marriott, Kaanapali Alii, and the Kahana Sunset. We recommend taking a life jacket or water wings (floaties) with you. Packing a small inflatable pool for use on your lanai or courtyard may provide a cool and safe retreat for your little one.

ENTERTAINMENT: Currently there are only two theaters, both located in Kahului. While your movie selections are limited, they are generally first run and the admission surprised us by being lower than at our local mainland theater. Two new theaters are in the planning and construction stages as we go to press. A three-screen theater is scheduled for the second level of the Wharf Shopping Center in Lahaina, and a single theater and bowling alley is planned for Kahana. There are a number of video stores which rent movies and equipment. Free "classic" movies are offered Wednesday nights at the Wailea Shopping Village under the stars on the Village Green. Bring a chair, mat or beach towel to sit on the ground. Give them a call at 879-4465 to verify the time and movie.

In the Lahaina/Kaanapali area is the colorful Sugar Cane Train. It runs a course several times a day along Honoapiilani Highway from Kaanapali to Lahaina through the sugar cane fields. Transportation can be purchased alone or in combination with a trip on the Lin Wa, a glass bottom boat. Disembarking from the train at the Lahaina terminal, you will board a red, double decker bus for the short drive to the Lahaina Harbor. The Lin Wa trip lasts over an hour and includes fish viewing and the option of a brief swim before returning to port. (See Land Tours for additional details). There is time for a stroll or a visit to the missionary homes before returning to the train for the trip home.

Flashlights can turn the balmy Hawaiian evenings into adventures! One of the most friendly island residents is the Bufo (Boof-oh). This large toad emerges at night to feed or mate and seems to be easier to spot during the winter months, especially after rain showers. While they can be found around most condominiums, Kawiliki Park (the area behind the Luana Kai, Laule'a and several other condominium complexes with access from Waipulani Road off South Kihei Road) seems to be an especially popular gathering spot. We also enjoy searching for the African snails with shells that grow to a hefty five inches.

The other Hawaiian creature that cannot go without mention is the gekko. This small lizard is a relative of the chameleon and grows to a length of three or four inches. They are most easily spotted at night when they seem to enjoy the warm lights outside your door. We have heard they each establish little territories where they live and breed so you will no doubt see them around the same area each night. They are very shy and will scurry off quickly. Sometimes you may find one living in your hotel or condo. They're friendly and beneficial animals and are said to bring good luck, so make it feel welcome.

If you headquarter your stay near the Papakea Resort, you might take an adventurous night-time reef walk. If an evening low tide does not conflict with your children's bedtime, put on some old tennis shoes and grab a flashlight. (Flashlights that are water-proof or at least water resistant are recommended.) The reef comes right into shore at the southern end of Papakea where you can walk out onto it like a broad living sidewalk. Try and pick a night when the low tide is from 9 – 11 p.m. (tide information is available in the Maui News or call the recorded weather report) and when the sea is calm. Searching the shallow water will reveal sea wonders such as fish and eels that are out feeding. Some people looked at us strangely as we pursued this new recreation, but our little ones thought it an outstanding activity. Shoes are a must as the coral is very sharp. Afterwards, be sure to thoroughly clean your shoes promptly with fresh water or they will become horribly musty smelling, as we learned the hard way.

The Maui Youth Theater is located in Kahului and presents about six plays a year. Your choice might include such favorites as Winnie the Pooh or the Wizard of OZ. Phone 871-7484 for information on performances.

Also located in Kahului is the Maui Zoo. Admission is free and, while only a limited number of animals make their home here, it makes a great stop off. Bring along a picnic lunch! For more information see WHERE TO STAY – WHAT TO SEE – Wailuku & Kahului.

Many restaurants offer a Keiki (children's) menu. There are also an assortment of Burger King's and McDonald's on the island. Paradise Fruits in Kihei has terrific yogurt shakes and healthy snacks or sandwiches along with a good selection of fresh fruits and vegetables. Inexpensive hamburgers and sandwiches are also available at the Azeka's Market take-out counter.

The annual Keiki Fishing Tournament is held sometime during July each year in Kaanapali. The large pond in the golf course is stocked with fish for the event.

The local bookstores offer a wealth of wonderful Hawaiian books for children. A young snorkeler might enjoy *Hawaiian Reef Fishes*, a coloring book by Lori Randall featuring forty reef fish with background information on each. The *Hawaiian Animal Life* coloring book by Sean McKeown has more than just pictures to color. The text presents interesting factual information designed to stimulate each child with a fundamental knowledge of Hawaii's birds, reptiles, amphibians and mammals. A number of colorful Hawaiian folk tales may be a perfect choice to take home for your children to enjoy, or as a gift. *My Travels in Hawaii* is a 56-page coloring and activity book that highlights scenic spots on all the islands. (See ORDERING INFORMATION).

Check with your resort concierge for additional youth activities. During the summer months, Christmas holidays and Easter, many of the resort hotels offer partial or full day activities for children.

TRAVEL TIPS FOR THE PHYSICALLY IMPAIRED

Make your travel plans well in advance and inform hotels and airlines when making your reservations that you are handicapped. Most facilities will be happy to accommodate. Bring along your medical records in the event of an emergency. It is recommended that you bring your own wheelchair and notify the airlines in advance that you will be transporting it. There are no battery rentals available on Maui. Other medical equipment rental information is listed below.

ARRIVAL AND DEPARTURE: On arrival at the Kahului airport terminal, you will find the building easily accessible for mobility impaired persons. Two parking areas are located in front of the main terminal for disabled persons. Restrooms with handicapped stalls (male and female) are also found in the main terminal. If you are unable to use the steps of the boarding ramps, you will need to be boarded with a special lift. Advance notification to the airlines is important.

TRANSPORTATION: There is no public transportation on Maui and taxi service can be spendy. The only two car rental companies providing hand controls are Avis and Hertz. See the Rental Car listing for phone numbers. They need some advance notice to install the equipment. The Maui Economic Opportunity Center operates a van with an electric lift for local residents, however, visitors can make arrangements with them by calling (808) 877-7651.

MEDICAL SERVICES AND EQUIPMENT: Maui Memorial Hospital is located in Wailuku (808-244-2036). There are also good clinics in all areas of the island. Check the local directory. Several agencies can assist in providing personal care attendants, companions, and nursing aides while on your visit. Maui Center for Independent Living (808-242-4966) provides personal care attendants, as does Aloha International Employment Service Health Care Registry (808-244-5223).

The following companies offer medical equipment rentals. Craft Drugs, Kaahumanu Center, Kahului (808-877-0111) can provide wheelchairs, walkers, disposable oxygen, etc., but there is no delivery. Lahaina Pharmacy, Lahaina Shopping Center (808-661-3119) has wheelchairs, crutches, canes, and walkers with delivery by special arrangement. Maui Rent, 349 Hanakai, Kahului (808-877-5827) has walkers, wheelchairs, and shower chairs. It is again recommended that you contact them well in advance of your arrival.

ACCOMMODATIONS: Each of the major island hotels offer one or more handicapped rooms including bathroom entries of at least 29″ to allow for wheelchairs. Due to the limited number of rooms, reservations should be made well in advance. Information on condominium accessibility is available from the Maui Commission of the Handicapped Office.

ACTIVITIES: None of the van tour companies currently offer wheelchair access. The Maui Easter Seal Society can provide information on recreational activities for the disabled traveler. Among the options are wheelchair tennis or basketball, bowling and swimming. Contact them in advance of your arrival at (808-242-9323). Wheelchair access to some of the tourist attractions may be limited. More information and phone numbers can be found in RECREATION AND TOURS.

Additional information can be obtained from the Commission of the Handicapped c/o State Department of Health, 54 High St., Wailuku, Maui 96793 (808-244-4441), or the Commission on the Handicapped, Old Federal Building, 335 Merchant St., #215, Honolulu, Hawaii 96813 (808-548-7606).

WEDDINGS - HONEYMOONS

If a Hawaiian wedding (or a renewal of vows) is in your dreams, Maui can make them all come true. While the requirements are simple, we have heard that some people have been given conflicting and confusing information. Here are a few tips, based on current requirements at time of publication, for making your wedding plans run more smoothly. The bride will need to have a rubella blood test and have the results certified by the lab and the physician. This can be done at home and brought with you. Both parties must be 18 years of age or have consent from both parents. Proof of age is required for anyone age 19 or under and evidence should be a certified copy of your birth certificate or baptismal record. A license must be purchased in person in the state of Hawaii. Call the Department of Health in Kahului (808-244-4313) for the name of a licensing agent in the area where you will be staying. The fee is currently $8. There is no waiting period once you have the license. Check with the Chamber of Commerce in Kahului for information regarding a pastor. Many island pastors are very flexible in meeting your needs, such as an outdoor location etc. The social director of the major resorts can often times assist you with your plans. For copies of current requirements and forms, write in advance to the State of Hawaii, Department of Health, Marriage License Section, 1250 Punchbowl St., Honolulu, Hi 96813 (808-548-5862).

Several independent companies are also available to handle all those important details. Our number one recommendation is ***Arthur's Limousine Service*** (808-661-5466), P.O. Box 11865, Lahaina, Maui, HI 96761. They can provide the ultimate in wedding fantasies or simple ceremonies. Top this off with transportation in their 28-foot stretch limo to your honeymoon hotel. Other agencies include Hawaiian Wedding Experience (808-667-6689), P.O. Box 11093, Lahaina, Maui, HI 96761 and Pierre of Lahaina Studios (808-667-7988), 129 Lahainaluna Rd., Lahaina, Maui, HI 96761.

Honeymoon packages are available from a number of Maui resorts. Prices vary depending on your length of stay and current air fares. Services might include your rental car, champagne, meals, sunset sails or sporting activities. Contact the complexes of your choosing for current honeymoon package rates.

HELPFUL INFORMATION

INFORMATION BOOTHS: Booths located at the shopping areas can provide helpful information and lots of brochures! Brochure displays are everywhere.

MAUI VISITORS BUREAU: (808-871-8691), 380 Dairy Rd. Kahului, Maui, HI 96732

TELEVISION: KBPC Cable Television, channel 7, is designed especially with tourists in mind. Information is provided on recreation, real estate, shopping, restaurants and other points of interest.

RADIO: KPOA 93.5 FM plays great old and new Hawaiian music, with a daily jazz program 8 p.m. to 1 a.m. Tune in and catch the local disk jockeys "talking story"!

PERIODICALS: Maui Star, Art to Onions, This Week Maui, Maui Gold, Rent A Car Drive Guide, Maui Island Guide Directory, The Kaanapali Guide, The Kihei/Wailea Guide, The Maui Island Guide, and A Taste of Maui are all free publications available almost everywhere. NOTE: Most of these free publications offer lots of advertising, however, they do have coupons which will give you discounts on everything from meals to sporting activities to clothing. It may save you a bit to search through these before making your purchases.

The Bulletin – This is primarily a T.V. guide which is published newspaper style and available at no charge. It does have features on some local events and is very popular among the residents. You may have a little more trouble locating a copy of this one.

Maui Beach Press – This free newspaper format weekly has informative local stories, maps, entertainment, and restaurant information.

Lahaina News – A small free weekly newspaper. It contains a television guide and local news.

Lahaina Sun – Lots of interesting tidbits about the happenings around West Maui. Free!

Maui News – This is the local Maui newspaper, published Monday thru Friday, and is available for 35 cents. A good source of local information.

SUN SAFETY: The sunshine is stronger in Hawaii than on the mainland, so a few basic guidelines will ensure that you return home with a tan, not a burn. Use a good lotion with a sunscreen, and reapply after swimming. Moisturize after a day in the sun. Wear a hat to protect your face. Exercise self-control and stay out a limited time the first day, remembering that a gradual tan will last longer. It is best to avoid being out between the hours of noon and three when it is the hottest. Be cautious of overcast days when it is very easy to become burned unknowingly. Don't forget that the ocean acts as a reflector and time spent in it equals time spent on the beach.

FOR YOUR PROTECTION: Do not leave valuables in your car, even in your trunk. Many rental car companies urge that you do not lock your car as vandals cause extensive and expensive damage breaking the locks. Many companies also warn not to drive on certain roads (Ulupalakua to Hana and the unpaved portion of Hwy. 34) unless you are willing to accept liability for all damages.

HELPFUL PHONE NUMBERS:

```
EMERGENCY:
    Police – Ambulance – Fire.................................911
NON-EMERGENCY POLICE:
    Lahaina............................................661-4441
    Hana...............................................248-8311
    Wailuku............................................244-6400
Poison Control......................................1-800-362-3585
Helpline (suicide & crisis center)........................244-7407
Red Cross..............................................244-0051
Consumer Protection....................................244-4387
Directory Assistance:
    Local..............................................(1) 411
    Inter-island.....................................1-555-1212
    Mainland.......................1-(area code)-555-1212
Customs.............................................. 877-6013
Hospital (Maui Memorial):
    Information......................................242-2036
    Emergency.......................................242-2343
Camping Permits:
    State Parks......................................244-4354
    County Parks.....................................244-9018
Maui Visitors Bureau....................................871-8691
Time of Day............................................242-0212
Information – County of Maui............................244-7866
Complaint Office – County of Maui.......................244-7756
Haleakala National Park Information.....................572-7749
Haleakala Park Headquarters............................572-9306
Haleakala Weather......................................877-5124
Ohe'o Headquarters.....................................248-8251
Carthaginian Whale Watch Report........................661-8527
Weather:
    Maui............................................. 877-5111
    Marine (also tides, sunrises, sunsets)...........877-3477
    Recreational Area................................877-5124
```

COSTS PER HOUR: Did you ever wonder what something was costing in relation to the time spent. This is what we came up with based on approximate lengths of time with average prices.

$190 /hr.	Parasail (based on $35 for a 10 to 12 min. ride)
$133	Maui helicopter tour (1½ hour trip)
$75	Sailboat charter (usually 4 to 8 hrs.)
$60	Rolls Royce limo service, per hour
$50	Fishing boat charter (8 hrs.)
$47	Round trip coach airfare LA to Maui (11 hrs.)
$43	Dinner for two at a top restaurant (2 hrs.)
$15	Horseback rides (up to $25 per hr.)
$13.50	Introductory scuba dive (3 hrs.)
$12.85	18 holes of golf at a resort course (3½ hrs.)
$11.85	Deep sea fishing – Shared boat (8 hrs.)
$11.25	Molokini snorkel trip (4 hrs.)
$10.60	Lanai snorkel/sail/tour (8 hrs.)
$ 9.30	Haleakala Bike trip (8 hrs.)
$ 7.29	First class hotel room ($175/day)
$ 6.25	Diver certification course (36 hrs.)
$ 6.20	Haleakala sunrise van tour (6 hrs.)
$ 4.80	Hana van tour (10 hrs.)
$ 3.10	Moderate condominium ($75/day)
$ 1.25	Rental car ($30/day)

GETTING THERE

The best air prices can generally be arranged through a reputable travel agent who can often secure air or air with car packages at good prices by volume purchasing. Prices can vary considerably, so comparison shopping is a wise idea.

The major American carriers that fly form the mainland to Hawaii (Honolulu) are:

AIR AMERICA – 1-800-247-2475, in Honolulu 808-833-4433. This newest arrival on the scene has only one L-1011 for their San Francisco – Honolulu route, so any mechanical difficulty will cause delays.

AMERICAN AIRLINES – 1-800-433-7300; in Los Angeles, 213-568-8999; in Honolulu, 808-526-0044. Has direct flights to Maui.

CONTINENTAL – 1-800-525-0280; in Honolulu, 808-836-7730.

DELTA AIR LINES – 1-800-221-1212. They fly out of Atlanta, stopping on the west coast, then direct flights to Maui.

HAWAIIAN AIRLINES – 1-800-367-5320; in Honolulu, 808-537-5100. Based on acquaintances, friends, and our own experiences, Hawaiian Airs lower fares must be tempered by the increased risk of flight changes, delays, cancellations, and reroutings.

NORTHWEST AIRLINES – 1-800-225-2525; in Honolulu, 808-955-2255.

TWA – 1-800-321-2000; in Honolulu, 808-241-6522.

UNITED AIRLINES – United has more flights to Hawaii from more U.S. cities than any other airline. They have no central 800 number, but do have one for each area in the United States. See your telephone directory. Their Honolulu number is 808-547-2211. They have direct flights to Maui.

The direct flights available on United, Delta, and American Airlines save time and energy by avoiding the otherwise necessary stopover on Oahu. Travel agents schedule at least an hour and a half between arrival on Oahu and departure for Maui to account for any delays, baggage transfers, and the time required to reach the inter-island terminal. If you do arrive early, check with the inter-island carrier. Very often you can get an earlier flight which will arrive on Maui in time to get your car, and maybe some groceries, before returning to pick up your luggage when it arrives on your scheduled flight. Alert! We were foiled by this terrific plan when we hopped onto an earlier flight only to find that it was a prop-jet and the flight was enough longer that we arrived at the same time we would have on our scheduled jet! Oh well!

The inter-island carriers that operate between Honolulu and Maui are:

ALOHA AIRLINES – They fly only jets – mostly 737's. Their Honolulu number is 808-836-1111, in Maui 808-244-9071. This airline tends to have more respect for its schedule than the others, and its personnel are more courteous.

HAWAIIAN AIRLINES – They fly DC9's, Dash 7's and prop planes. The Honolulu number is 808-537-5100, in Maui 808-244-9111, and from the mainland 1-800-367-5320. They service both the Kahului and Kapalua West Maui Airports.

MID PACIFIC AIRLINES – They fly only turbo-prop planes. The Honolulu number is 808-836-3313, and from the mainland 1-800-367-7010. As we go to press Mid Pacific has suspended all operations, including answering the phone. With business reorganization they hope to reopen but no date has been set.

PRINCEVILLE AIRWAYS – They fly 18 passenger twin engine turbo-prop aircraft. They service the Kahului, Hana, and Kapalua West Maui Airports on Maui, as well as to all other islands. From Hawaii the toll free number is 1-800-652-6541, and from the mainland 1-800-323-3343.

Most visitors arrive via the Kahului Airport, direct or inter-island, which is only a 20 minute drive to the Kihei-Wailea-Makena areas, but a 45/60 minute drive to the Kaanapali/Kapalua areas. If your destination is West Maui from Oahu, Kauai, or Hawaii, it might be more convenient to fly into the new Kapalua West Maui Airport. However, the airport is serviced only by a few airlines. Restrictions allow only prop-jets to land here which means the flight is lower, slower, and louder, but more scenic.

One luxurious way to see the islands is aboard one of the American Hawaii Cruises ships, the *Independence* or *Constitution*. These comfortable 700 foot ships provide adequate accommodations and friendly service during the seven day sail around the islands. They come into port at each of the major islands for a day of touring. About half the crew are from Hawaii. For additional information write American Hawaii Crusies, 550 Kierny St., San Francisco, CA 94108. Phone 1-800-227-3666 U.S. or from Canada phone collect (415) 392-9400.

GETTING AROUND

FROM THE AIRPORT: After arriving, there are several options. Taxi cabs, because of the distances between areas, can be very costly (i.e., $30 from Kahului to Kaanapali). There are several bus/limo services available also. The limited around-the-island public transportation that did exist has been terminated at this time with no plans to reinstate it. There are some local area shuttles. The best option may be a rental car unless your resort provides transportation.

The Grayline (877-5507) (1-800-367-2420) provides the Kahului Airport with service to Lahaina and Kaanapali. Baggage is charged per piece. The shuttle currently departs 10:15, 11:45, 1:15, 2:45, and 4:15. Check in at the airport desk (call to verify current schedules and price). Service from Kahului to Kihei/Wailea is $8.32 per person and to Kapalua $17.50 per person. Private limousines are available with reservations and a two seat minimum.
Mita Inc. (871-4622) is a local taxi company based at the Kahului Airport. They can provide service from the Kahului Airport to the Lahaina area for $30, Kaanapali $35, and to the Kihei-Wailea area for about $18 – $22. Classy Taxi uses a 1928 Model A and a 1904 Oldsmobile (878-2211 and 661-2211).

LOCAL TRANSPORTATION: If you don't choose a rental car, you will find limited public transportation.

The Kaanapali trolley runs through the Kaanapali Beach Resort area daily between 7 a.m. and 11 p.m. and is now FREE! The trolley takes Kaanapali guests to Lahaina with pickups at Whalers Village and the resorts.

In the Wailea Resort area a complimentary shuttle runs every 15–20 minutes between 6:30 a.m. and 10:30 p.m. making stops at the tennis center, golf course, shopping centers, the Stouffer Wailea Beach Resort and the Maui Inter-Continental Hotel.

Kapalua has a shuttle running between 6:15 a.m. and midnight between the condos and the hotel. Call the front desk to request it. Most van tours offer pickup at your hotel or condo.

Travel in style with one of the following limo services: Arthur's Limousine Service ★ (669-5466) or (242-6772), HRH Services and Limousines (242-4377), Kihei Limousine (879-7601) or Silver Cloud Limousine Service (669-8580).

RENTAL CARS AND TRUCKS: It has been said that Maui has more rental cars per mile of road than anywhere in the nation. This is not surprising when you realize that Maui has virtually no mass transit, a population of only 78,000 (1986 figures), and over two million visitors per year. Recently, shuttles have been initiated to help eleviate this problem. A choice of more than 30 car rental companies offer luxury or economy and new or used models. Some are local island operators, others are nation-wide chains, but all are very competitive. The rates may vary between high and low season and the best values are during price wars, or super summer discount specials.

Despite the recent Lahaina/Kaanapali rush hour traffic congestion, a rental car is still the best and sometimes only way to get around the island, and for your dollar a very good buy. Prices for compacts range from $13.95 to $20.95/day, mid-size from $20.95 to $34.95, vans from $45.95, and jeeps from $30. The least expensive choice is a late-model compact, with stick shift and no air conditioning. Often these cars are only 2 – 3 years old and in very good condition. Also available from specialty car rental agencies are a variety of luxury cars. A Porsche or Mercedes will run $200 plus per day. Currently there are no companies which rent camping equipment. Vans are available from a number of agencies, but camping in them is not allowed.

Many of the rental companies have booths just outside the main terminal building at the Kahului Airport. There is also a large courtesy phone board in the main terminal (not at the United terminal). This free phone is for those rental agencies not having an airport booth, or regular shuttle service, so that you can call for a pick up. A pay phone is available in the United terminal. A few agencies will take your flight information when your car reservation is made and will meet you and your luggage at the airport with your car.

The policies of all the rental car agencies are basically the same. Most require a minimum age of 21 to 25 and a maximum age of 70. All feature unlimited mileage with you buying the gas (it runs 35 to 40 cents per liter). A few require a deposit or major credit card to hold your reservation. Insurance is an option you may wish, which can run an additional $5 – $10 a day. A few agencies will require insurance for those under age 25. Add to the rental price a 4% sales tax.

Most of the car rental agencies strongly encourage you to take the additional insurance coverage. We suggest you check with your own insurance company before you leave to verify exactly what your policy covers. Hawaii is a no-fault state and without the insurance, you are required to take care of all the damages before leaving the island.

A few of Maui's roadways are rough and rugged. The rental agencies recommend that cars not traverse these areas (shown on the map they distribute) and that if these roads are attempted, you are responsible for any damage.

As a starting point, we would suggest you call Tropical Rent-A-Car as one possible choice. They have very competitive prices and we have always been pleased with their service.

* Indicates the company has some, if not all, late model cars.

RENTAL CAR LISTING:

AAA SCOOTER & JEEP *
Lahaina 661-0606

ALAMO RENT A CAR
1-800-327-9633
Kahului 877-3466

ANDRES RENT A CAR *
Kahului 877-5378

ARTHUR'S
LIMOUSINE SERVICE
1-800-628-4288
Lahaina 661-5466

ATLAS U DRIVE
1-800-367-5238
Kahului 387-7208

AVIS
1-800-331-1212
Kahului 871-7575
Kaanapali 661-4588

BUDGET
1-800-527-0700
Kaanapali 661-5920
Wailea 879-9150
Kahului 871-8811

CHARTON U DRIVE
Kahului 877-7836
Kaanapali 661-3489

CONVERTIBLES HAWAII
1-800-367-5230
Kahului 877-6543

DOLLAR RENT A CAR
1-800-926-4200
Kahului 877-6526
Kaanapali 661-3037
Kapalua 669-7400

EL CHEAPO *
Kahului 877-5851

FORD RENT A CAR
Wailuku 244-3994

HERTZ
1-800-654-8200
Kahului 877-5167

ISLAND AUTO LEASING
Kahului 877-0031

KAMAAINA
RENT A CAR *
Kahului 877-5460

KIHEI HOLIDAZE
Kihei 879-1905

KIHEI RENT A CAR *
Kihei 879-7257

KLUNKERS USED CARS *
Kahului 877-3197

LUXURY SPORTS
CAR RENTAL
1-800-628-4288
Lahaina 661-5646
Kihei 879-8977

MAUI MISER
RENT A CAR *
Kahului 871-2666

MAUI RENT A JEEP
Kahului 877-6626

MAUI SAILING
CENTER
Kihei 879-6260
Jeep rentals only

NATIONAL
1-800-227-7368
Kahului 877-5347
Kaanapali 667-9737

PACIFIC
RENT A CAR
Kahului 877-3065

PARADISE RENT *
A USED CAR
Kihei 879-8788

PRACTICAL
USED CAR RENTAL *
Kahului 871-2860

RAINBOW *
Lahaina 661-8734

RENT A WRECK *
1-800-367-5230
Kahului 877-5600

ROBERTS
Kahului 877-6226

SEARS RENT A CAR *
Kahului 877-7764
Lahaina 661-3546

SUNSHINE
RENT A CAR *
1-800-367-2977
Kahului 871-6222

SURF RENT A CAR *
(flat beds, pick-ups)
Wailuku 244-5544

THRIFTY
1-800-367-2277
Kahului 871-7596
Kaanapali 667-9541

TOM'S RENT A CAR
1-800-367-5224
Kahului 871-7721

TRANS MAUI
RENT A CAR *
1-800-367-5228
Kahului 877-5222

TRAVELERS
RENT A CAR
Kahului 877-7604
Kaanapali 877-7604

24 KARAT CARS
Kaanapali 667-6289

TROPICAL
RENT A CAR
1-800-367-5140
Kahului 877-0002
Kaanapali 661-0061

UNITED CAR RENTAL *
Kahului 871-7328
Lahaina 667-2688

UPTOWN SERVICE
Wailuku 244-0869

VIP CAR RENTAL
Kahului 877-2054

WORD OF MOUTH
RENT A CAR *
Kahului 877-2436

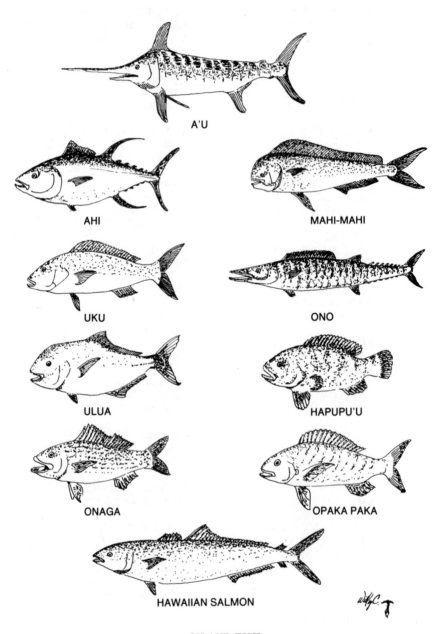

A'U

AHI

MAHI-MAHI

UKU

ONO

ULUA

HAPUPU'U

ONAGA

OPAKA PAKA

HAWAIIAN SALMON

ISLAND FISH

A FEW WORDS ABOUT FISH

Whether cooking fish at your condominium or eating out, the names of the island fish can be confusing. While local shore fishermen catch shallow water fish such as Goatfish or Papio for their dinner table, commercial fishermen angle for two types. The steakfish are caught by trolling in deep waters and include Ahi, Ono, and Mahi. They sometimes provide a healthy struggle before being landed. The more delicate bottom fish include Opakapaka and Onaga which are caught with lines dropped as deep as 1,500 feet to ledges or shelves off Maui's west shoreline. Here is a little background on the popular fish you might find on your dinner plate.

A'U – The broadbill swordfish averages 250 pounds in Hawaiian waters. The broadbill is hard to locate, difficult to hook, and a challenge to land. It would be classified as a steakfish.

AHI – The yellow fin tuna (Allison tuna) is caught in deep waters off the Kauai coast. The pinkish red meat is firm yet flaky. This fish is popular for sashimi. They weigh between 60 and 280 pounds.

ALBACORE – This smaller version of the Ahi averages 40 – 50 pounds and is lighter in both texture and color.

AKU – This is the blue fin tuna.

EHU – Orange snapper

HAPU – Hawaiian sea bass

KAMAKAMAKA – Island catfish is a very tasty and popular dish, however, a little difficult to find at most restaurants.

LEHI – The Silver Mouth is a member of the snapper family with a stronger flavor than Onaga or Opakapaka and a texture resembling Mahi.

MAHI – Although called the dolphin fish, this is no relation to Flipper or his friends. It is caught while trolling and weighs between 10 and 65 pounds. This is a seasonal fish which causes it to command a high price when fresh. BEWARE, while excellent fresh, it is often served in restaurants having arrived from the Philippines frozen and is far less pleasing. A clue as to whether fresh or frozen may be the price tag. If it runs less than $10 it is probably the frozen variety. Fresh Mahi will run $14 – $20 a dinner. This fish has excellent white meat that is moist and light. It is very good sauteed.

MU'U – We tried this mild white fish at the Makawao Steak House. They serve it quite often, and we were told there is no common name for this fish.

ONAGA (ULA) – Red snapper is a local favorite. Caught in holes that are 1,000 feet or deeper, this fish has an attractive hot pink exterior with tender, juicy, white meat inside.

ONO – Also known as Wahoo. The word ONO means "very good" in Hawaiian. A member of the Barracuda family, its white meat is flaky and moist. It is caught at depths of 25 – 100 fathoms while trolling and weighs between 15 and 65 pounds.

'OPAE – Shrimp

OPAKAPAKA – Otherwise known as pink snapper and one of our favorites. The meat is very light and flaky with a delicate flavor.

PAPI0 – This is a baby Ulua which is caught in shallow waters and weighs 5 – 25 pounds.

UKU – The meat of this grey snapper is light, firm and white with a texture that varies with size. It is very popular with local residents. This fish is caught off Kauai, usually in the deep Paka Holes.

ULUA – Also known as Pompano, this fish is firm and flaky with steaklike, textured white meat. It is caught by trolling, bottom fishing, or speared by divers and weighs between 15 and 110 pounds.

GROCERY SHOPPING

To give you an idea of what to expect at the supermarket, here are some grocery store prices. Bread $1.05 – $2.49, chicken $1.09 /lb., hamburger $1.39 – $2.99 /lb., mayonnaise $1.69 – 2.15, Starkist Tuna $1.33, disposable diapers 12-24 count size $4.99 – $6.99, 32 oz. ketchup $2.49, 2% milk $1.72 half gallon.

The three major grocery stores in Kahului are Foodland, Safeway, and Star Market. In Lahaina you can choose between Foodland or Nagasako at the Lahaina Shopping Center or the new Safeway at the Cannery Shopping Center. In Kihei the major markets are Foodland, Azeka's, and Star Market. These larger stores offer the same variety as your hometown store and the prices are better than at the small grocery outlets. In Hana there is, of course, Hasegawa as well as the Hana Ranch Store.

A few of the more unusual or specialty markets include: ***Paradise Fruits*** ★ in Kihei (open 24 hours) offers an open-air market with a variety of fresh fruits and vegetables which are also available for shipment home. ***Azeka's Market*** (879-0611) at Azeka's Place in Kihei can provide you with those world famous Azeka (Kalbi) ribs for cooking. **The Farmers' Market** is a group of people who bring produce down from the Kula area. They set up roadside shopping, and you can't find it fresher. Their locations seem to change each time we visit. Just look for the green sandwich board signs that are set up roadside, or look for a brochure in the shopping center information racks. ***Take Home Maui*** (661-8067) is located just off Front Street in Lahaina and offers a limited selection of fruits

Foodland, Starmart, Safeway

and vegetables for shipment home. *The Fish Co.* (244-9633 or 242-6532) is located near the dock at Maalaea Harbor, open Mon. – Sat. 10 – 5. They offer a wonderful selection of fresh island fish.

Local grocery shopping is a little more adventuresome. The largest local stores are in Wailuku and Kahului. In addition to the regular food staples, they have wonderful selections of local foods such as marinated seafoods and often have deli sections which feature local favorites and plate lunches. *Takamiya's* at 359 N. Market St. in Wailuku has a huge deli section with perhaps more than 50 cooked foods and salads as well as very fresh meats. *Ah Fook's* at the older Kahului Mall has a smaller deli section with plate lunches running about $3. *Ooka's* is the largest of the three. The packed parking lot and crowded aisles prove its popularity! Its prices are the best, and they run local coupons in mailings to island residents which add to the savings. Lots of selections in sundry items, as well as seafood and meats.

ANNUAL MAUI EVENTS

FEBRUARY
- Marine/Art Expo runs two months at the Maui Inter-Continental Hotel

MARCH
- Annual Maui Marathon from Wailuku to Lahaina, sponsored by the Valley Isle Road Runners
- Annual Kukini Run along the Kahakuloa Valley Trail
- The 26th is Prince Kuhio Day, a state holiday.
- LPGA Womens Kemper Open at the Kaanapali Golf Course

MAY
- May Lei Day celebration in Wailea (check with the Inter-Continental Hotel for their events)
- Seabury Hall in Makawao sponsors their annual craft fair the Saturday prior to Mother's Day

JUNE
- Obon Season (late June through August) – Bon Odori festivals are held at the many Buddhist temples around the island. They are announced in the local newspapers and the public is invited.
- King Kamehameha Day Celebration
- Maui Upcountry Fair

JULY
- Annual 4th of July Rodeo & Parade in Makawao
- Canoe races at Hookipa State Park
- Maui Jaycees Carnival at Kahului Fairground
- Annual Sausa Cup races in Lahaina, sponsored by the Lahaina Yacht Club
- Victoria to Maui Yacht Race
- Kapalua Wine Symposium
- Keiki Fishing Tournament at Kaanapali

GENERAL INFORMATION
Weather

AUGUST
- Kapalua Music Festival (a week of Hawaiian & classical music)
- Run to the Sun Marathon, a grueling trek from sea level up to the 10,000 foot level of Haleakala Crater
- The 21st is Admissions Day, a state holiday.

SEPTEMBER
- Maui County Rodeo in Makawao
- Aloha Week Festival
- Labor Day Fishing Tournament
- Wailea Speed Crossing, a windsurfing regatta across the seven mile stretch of Pacific to Molokini and back. Sponsored by the Maui Inter-Continental

OCTOBER
- Maui County Fair at the Kahului Fairgrounds
- Open Pro-Am Golf Championship
- Parade and Halloween festivities in Lahaina

NOVEMBER
- Na Mele O'Maui Festival at Lahaina & Kaanapali Beach Resorts
- Kapalua International Championship of Golf
- Queen Kaahumanu Festival at the Maui High School
- Sand Castle contest, check for current beach location in Kihei, usually held Thanksgiving weekend
- Thanksgiving weekend Santa arrives at Kaahumanu Mall

DECEMBER
- Kapalua/Betsy Nagelsen Pro-Am Tennis Invitational
- Christmas House at Hui Noeau, near Makawao, is a non-profit organization featuring pottery, wreaths, and other artwork

For exact dates of these events, write to the Hawaii Visitors Bureau, 2270 Kalakaua Avenue #801, Honolulu, Hawaii 96815, and request the Hawaii Special Events Calendar. The calendar also gives non-annual information and the contact person for each event. Check the local papers for dates of additional events.

WEATHER

When one thinks of Hawaii, and especially Maui, one visualizes bright sunny days cooled by refreshing trade winds, and this is the weather at least 300 days a year. What about the other 65 days? Most aren't really bad – just not perfect. Although there are only two seasons, summer and winter, temperatures remain quite constant. Following are the average daily highs and lows for each month and the general weather conditions.

January	80/64	May	84/67	September	87/70
February	79/64	June	86/69	October	86/69
March	80/64	July	86/70	November	83/68
April	82/66	August	87/71	December	80/66

Summer: May thru mid October, 80 degree days, 70 – 80 degree nights. Tradewinds are more consistent keeping the temperatures tolerable, however, when the trades stop, the weather becomes hot and sticky. Kona winds are less frequent. 13 hours of daylight.

Winter: Mid October thru April, 70 – 80 degree days, 60 – 70 degree nights. Tradewinds are more erratic, vigorous to none. Kona winds are more frequent causing wide-spread cloudiness, rain showers, mugginess and even an occasional thunderstorm. 11 hours of daylight.

Summer type wear is suitable all year round. However, a warm sweater or light-weight jacket is a good idea for evenings and trips such as to Haleakala.

If you are interested in the types of weather you may encounter or are confused by some of the terms you hear, read on. For further reference con ,ult *Weather in Hawaiian Waters*, by Paul Haraguchi, 99 pages, available at island bookstores.

TRADE WINDS: Trade winds are an almost constant wind blowing from the northeast through the east and are caused by the Pacific anti-cyclone, a high pressure area. This high pressure area is well developed and remains semi-stationary in the summer causing the trades to remain steady over 90% of the time. Interruptions are much more frequent in the winter when they blow only 40 to 60% of the time. The major resort areas of East and West Maui are situated in the lee of the West Maui Mountains and Haleakala respectively. Here they are sheltered from the trades and the tremendous amount of rain (400 plus inches per year) they bring to the mountains.

KONA WINDS: The Kona Wind is a stormy, rain-bearing wind blowing from the south-west, or basically from the opposite direction of the trades. It brings high and rough surf to the resort side of the island – great for surfing and boogieboarding, bad for snorkeling. These conditions are caused by low pressure areas northwest of the islands. Kona winds strong enough to cause property damage have occurred only twice since 1970. Lighter non-damaging Kona winds are much more common, occurring usually two to five times almost every winter (November thru April).

KONA WEATHER: Windless, hot and humid weather is referred to as Kona weather. The interruption of the normal trade wind pattern brings this on. The trades are replaced by light and variable winds and, although this may occur any time of the year, it is most noticeable during the summer when the weather is generally hotter and more humid, with fewer localized breezes.

KONA LOW: A Kona low is a slow-moving, meandering, extensive low pressure area which forms near the islands. This causes continuous rain with thunderstorms over an extensive area and lasts for several days. November through May is the most usual time for these to occur.

HURRICANES: Hawaii is not free of hurricanes. However, most of the threatening tropical cyclones have weakened before reaching the islands, or have passed harmlessly to the west. Their effects are usually minimal causing only high surf on the eastern and southern shores of some of the islands. At least 21 hurricanes or tropical storms have passed within 300 miles of the islands in the last 33 years, but most did little or no damage. Only Hurricane Dot of 1959 and Hurricane Iwa of 1982 caused extensive damage. In both cases, the island of Kauai was hit hardest, with lesser damage to southeast Oahu and very little damage to Maui.

TSUNAMI: A tsunami is an ocean wave produced by an undersea earthquake, volcanic eruption, or land slide. Tsunamis are usually generated along the coasts of South America, the Aleutian Islands, the Kamchatka Peninsula, or Japan and travel through the ocean at 400 to 500 miles an hour. It takes at least 4 ½ hours for a tsunami to reach the Hawaiian Islands. A 24-hour Tsunami Warning System has been established in Hawaii since 1946. When the possibility exists of a tsunami reaching Hawaiian waters, the public will be informed by the sound of the attention alert signal sirens. This particular signal is a steady one minute siren, followed by one minute of silence, repeating as long as necessary. Immediately turn on a TV or radio; all stations will carry CIV-Alert emergency information and instructions with the arrival time of the first waves. Do not take chances – false alarms are not issued. Move quickly out of low lying coastal areas that are subject to possible inundation.

The warning sirens are tested throughout the state on the first working Monday of every month at 11 a.m. The test lasts only a few minutes and CIV-Alert announces on all stations that the test is underway. Since 1813, there have been 112 tsunamis observed in Hawaii with only 16 causing significant damage.

Tsunamis may also be generated by local volcanic earthquakes. In the last 100 years there have been only six, with the last one November 29, 1975, affecting the southeast coast of the island of Hawaii. The Hawaiian Civil Defense has placed earthquake sensors on all the islands and, if a violent local earthquake occurs, an urgent tsunami warning will be broadcast and the tsunami sirens will sound. A locally generated tsunami will reach other islands very quickly, therefore, there may not be time for an attention alert signal to sound. Any violent earthquake that causes you to fall or hold onto something to prevent falling is an urgent warning, and you should immediately evacuate beaches and coastal low-lying areas.

TIDES: In Hawaii, the average tidal range is about two feet. Tide tables are available daily in the Maui News or by calling the marine weather number, 877-3477.

SUNRISE AND SUNSET: In Hawaii, day length and the altitude of the noon sun above the horizon do not vary as much throughout the year as at the temperate regions because of the island's low latitude within the sub-tropics. The longest day is 13 hours 26 minutes (sunrise 5:53 a.m., sunset 7:18 p.m.) at the end of June, and the shortest day is 10 hours 50 minutes (sunrise 7:09 a.m. and sunset 6:01 p.m. at the end of December). Daylight for outdoor activities without artificial lighting lasts about 45 minutes past sunset.

Where to Stay — What to See

INTRODUCTION

Maui has more than 12,000 hotel rooms and condominium units in vacation rental programs, with the bulk of the accommodations located in two areas. These are West Maui, a 10 mile stretch between Lahaina and Kapalua, and East Maui, which is also about ten miles of coastline between Maalaea and Makena. On the northern side, there are four properties near the Kahului Airport, several complexes in Hana and two in upcountry. This chapter contains a list of essentially all of the condominiums that are in rental programs, as well as the island's hotels.

HOW TO USE THIS CHAPTER: For ease in locating information, the properties are first indexed alphabetically following this introduction. In both East and West Maui, the condominiums have been divided into groups that are geographically distinct and are laid out (sequentially) as you would approach them arriving from the Kahului area. These areas also seem to offer similar price ranges, building style, and beachfronts. At the beginning of each section is a description of the area, sights to see, shopping information, and a sequential listing of the complexes. For each complex, we have listed the local address and/or P.O. Box, and various rental agents handling units at this property. The prices listed are generally the lowest available. At the end of the accommodations chapter is an alphabetical list of all the rental agents and the properties they handle. We have chosen to list prices and, while these were the most current available at press time, they are subject to change without notice. As island vacationers ourselves, we found it important to include this feature rather than just giving you broad catagories such as budget or expensive. After all, one person's "expensive" may be "budget" to someone else!

For the sake of space, we have made use of some abbreviations. The size of the condominiums are abbreviated as studio (S BR), one bedroom (1 BR), two bedroom (2 BR) and three bedroom (3 BR). The number in parenthesis refers to the number of people that can occupy the unit for the price listed. Occasionally we have a listing such as (2, max 5). This means that the price is for two people, but there are enough beds for a maximum of five people to occupy this unit. The description will tell you how much it will be for additional person over two, i.e. each additional person $6/night. Some facilities consider an infant as an extra person, others will allow children free up to a specified age. The abbreviations o.f., g.v., and o.v. refer to oceanfront, gardenview and oceanview units. The prices are listed with a slash dividing them. The first price listed is the high season rate, the second price is the low season rate. A few have a flat yearly rate so there will be only be a single rate.

41

Condos are abundant, and the prices and facilities they offer can be quite varied. We have tried to indicate our own personal preferences by the use of a ★. We felt these were the best buys or special in some way. However, it is impossible for us to view all the units within a complex and since condominiums are privately owned, each unit can vary in its furnishings and its condition.

WHERE TO STAY: As for choosing the area of the island in which you stay, we offer these suggestions. The Lahaina and Kaanapali areas offer the visitor the hub of the island's activities, but accommodations are a little more costly. The beaches are especially good at Kaanapali. The values and choice of condos are more extensive a little beyond Kaanapali in the Honokowai, Kahana (Lower Honoapiilani Hwy. area) and further at Napili. However, there are fewer restaurants here and slightly cooler temperatures. Some of the condominiums in this area, while very adequate, may be little overdue for redecorating. While many complexes are on nice beaches, many are also on rocky shores. Kapalua offers high class and high price condominium and hotel accommodations. Kihei and Wailea are a half-hour drive from Lahaina and offer some attractive newer condo units at excellent prices. Many Maui vacationers feel that Kihei offers better weather in the winter months. It is much quieter and, while there are not as many restaurants, there are some excellent ones. The beaches here are plentiful and accessible as well as being beautiful and well kept, suitable for a variety of water activities. We suggest reading the introductory section to each area for additional information.

HOW TO SAVE MONEY: Maui has two "price" seasons. High or "in" season and low or "off" season. Low season is generally considered to be April 15 to December 1, and the rates are discounted at some places as much as 30%. Different resorts and condominiums may vary these dates by as much as two weeks and a few resorts are going to a flat, year round rate. Ironically, some of the best weather is during the fall when temperatures are cooler than summer and it is less rainy than the spring months. (See GENERAL INFORMATION – weather for year round temperatures).

For longer than one week, a condo unit with a kitchen or kitchenette can result in significant savings on your food bill. While this will give you more space than a hotel room and at a lower price, you may give up some resort amenities (shops, restaurants, maid service, etc.) There are several large chain grocery stores around the island with fairly competitive prices, although most things at the store will run slightly higher than on the mainland. (See GENERAL INFORMATION – Shopping.)

Money can be saved by using the following tips when choosing a place to settle. First, it is less expensive to stay during the off or low season. Second, there are some areas that are much less expensive. Although Kahului has some very inexpensive motel units, we can't recommend this area as a place to headquarter your stay. The weather is wetter in winter, hotter in summer, generally windier than the other side of the island, and there are few good beaches. The several older hotels in Wailuku have not been included as they seemed a little too rugged. There are some good deals in the Maalaea and Kihei areas, and the northern area above Lahaina has some older complexes that are reasonably good values. Third, some condo type units without kitchens are less expensive, but you must weigh the cost savings versus doing your own cooking. Fourth, there are some pleasant condo units either across the road from the beach or on a rocky, less attractive beach. This can represent a tremendous savings, and there are always good beaches a short walk or drive away. Fifth, hotel rooms or condos with garden or mountain views are less costly than oceanview or oceanfront rooms. We find the mountain view, especially in Kaanapali to be, in fact, superior. Not only are the mountains gorgeous, but your room does not get full day sunlight and stays cooler.

There is a growing trend to offer only limited maid service in the condominiums, perhaps only on check out or once a week. Additional maid service is usually available for an extra charge. Rooms without telephones or color televisions usually have lower prices and a few condominiums do not have pools. A few words of caution, condominium units within one complex can differ greatly and, if a phone is important to you, ask! More complexes are adding phone service to their rooms, however, there are still many that have only a courtesy phone or a pay phone at the office. Some may add 50 – 75 cents per in-room local call, others have no extra charge. Some units have washers and dryers in the rooms, while others do not.

Travel agents will be able to book your stay in the Maui hotels and also in most condominiums. If you prefer to make your own reservation, we have listed the various contacts for each condominium and endeavored to quote the best price generally available. Rates vary between rental agents, so check all those listed for a particular condominium. We have indicated toll free 800 numbers when available. For additional Canadian toll free numbers check the rental agent list. Look for an 808 area code preceding the non-toll free numbers. You might also check the classified ads in your local newspaper for owners offering their units, which may be a better bargain.

Although prices can jump (and have done so in recent years), most go up only 5 – 10% per year. Prices listed do not include sales tax.

GENERAL POLICIES: All listings are condominiums unless specified as a (Hotel). Condominium complexes require a deposit, usually equivalent to one or two nights stay, to secure your reservation and insure your room rate from price increases. Some charge higher deposits during winter or over Christmas holidays. Generally a 30 day notice of cancellation is needed to receive a full refund. Most require payment in full either 30 days prior to arrival or upon arrival and a great many do not accept credit cards. The usual minimum condo stay is 3 nights with some requiring one week in winter. Christmas holidays may have steeper restrictions with minimum stays as long as two weeks, payments 90 days in advance and heavy cancellation penalties. It is not uncommon to book as much as two years in advance for the Christmas season. The minimum stay in condominiums is generally three nights. ALL CONDOMINIUMS HAVE KITCHENS, T.V.'S. AND POOLS UNLESS OTHERWISE SPECIFIED. Monthly and often times weekly discounts are available. Room rates quoted are generally for two. Additional persons run $8 – $10 per night per person with the exception of the high class resorts and hotels where it may run as much as $25 – $35 extra. Many complexes can arrange for crib rentals. (See GENERAL INFORMATION – Traveling with Children). We have tried to give the lowest rates generally available, which might not be through the hotel or condo office, so check with the offices as well as the rental agents. When contacting condominium complexes by mail, be sure to address your correspondence to the attention of the manager. The managers of several complexes do not handle any reservations and we have indicated to whom you should address reservation requests. If two addresses are given, use the P.O. Box or R.R. rather than street address.

CONDOMINIUM & HOTEL INDEX

BED AND BREAKFAST

An alternative to condominiums and hotels are the Bed and Breakfast organizations. They offer homes around the island, and some very reasonable rates. "Bed & Breakfast Hawaii" is among the best known. To become a member and receive their directory, which also includes the other islands, contact: Bed and Breakfast Hawaii, Directory of Homes, Box 449, Kapaa, Hawaii 96746. Another organization, "Bed and Breakfast Maui Style" can be reached at P.O. Box 886, Kihei, Maui 96753 (808-879-7865) or (808-879-2352). "Go Native Hawaii" also features bed and breakfast vacations, contact them at P.O. Box 13115, Lansing, MI 48901, phone (517-349-9598).

PRIVATE RESIDENCES

PREMIER CONNECTION
310 Market Street, Suite 2, Wailuku, Maui, Hi 96793. (808-244-4877) Privacy, elegance, and the ultimate in luxury, can be provided by Rob Dorman and his staff for your stay on Maui. A variety of exceptional hotel suites, homes or mansion-like dwellings are available for short or long term stays. Prices reflect the quality of the accommodations and location, which run $200 to $2,000 per day. They can also arrange transportation, tours, flowers and such.

PACIFIC ISLAND ADVENTURES
4218 Waialae Avenue, Suite 203-A, Honolulu, HI 96816. (808-735-9000) (1-800-522-3030) Offers a limited number of homes on all the islands. Most require a seven day minimum stay. Daily rates for three, four, five and even six bedroom homes range from $200 – $1,500 per day.

HANA BAY VACATION RENTALS
Suzanne and Stan Collins offer eight homes in the Hana area. Contact Hana Bay Vacation Rentals, P.O. Box 318, Hana, Maui, HI 96713. (808-248-7727)

ALAELOA
Contact manager, 20 Alaeloa #8, Lahaina, Maui, Hi 96761. (808-669-6259) This is a residential area of 46 homes. Several are available for rent with a 30 day minimum stay. They are generally two bedroom homes with ocean view and are priced $2,500 per month and up. A small private cove with beautifully clear water, sandy beach and pavilion for guest use is located at the bottom of a steep walkway. Excellent swimming and snorkeling. No public access.

LONG-TERM STAYS

Almost all condo complexes and rental agents offer the long term visitor moderate to substantial discounts for stays of one month or more. Private homes can also be booked through the agents listed above.

LAHAINA

INTRODUCTION

As you leave the Kahului area on Hwy. 38, you plunge immediately into miles of sugar cane. The rugged and deeply carved valleys of the West Maui mountains are on the right, and on the left the dormant volcano of Haleakala. Its broad base and seemingly gentle slopes belie its 11,000 foot height, and no hint of its enormous moon-like crater is discernible from below. The mountains are so distinct and sharp edged they appear to have been cut out with giant scissors. The drive across the isthmus ends quickly as you pass Maalaea Harbor where the gently swaying sugar cane gives way to rugged sea cliffs and panoramic Pacific vistas. Across the bay is East Maui and in the distance the islands of Kahoolawe and Lanai. Construction of this road was to accommodate the new resort developments at Kaanapali that began in the 1960's. Traffic must have been far different on the old road which is still visible in places along the craggy cliffside. The tunnel, built in 1951, is the only one on Maui. Just beyond it are enormous metal chain blankets hanging along the rocky cliffs above the road. Termed a protective measure by some and an eyesore by others, they were installed in 1987.

As you descend from the cliffs the first glimpse of the tropical and undeveloped West Maui coastline is always a thrill. Stretching as far as the eye can see are sugar cane fields hugging the lower slopes of the mountains and a series of narrow, white sand beaches lined by kiawe trees and coconut palms. For several miles the constant stream of traffic is the only clue to the populated areas ahead. Olowalu is the first sign of civilization. It is merely a hamlet along the roadside, an unusual location perhaps for one of the island's best restaurants, Chez Paul. The public beaches continue to line the highway and the unobstructed view of the ocean may reward the observant with a whale sighting during the December to April humpback season.

A few homes to the left and the monolithic smoke stack of the Pioneer Mill announce your arrival to Lahaina, the now bustling tourist center of Maui. It has maintained the aura of more than a century ago when it was the whaling capitol of the world. Located about a 45 minute drive from the Kahului Airport (depending on traffic), this coastal port is noted for its Front Street which is a several block strip of shops and restaurants along the waterfront. The Lahaina Harbor is filled with boats of varying shapes and sizes, eager to take the visitor afloat for a variety of sea excursions.

The oldest accommodations on the island are located here. Still popular among many a visitor it offers nostalgic and rustic atmosphere, and very reasonable prices. Other accommodations include a luxuriously expensive condominium complex and two charming new country inns. Although several complexes are located oceanfront, the beaches in Lahaina are fronted by a close-in reef which prohibits swimming. Only Puamana has a beach suitable for swimming. If you want to be in the midst of the action on Maui, you might want to investigate staying in this area.

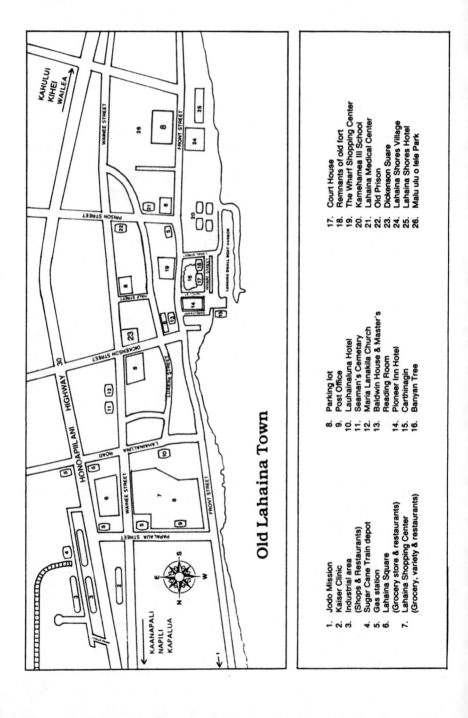

Old Lahaina Town

1. Jodo Mission
2. Kaiser Clinic
3. Industrial area
   (Shops & Restaurants)
4. Sugar Cane Train depot
5. Gas station
6. Lahaina Square
   (Grocery store & restaurants)
7. Lahaina Shopping Center
   (Grocery, variety & restaurants)

8. Parking lot
9. Post Office
10. Lauhainaluna Hotel
11. Seaman's Cemetary
12. Maria Lanakila Church
13. Baldwin House & Master's
    Reading Room
14. Pioneer Inn Hotel
15. Carthinagin
16. Banyan Tree

17. Court House
18. Remnants of old fort
19. The Wharf Shopping Center
20. Kamehamea III School
21. Lahaina Medical Center
22. Old Prison
23. Dickenson Suare
24. Lahaina Shores Village
25. Lahaina Shores Hotel
26. Malu ulu o lele Park

BEST BETS: **Puamana** – A nice residential type area of two-plex and four-plex units, some oceanfront. **Lahaina Shores** – A moderately priced colonial style high rise within walking distance of Lahaina shops. **Plantation Inn** and **Lahaina Hotel** – Two tastefully done new bed and breakfast hotels with all the elegance of bygone days.

WHAT TO DO AND SEE

There is much to see and do in busy Lahaina town. The word Lahaina means "merciless sun." It does tend to become quite warm, especially in the afternoon. Parking can be somewhat irksome. Several all day lots are located near the corner of Wainee and Dickenson (only a couple blocks off Front Street) and charge $3 for all day. One nearer to Front Street charges $7 per day. The inexpensive lots fill up early in the day. The Lahaina Shopping Center has a three hour (free) parking area, but it is always very crowded. If you don't mind a short walk, free parking is available across the road from the Lahaina Shores Village. (See the Lahaina map for locations of other parking areas). On-street parking is very limited and if you are fortunate enough to find a spot, many are only for one hour. BEWARE, the police here are quite prompt and efficient at towing.

Now that you have arrived, let's get started. Historical memorabilia abounds in Lahaina. The historical landmarks have all been identified by numbered markers. A free pamphlet is available at the historical sites in Lahaina (Baldwin House, Carthaginian, Masters Reading Room, and Wo Hing Temple) for your own self-guided tour. Following is a brief discussion of the most interesting and significant, not to be missed, sites. You may be able to purchase admission at a package price. Check at the Wo Hing Temple, Carthaginian or Baldwin House for more information on this option.

The Banyan Tree is very easy to spot at the south end of Lahaina adjacent to Pioneer Inn on Front Street. Planted on April 24, 1873 by Sheriff William Owen Smith, it was to commemorate the 50th anniversary of Lahaina's first Protestant Christian Mission.

The stone ruins of **the old fort** can be found harborside near the Banyan Tree. The fort was constructed in the 1830's to protect the missionarys' homes from the whaling ships and the occasional cannon ball that would be shot off when the sailors were aroused. The fort was later torn down and the coral blocks reused elsewhere. A few blocks have been excavated and the corner of the fort was rebuilt as a landmark in 1964. On the corner near the Pioneer Inn is a plaque marking the site of the 1987 Lahaina Reunion Time Capsule, which contains newspapers, photos and other memorabilia.

Pioneer Inn, built in 1901, is the distinguished green and white structure just north of the Banyan Tree. It was a haven for inter-island travelers during the early days of the 20th century. Having survived the dry years of prohibition, it added a new wing in 1966 along with a center garden and pool area. Two restaurants operate here and accommodations are available in the original and the newer structure. (See RESTAURANTS – Lahaina and WHERE TO STAY – Lahaina for additional information).

The Lahaina Courthouse was built in 1859, at a cost of $7,000, from wood and stone taken from the palace of Kamehameha II. You'll find it located near the Lahaina Harbor. After years of planning, it now appears the Lahaina Restoration and Preservation Foundation will begin renovations to restore and convert it into a museum featuring Lahaina's plantation era, and the importance of the reign of Kamehameha III on the Hawaiian Islands. The first floor would also house an information center.

In front of Pioneer Inn is the **Lahaina Harbor**. You can stroll down and see boats and visit stalls where a wide variety of water sports and tours can be arranged. (See RECREATION AND TOURS - Sea Excursions.) **The Carthaginian** is anchored in the harbor and is actually a replica of the first Carthaginian, which went aground in 1920 during an attempt to tow it to Honolulu. The Carthaginian has been used in the filming of several movies, including *Hawaii*. It is open for public inspection daily from 9 to 4:30, with admission $2.00 for adults and accompanying children free.

The Hauola Stone or Healing Rock can be found near the Lahaina Harbor. Look for the cluster of rocks marked with a visitors bureau warrior sign. The rock, resembling a chair, was believed to have healing properties, which could be gained by merely sitting in it with feet dangling in the surf. Here you will also find remnants of the **Brick Palace** of Kamehameha the Great. Vandals destroyed the display which once showed examples of the original mud bricks.

The Baldwin House is across Front Street from Pioneer Inn. Built during 1834-1835, it housed the Reverend Dwight Baldwin and his family from 1837 to 1871. Tours are given every 15 minutes between the hours of 9:30 and 4:30. Adults are $2, no charge for children. The empty lot adjacent was once the home of Reverend William Richards, and a target of attack by cannonballs from angry sailors during the heyday of whaling. On the other side of the Baldwin Home is the Master's Reading Room. Built in 1833, it is the oldest structure on Maui. Its original purpose was to provide a place of leisure for visiting sea captains. It is not open to the public at this time.

Whale watching is always an exciting pastime in Lahaina. The whales usually arrive in November and December and breed in the warm waters off Maui for several months. At the desk of the Carthaginian you will find a chart showing where whale sightings have occurred this season. There is also a number to call to report any sightings you make. WHALE WATCH HOTLINE at 879-6530, or the CARTHAGINIAN WHALE WATCH REPORT at 661-8527. Whale watching excursions are available. (For more information see RECREATION AND TOURS.)

The Old Jail (Hale Paaho) is located on Prison Street, just off Wainee and only a short trek from Front Street. The remains of the old jail were reconstructed in 1959. Originally it was built in 1852 to house the unruly sailors from the whaling vessels and to replace the old fort. The prison house was built first, followed a few years later by the coral walls (the blocks taken from the old fort). The Lahaina Restoration Foundation is reconstructing the gate house to its original state. While not completed as we go to press, we are told the area will be available for group functions, have kitchen facilities and modern restrooms.

Construction of the **Waiola Church** began in 1828 on what was then called the Wainee Church. Made of stone and large enough to accommodate 3,000 people, the church unfortunately, did not survive the destructive forces of nature and man. The current structure dates from only 1953. In the neighboring cemetery you will find tombs of several notable members of Hawaiian royalty, including Queen Keopuolani, wife of Kamehameha the Great and mother of Kamehameha I and II. The church is located on Wainee and Shaw Streets.

Maria Lanakila Church is on the corner of Wainee and Dickenson. Built in 1928, it is a replica of the 1858 church. Next door is the Seamans' Cemetery.

Hawaiian Experience Theatre will open in 1988 on Front Street at the site of the old Queen's Theatre. Each day there will be 13 showings of a 45 minute movie which emphasizes the Hawaiian culture and history. While the exterior will resemble a 1920's era cinema, a unique feature of this 150 guest facility will be the 60 by 30 foot screen which will encircle the viewer both around and above. The effect is a very realistic feeling for the feature film *Hawaii: Island of Gods*. Admission to this million dollar movie extraordinaire will be $5 for adults (student discounts). The first of these "experience theatres", which opened in Alaska, has proven so popular that it has become a top state tourist attraction.

The Wo Hing Temple on Front Street opened following restoration in late 1984. Built in 1912, it now houses a museum which features the influence of the Chinese population on Maui. Hours are 9-9 with an admission donation. The adjacent cook house has become a miniature theatre which features movies filmed by Thomas Edison during his trips to Hawaii in 1898 and 1906.

The **Whaling Museum** is located at the back of the Crazy Shirts shop on Front Street. No admission is charged.

The Sugar Cane Train is just outside Lahaina and will transport you between Kaanapali and Lahaina. One way for adults is $4.25, and children $2.00. Round trip for adults runs $6.50 and children $3.25. "Babes in arms are free." Special package options include train trips combined with lunch in Lahaina, a visit to the Baldwin House and the Carthaginian, or a trip in the glass bottom boat, the Lin Wai. Make your plans early as space is limited and sometimes the return trips are booked. The red double decker bus stops at the Wharf Shopping Center and in front of the Pioneer Inn to transport you to the Sugar Cane Depot.

The Lahaina Jodo Mission is located on the Kaanapali side of Lahaina, on Ala Moana Street near the Mala Wharf. The great Buddha commemorated the 100th anniversary of the Japanese immigration to the islands which was celebrated at the mission in 1968. None of the buildings are open to the public. The public is welcome to attend their summer O'Bon festivals. Check the papers for dates and times.

The oldest printing house west of the Rockies is located just outside of Lahaina on Lahainaluna Road. **Hale Pa'i** is open daily from 10 a.m. to 4 p.m. Phone 667-7040. Donations are appreciated.

Just outside Lahaina at Olowalu you can find some good examples of early **Hawaiian petroglyphs**. These rock carvings are believed to be the Hawaiian's first attempt at a written language. To reach the site you need to locate the dirt road on the Lahaina side of the Olowalu Store. Turn toward the mountains at a large silver-gray water tank and follow it up through the cane fields 3/10 of a mile. Look for cliffs on the right and some broken down wood stairs leading up to a walkway (to the right of the unsafe stairs). The petroglyphs are easily visible, along with other graffiti. The area is under the auspices of the Lahaina Restoration Foundation and they have hopes of restoring and preserving this historical landmark.

WHERE TO SHOP

Shopping is a prime fascination in Lahaina and it is such a major business that it breeds volatility. Shops change frequently, sometimes seemingly overnight, with a definite "trendiness" to their merchandise. It was a few years back that just about every other shop was a scrimshaw store or factory. Visitors could watch artisans creating pieces up close and personal. The next few years found the transformation to T-shirt stores. There still are many of these, but the clothing stores are diminishing in numbers. The theme now is art, art, art, with galleries springing up on every corner. It's a wonderful opportunity to view the fine work of the many local artists with no admission charge! Original oils, watercolors, acrylics, and carvings are on display, as well as fine quality lithographs.

Here are some shops that are unusual or favorites of ours and may be of interest to you.

Lahaina Galleries, 17 Lahainaluna Rd., and 728 Front Street, plus galleries in Kaanapali and Kapalua. Begun in 1976, they do a very good business. The art falls in the $500 – $30,000 range. Not all their pieces are by local artists, however, these are the most popular sellers.

The Harris Collection at 124 Lahainaluna Rd. (661-5556) features works in ceramics and bronze by many local Maui artists.

The Lahaina Print Sellers is located on the second floor of the Wharf Shopping Center, with other locations at Whaler's Village in Kaanapali, Wailea Shopping Center and at the Seaman's Hospital in Lahaina. They specialize in framed antique maps and old prints from around the world. It's an interesting place to browse. The items differ at each location. (Whaler's Village 667-7617 or 661-3579 at the Wharf.)

Island Sandals is tucked away in a niche of the Wharf Shopping Center near the postal center at 658 Front Street, Space #125, Lahaina, Maui, Hi 96761. (661-5110). Michael Mahnensmith is the proprietor and creator of custom-made sandals. He learned his craft in Santa Monica from David Webb who was making sandals for the Greek and Roman movies of the late 50's and early 60's. He rediscovered his sandal design from the sandals used 3,000 years ago by the desert warriors of Ethiopia. He developed the idea while living in Catalina in the 1960's and copyrighted it in 1978. The shoes are all leather, which is porous and keeps the feet cool and dry, with the exception of a non-skid synthetic heel. They feature a single strap which laces around the big toe, then over and under the foot, and around the heel, providing for comfort and good arch support. As the sandal breaks in, the strap stretches and you simply adjust the entire strap to maintain proper fit (which makes them feel more like a shoe than a sandal). This custom footwear can be fitted in the morning and ready for an afternoon pickup. The charge is $62 for the right shoe and the left shoe is free. Anyone who gets shoes from Island Sandals becomes an agent and is authorized to trace foot prints of others. Commissions are automatic when your sales reach the "high range." (However, you must like coconuts and bananas.) Michael stresses the importance of good footwear while on Maui, so stop in upon your arrival, or they can be ordered by sending a tracing of your foot and big toe (or having an authorized agent do so) along with $62 to Island Sandals. Michael also can assist with leather repair of your shoes, purses, bags, or suitcases.

Seegerpeople at the Wharf has an interesting photographic twist. Located in the lower level corner, they have on display hundreds of samples of their work. After a photographic sitting that lasts about half an hour with a dozen poses, selections are made. The prints are first adhered to a heavy plastic board, then to white plastic, after which the photographs are cut out closely around the head and body. This results in miniature people that can be creatively arranged and mounted on stands. They're not cheap, but they sure are fun. We enjoyed just looking at all their samples! A sitting, three mounted poses, and the stand runs about $100.

A three screen movie theater is scheduled to be added to the second level of the *Wharf Shopping Center*. Seating capacity will be for 330 people with parking space provided behind Burger King for 55 cars. The shopping center has also introduced "Aloha Friday" – a free show each Friday at 6:30.

Dan's Green House is located at 133 Prison Street (661-8412). A variety of beautiful tropical birds are for sale as well as an array of plants for shipping home. Their specialty is the Fuku-Bonsai "Lava Rock" plants. These bonsai are priced from $13 and are well packaged to tolerate the trip home.

Claire the Ring Lady is at 858-4 Front Street (667-9288). Claire, who learned her craft in Florence, can take your stone, (or choose one of hundreds of hers) and make it up to your specifications.

The Sea Breeze at 855 Front Street (661-0863), doesn't feature classy atmosphere, but it has been around for awhile. Its prices tend to be a little less for many of the tourist items than the other shops along the waterfront.

You will find the rebirth of the aloha shirt at **Kula Bay**, 120 Lahainaluna Road just off Front Street (667-5852). Stop by and have Charles Reeb show you their 100% cotton, made in the U.S.A., slacks, shorts and shirts. They've taken original patterns of aloha shirts from the 1930's, and 40's, updated and subdued the colors and then recreated them on comfortable all cotton fabric. Many of the shirts have coconut buttons! They are also available in solid colors. Check out the hammock upstairs. This is the first of ten planned shops throughout the islands.

An area slightly removed from Lahaina's Front Street is termed the industrial area. You'll find it located near the depot for the Sugar Cane Train. Besides Hilo Hattie's, there are a number of interesting shops. **The Bakery** is a personal favorite for some really fine pastries and breads. **MGM, Maui Gold Manufacturing** (661-8981) not only does standard repairs, but designs outstanding jewelry pieces. They can design something to your specifications, or choose a piece from one of their many photograph books. A limited number of pieces are ready made for sale as well. **J.R.'s Music Shop** (661-0801) has a large selection of Hawaiian tapes and records as well as just about any other type of music. They are located on the back side of The Bakery building. **Hilo Hattie's** offers a huge selection of tourist aloha wear and provides a free shuttle from the Wharf Shopping Center on Front Street in Lahaina.

Dickenson Square (On Dickenson St. off Front St.) is a new mall which bears a strong resemblance to Pioneer Inn. A clothing shop, several small shops, a quick stop grocery, and a new Nautilus center are located here, however, the main attraction is its historic architecture.

505 Front Street is a short walk past the Banyan Tree. Originally developed to be condominiums, it is now converted to shops and restaurants. The Old Lahaina Luau is held on the beachfront here.

The most dramatic new development to arrive on Maui is **The Cannery** which opened in 1987. This enclosed air conditioned mall is anchored by Safeway and Longs Drug Store (with a variety satellite stores, several small food outlets, and a restaurant.) The surfing display at **Hobie Sports** is interesting. A large parking area makes for convenient access. It's easy to spot as you leave Lahaina heading for Kaanapali. The original structure, built in 1920, was used as a pineapple cannery until its closure in 1963.

Construction is underway for West Maui's newest shopping center. As yet without a name, it will be located across from the Lahaina Shopping Center. The 150,000 square feet of retail space is scheduled to be completed by the summer of 1989.

BE FOREWARNED!!! If you have the time, do a lot of window shopping before you buy. The prices can vary significantly on some items from one store to another.

ACCOMMODATIONS - LAHAINA

Puamana   Plantation Inn
Lahaina Shores   Lahaina Hotel
Pioneer Inn   Lahaina Roads
Maui Islander   Puunoa

PUAMANA ★
P.O. Box 515, Lahaina, Maui, HI 96761. (808-667-2551) 1-800-367-5630
Agents: Whaler's Realty 1-800-367-6532, Jarvinen 1-800-421-0767

1 BR (4) $100– 60 / 95–150	3-night minimum
2 BR (6) 165–225 / 155–210	Limited maid service
3 BR (8) 190–270 / 175–260	Weekly & monthly discounts

228 units in a series of duplexes and four-plexes in a garden setting, this large oceanside complex resembles a residential community much more than a vacation resort. The wide variation in price reflects location in the complex, oceanfront to gardenview. Condo/car packages are also available.

LAHAINA SHORES
475 Front Street, Lahaina, Maui, HI 96761. (808-661-3309) 1-800-367-2972
Agent: Maui 800 1-800-367-5224, Rainbow Reservations 1-800-367-6092,
Whaler's Realty 1-800-367-5632, Kumulani 1-800-367-2954

Studio	$ 89– 99 / $ 82– 90	Mtn.v.–o.v.
1 BR	120–140 / 130–140	o.v.–o.f.
Penthouse	155–175 / 165–175	Mtn.v.–o.f.

Extra persons are $9/day, children under 6 no charge. 200 oceanfront units in this building of Victorian style offer air conditioning, lanais, kitchens, daily maid service, and laundry facilities on each floor. The beach here is fair and the water calm due to offshore reefs, but too shallow and corally for swimming. Lahaina proper is only a short walk away, plus this complex neighbors the Lahaina Shores Village which offers several restaurants and a small grocery store.

PIONEER INN   (Hotel)
658 Wharf St., P.O. Box 243, Lahaina, Maui, HI 96764.   (808-661-3636)
Agent: Maui 800 1-800-367-5224

Original building: shared bath, single $18, double $21, private bath, single
$22-24, double $25-27. New wing: lanais, private bath, air conditioning. Single
$36 outside, $39 courtyard. Double $39 outside, $42 courtyard, $52 superior.

If you want rustic, this is it, and the prices can't be beat. The original building
was constructed in 1901 as accommodations for interisland travelers. Pioneer Inn
has been a Lahaina landmark ever since. Many of the units in the old building
have shared baths and the furnishings are Spartan. Don't let the "new" in new
wing give you ideas of grandeur. This wing was added in 1966 and is a little more
modern, with each having a private bath. Here you are in the hub of activity in
Lahaina and sounds of the music downstairs will lull you to sleep. If you had
been a guest back in 1901, you would have been required to adhere to the following bizarre "house rules": "You must pay you rent in advance. You must not let
you room go one day back. Women is not allow in you room. If you wet or burn
you bed you going out. You are not allow to gambel in you room. You are not
allow to give you bed to you freand. If you freand stay overnight you must see
the mgr. You must leave you room at 11 am so the women can clean you room.
Only on Sunday you can sleep all day. You are not allow in the down stears in the
seating room or in the dinering room or in the kitchen when you are drunk. You
are not allow to drink on the front porch. You must use a shirt when you come to
the seating room. If you cant keep this rules please dont take the room".

MAUI ISLANDER   (Hotel)
660 Wainee St., Lahaina, Maui, HI 96761. (808-667-9766)
Agents: Maui 800 1-800-367-5224, Jarvinen 1-800-421-0767

Room-no kitchen (2) $82/72,   Studio (4) $94/84,   1 BR (4) $106/96

2 & 3 BR suites are available by combining 1-bedroom suites with connecting
studio rooms. This complex is located only a short walk from Lahaina, yet far
enough away to be peaceful. Daily maid service, pool, telephones, laundry
facilities, television, tennis courts.

PLANTATION INN ★
174 Lahainaluna Rd., Lahaina, Maui, HI 96761 (808-667-9225) 1-800-433-6815

Deluxe double with breakfast $95, front double with breakfast $109, suite with
breakfast $129, 3-bedroom poolside cottage/no breakfast $140. Optional dinner
$15 per person.

It's wonderful to see this kind of development in Lahaina. This new building has
all the charm of an old inn, while all the benefits of modernization. Filled with
antiques, hardwood floors, and stained glass, they also offer air conditioning,
refrigerators and even VCR's. Located a block from the ocean in the heart of
Lahaina, it also has a 12 foot deep tiled pool, and a spa. Developed by the owners
of Central Pacific Divers, they of course offer diving packages. An added bonus
is the outstanding Gerard's Restaurant which has relocated to the lobby and provides guest breakfasts and the option for dinner as well.

LAHAINA HOTEL (Hotel)
127 Lahainaluna Rd., Lahaina, Maui, HI 96761. (808-487-9919)

Rick Ralston, who also owns Crazy Shirts, has undertaken renovations at this ideally situated location. The transformation should be dramatic. Gone are the $25 a night "rustic" units. The new hotel will have 13 rooms for double occupancy priced "moderately expensive." Air conditioned and a turn-of-the-century motif. The plans include a restaurant and bar on the ground level which will provide a morning repast for this new "bed and breakfast" type establishment. Completion is expected for fall 1988. (As we go to press the only phone number is the central office of Crazy Shirts on Oahu, which is listed above.)

LAHAINA ROADS
1403 Front St., Lahaina, Maui, HI 96761. (808-661-3166) 1-800-624-8203

1 BR (2,max 4) $85/60,   2 BR (2,max 6) $109/82,   Penthouse (4) $170/120

Additional person $6/night, 7-night/3-night minimum, NO CREDIT CARDS. Maid service available upon request. 42 oceanview units, covered parking and elevator to upper levels. Microwaves, washer/dryer, cable tv.

PUUNOA
45 Pali Kai Place, Lahaina, Maui, HI 96761
Agents: Classic Resorts (808-667-1400) 1-800-642-MAUI

2 BR 3 bath o.f. (6) $480/450,   3 BR, 4 bath with loft (8) $600 –660 / 500–550

3-night deposit. Amenities include full size swimming pool, jacuzzi, his and hers sauna, and paddle tennis courts. Units include laundry rooms, lanais, master bath with jacuzzi, full bar and daily maid service. These ten luxury units are located on Puunoa Beach in a residential area just north of Lahaina. The beachfront has a coral reef which makes for calm conditions for children, but swimming or snorkeling are poor due to the shallowness and coral.

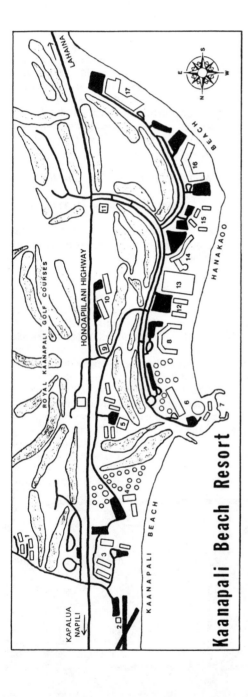

Kaanapali Beach Resort

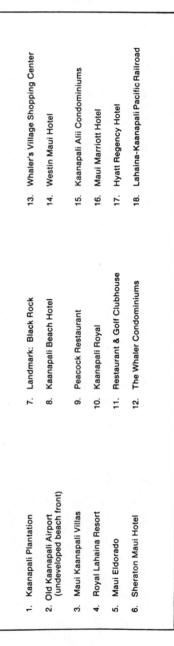

1. Kaanapali Plantation
2. Old Kaanapali Airport
   (undeveloped beach front)
3. Maui Kaanapali Villas
4. Royal Lahaina Resort
5. Maui Eldorado
6. Sheraton Maui Hotel

7. Landmark: Black Rock
8. Kaanapali Beach Hotel
9. Peacock Restaurant
10. Kaanapali Royal
11. Restaurant & Golf Clubhouse
12. The Whaler Condominiums

13. Whaler's Village Shopping Center
14. Westin Maui Hotel
15. Kaanapali Alii Condominiums
16. Maui Marriott Hotel
17. Hyatt Regency Hotel
18. Lahaina-Kaanapali Pacific Railroad

KAANAPALI

INTRODUCTION

The drive through Lahaina is quick (unless it's rush hour). All that is really visible are a couple gas stations, the old mill, a few nondescript commercial buildings, some backyards, and a Pizza Hut. Old Lahaina and the waterfront cannot be seen as they are a couple of large blocks off to the left. As you leave Lahaina, the vista opens with a view of the Hyatt Regency and the beginning of the Kaanapali Beach Resort three miles off in the distance. The resort is beautifully framed by the West Maui mountains on the right, the peaks of Molokai appearing to be another part of Maui in the background, the island of Lanai off to the left, and of course, the ocean. The name Kaanapali means "rolling cliffs" or "land divided by cliffs" and refers to the wide, open ridges that stretch up behind the resort toward Pu'u Kukui, West Maui's highest peak. The beaches and plush resorts here are what many come to Hawaii to find.

Kaanapali is an Amfac Development that began in the early 1960's with the first hotels, the Royal Lahaina and the Sheraton, opening in late 1962 and early 1963 respectively. The newest development is the transformation of the Maui Surf Hotel into the spectacular new Westin Maui Resort. The Kaanapali Resort, 500 acres along three miles of prime beachfront, is reputed to be the first large-scale planned resort in the world. There are six beachfront hotels and seven condominiums which total more than 5,000 rooms and units, two golf courses, 37 tennis courts, and a shopping village.

Now that the Kaanapali Airport has been closed, there are another 700 acres in the works for future development. The resort boasts the most convention space of any of the neighboring islands, with the Marriott, Westin Maui and the Hyatt Regency being popular convention locations. All the hotels are located beachfront, although some of the condos are situated above the beach in the golf course area. All are priced in the luxury range. The wide avenues and the spaciousness of the resorts lush green and manicured grounds are most impressive. No on-street parking and careful planning has successfully given this resort a feeling spaciousness. Nestled between a pristine white sand beach and scenic golf courses with a mountain range beyond, this may be the ideal spot for your vacation.

This may be paradise, but traffic congestion between Kaanapali and Lahaina may remind you more of L.A. Nonsynchronized traffic lights, roads designed for 20 years ago, and greatly increased traffic, have caused the four mile transit through Lahaina to Kaanapali (or Kaanapali to Lahaina) to consume over an hour during the afternoon rush (most other times there is only light traffic). Of deep concern to the government and residents alike, plans are underway to widen the road or create a by-pass. With the speed of bureaucracy though, actual development may be a few years away. The best tip is to avoid what seems to be the worst time of day, between 4 and 6 p.m.

BEST BETS: ***Hyatt Regency Maui*** – An elegant and exotic setting with a wonderful selection of great restaurants. ***Marriott*** – Beautiful grounds with a nice pool area and attractively decorated rooms. ***Westin Maui*** – A gorgeous new resort and a pool aficionados paradise. ***Kaanapali Alii*** – One of only three condominiums that are oceanfront. Luxurious, expensive and spacious. (Our choice to purchase with future lottery winnings!).

WHAT TO DO AND SEE

The Hyatt Regency and ***The Westin Maui*** must be put at the top of everyone's list of things to see. Few hotels can boast that they need their own wildlife manager, but upon entry you'll see why they do. Without spoiling the surprises too much, just envision the Hyatt with palm trees growing through the lobby, peacocks strolling by, and parrots perched amid extraordinary pieces of oriental art. The lagoon and black swans are spectacular. The pool area occupies two acres and features two swim-through waterfalls and a cavern in the middle with a swim up bar. A swinging bridge is suspended over one of the two pools and a huge slide offers added thrills for hotel guests. The newest project at Kaanapali is the Westin Maui. To appreciate this property, a little background may be necessary. The Maui Surf was the original hotel with the single curved building and a large expanse of lush green lawn and two pools. The transformation has been extraordinary. The pool areas are unsurpassed, with five swimming pools on various levels fed by waterfalls and connected by two slides. There are exotic birds afloat on the lagoons which greet you upon your arrival and glide gracefully by two of the hotel's restaurants. The oriental art collection surpasses even the Hyatts. Both resorts feature glamorous shopping arcades, with prices to match of course. Both developments were designed by the remarkable, champion hotel builder of Hawaii, Chris Hemmeter.

WHERE TO SHOP

Whaler's Village Shopping Center is located in the heart of Kaanapali. It offers several small shops for grocery items, as well as a bounty of jewelry and clothing shops, and several restaurants. A new multi-level parking structure is adjacent to the mall and parking is $1 for the first two hours or fraction thereof, and 50 cents for each additional half hour, with a $10 maximum charge. Restaurants can provide validation. The Whaling Museum, on the upper level, is free. (Donations are welcomed.) Historian Conrad Justel gives lectures on topics from scrimshaw to the life of a sailor. Call for times at 661-5992. Private group lectures are also a possibility. Near the front of the complex is a complete whale skeleton displayed along with models and information on many different whales. Waldens has a very good bookstore here with an excellent selection of Hawaiian literature. The mall is a pleasant place for an evening stroll and shop browsing, before or after dinner, followed by a seaside walk back to your accommodations on the paved beachfront sidewalk.

ACCOMMODATIONS - KAANAPALI

Hyatt Regency	Kaanapali Beach Hotel	Kaanapali Plantation
Marriott	Sheraton	International Colony Club
Kaanapali Alii	Royal Lahaina Resort	Maui Eldorado
Westin Maui	Maui Kaanapali Villas	Kaanapali Royal
The Whaler		

HYATT REGENCY ★ (Hotel)
200 Nohea Kai Drive, Lahaina, Maui, HI 96761. (808-661-1234) 1-800-228-9000

Terrace rooms $190, golf/mtn.v. $220, o.f. $260-290,
Golf suite $275, Regency Club* (mtn.v.) $320, (o.f.) $350, Ocean Suite $400
Deluxe Suite $750, Regency Suite $1,000, Presidential $2,000.

This magnificent complex is located on 18 beachfront acres and offers 815 rooms and suites. The beach here is beautiful, but has a steep drop-off. Adjoining Honokaoo Beach Park has a gentler slope into deeper water. *The Regency Club consists of certain floors that feature special services, including continental breakfast, evening cocktails and appetizers, and a complimentary health club membership. Room rates are based on single/double occupancy (for additional persons 13 years or older $25 charge per night/Regency Club level $45 charge per night.) 3 adults or 2 adults 2 children maximum per room. Numerous fine restaurants and an outstanding pool area are featured as well as an array of fine shops. Restaurants include Swan Court, Lahaina Provision Company, The Pavilion and Spats II. It's worth coming here just to look around!

MARRIOTT ★ (Hotel)
100 Nohea Kai Drive, Lahaina, Maui, HI 96761. (800-228-9290) 1-808-667-1200

Mtn./oceanview $185	Oceanview $210-225	Deluxe oceanview $250

This 720 room complex has a large, open lobby in the middle featuring an array of fine shops, as well as a physician's office. On site restaurants are Nikko's Steak House, Lokelani's, and the Kau Kau Bar.

KAANAPALI ALII ★
50 Nohea Kai Dr., Lahaina, Maui, HI 96761. 1-800-367-6090
Agents: Classic Resorts 1-800-642-MAUI, Condo Resorts 1-800-854-3823, Whaler's Realty 1-800-367-5632.

1 BR (2) gardenview $190/180	oceanview $230/215	
2 BR (4) gardenview $245/235	oceanview $285/270	oceanfront $360/345

Extra person $15/night, 3-night minimum. This is the newest condo development in Kaanapali. All 264 units are very spacious and beautifully furnished, with air conditioning, microwaves, washer/dryer, and include daily maid service. The 1-bedroom units have a den, which actually makes them equivalent to a 2-bedroom. Three lighted tennis courts, pool (also a children's pool), and exercise room. No restaurants on the property, but shops and restaurants are in easy walking distance. They charge for local phone calls from room. Cribs $10.

WESTIN MAUI ★ (Hotel)
2365 Kaanapali Parkway, Lahaina, Maui, Hi 96761. (808-667-2525)
Westin Central Reservations 1-800-228-3000.

Courtyard $180   Golf/Mtn. view $215   Oceanview $235   Oceanfront $275
Royal Beach Club $335   Suites $400 – $1,500

Rates are based on single or double occupancy. Third person add $20 (maximum
3 persons to a room). Family Plan offers no extra charge for children 18 or under
sharing the same room as parents. A 25% discount from room rate is available
for additional rooms occupied.

Under the direction of Chris Hemmeter, champion hotel builder in Hawaii, this
new resort offers 762 deluxe rooms, including 28 suites. The Westin Maui has an
ocean tower of 11 stories with 556 guest rooms and a beach tower with 206 guest
rooms and suites. Guest rooms are provided for those with disabilities as well as
non-smoking floors. The rooms have been designed in comfortable hues of
muted peach and beige. The top two floors of the new tower, house the Royal
Beach Club, which offers guests complimentary continental breakfast, afternoon
cocktails, reserved seating in the pool area and a guest relations coordinator.
While there are no tennis facilities on property, a shuttle provides convenient access to the nearby Royal Lahaina Tennis Center. Conference and banquet
facilities are available as well as an array of gift, art, and fashion shops. The
focal point of this resort is the "aquatic complex" which uses 650,000 gallons of
water for its meandering streams, many waterfalls and 25,000 square foot pool
area complete with two waterslides and a swim up jacuzzi tucked neatly away in
its own grotto. The pool areas are spacious and well arranged so that lounge
chairs are not packed tightly together. Nine restaurants and lounges overlook the
ocean, waterfalls and pools. The hotel spa includes complete exercise and weight
rooms, with steam, sauna and whirlpool baths. Tour the grounds with a guide to
learn more about the Westin's family of birds and their tropical surroundings.
(Three curators see to their care.) The artwork would put a museum to shame and
each piece was carefully selected and put in place by Chris Hemmeter. Numerous
nooks with comfortable chairs and more artwork provide intimate conversation
areas. Parents may appreciate the resort's Camp Keiki which offers activities and
care for children during summer, Easter and Christmas vacations.

THE WHALER ★
2481 Kaanapali Parkway, Lahaina, Maui, Hi 96761. (808-661-4861) Managed by
Village Resorts 1-800-367-7052. Agents: Condo Resorts 1-800-854-3823,
Maui Network 1-800-367-5221, Whaler's Realty 1-800-367-5632

S BR 1 bath (2)   o.v. $165/150   g.v. $150/135
1 BR 1 bath (4)   o.v. 205/195   g.v. 185/175
1 BR 2 bath (4)   o.v. 210/200   g.v. 190/180   o.f. $250/235
2 BR 2 bath (6)   o.v. 290/275   o.f. 345/325

Cribs $5 per night. $200 deposit, 3-night minimum, balance on check-in. 2-week
refund notice. Choice location in the heart of Kaanapali next to the Whaler's
Village Shopping Center and on an excellent beach front. Underground parking.

KAANAPALI BEACH HOTEL   (Hotel)
2525 Kaanapali Parkway,(P.O. Box 637), Lahaina, Maui, HI 96761.
(808-661-0011)   Agent: Amfac 1-800-227-4700 (Calif. 1-800-622-0838)

Standard garden $115 Superior courtyard $145 Deluxe $160 Deluxe o.v. $175
2 BR deluxe o.f. $210   Junior Suite (4) $175   Grosvenor Suite $300

Extra persons $15/night. 431 units located on the beach next to the Sheraton and
Black Rock and nearby Whaler's Village Shops. Air conditioning. Tennis
available at nearby Royal Lahaina. Try their whale-shaped swimming pool!
Restaurants on site include the Kaanapali Beach Hotel Koffee Shop and the Tiki
Terrace Restaurant. This hotel seems to be very popular for group tours.

SHERATON HOTEL   (Hotel)
2605 Kaanapali Parkway. (808-661-0031) 1-800-325-3535

Gardenview $170/150   Partial oceanview $195/175   Oceanview $215/200
Oceanfront cottages $250/225   Oceanview suites $350 - $750

Extra adults $25/night. This 511 unit hotel winds around the side of Black Rock
and was one of the first completed in Kaanapali. There are also eight-unit cottages on the grounds. The hotel is continuing to do some much needed updating
and renovations of the rooms. The beachfront here is excellent for snorkeling
and everyone comes here to enjoy the nearly tame fish. The only problem is finding a place to park if you're not staying here. The complex features a variety of
shops. Restaurants include The Discovery Room and Black Rock Terrace.

ROYAL LAHAINA RESORT ★
2780 Kekaa Drive,(P.O. Box 668) Lahaina, Maui, HI 96761. (808-661-3611)
Agent: Amfac 1-800-227-4700 (Calif. 1-800-622-0838)

Std. $115   Superior $155   Deluxe $180   Deluxe o.f. $200   Garden cottage $155
Oceanfront cottage $210   1 & 2 BR suites also available $375 - $950

514 units located on excellent Kaanapali Beach just north of Black Rock. All cottage suites have kitchens. Sailing Activities Center, 10 tennis courts, three swimming pools. Restaurants on the property include Royal Ocean Terrace, which
features a very good Sunday Brunch, and Chopsticks Restaurant. Nightly luaus
in the luau gardens.

MAUI KAANAPALI VILLAS
2805 Honoapiilani Hwy., Lahaina, Maui, 96761 (808-667-7791)   Agents:
Aston 1-800-367-5124, Whaler's Realty 1-800-367-5632, Kumulani
1-800-367-2954

Room with refrigerator $129/109   Studio with kitchen $129-155 / $119-135
1 BR with kitchen $165-195 / $145-175

Extra person $10. Located beachfront at Kaanapali, this was a part of the Royal
Lahaina Resort, and before that the Hilton. It was refurbished and converted into condominiums.

KAANAPALI PLANTATION

150 Puukolii Rd.,(PO Box 845) Lahaina, Maui, HI 96761 (808-661-4446)
Agents: Whaler's Realty 1-800-367-5632

1 BR (2,max 2) $ 85	Extra persons $10/night
2 BR (2,max 4) 95	7-day/3-day minimum
3 BR (2,max 6) 105	$150 deposit, 10-day refund notice

$10/night discount for 2-week stay or longer. Maid service every third day. NO CREDIT CARDS. 62 units in a garden setting situated on a hillside with ocean-view. Each unit has at least two baths, washer/dryers, ice makers, phones, and complimentary daily paper. No air conditioning, only ceiling fans. Tennis courts, BBQs, shuffleboard, and pool table in this complex which overlooks the Royal Kaanapali Golf Course.

INTERNATIONAL COLONY CLUB

2750 Kalapu Dr., Lahaina, Maui, HI 96761 (808-661-4070) 1-800-367-8047 ext. 419

1 BR (2) $85   2 BR (2) $95   Extra persons over age 2 $10/night

4-day minimum, longer during December holidays. $150 deposit refundable with 2 week notice prior to check-in. 44 individual low rise cottages with ocean view, terraces or lanais, and phones; only some have washer/dryers, but coin-op laundry is on premises. Maid service. Two swimming pools. One block to Kaanapali Beach. NO CREDIT CARDS.

MAUI ELDORADO

2661 Kekaa Drive, Lahaina, Maui, Hi 96761. (661-0021) 1-800-367-2967
Canada 1-800-663-1118.   Agents: Whaler's Realty 1-800-367-5632,
Maui 800 1-800-367-5224, Jarvinen 1-800-421-0767

S BR (1-2) $ 97–124 / 83–110	5-day minimum
1 BR (1-4) 127–149 / 113–135	Weekly/monthly discounts
2 BR (1-6) 179–229 / 167–216	Cribs $10/day

204 air conditioned units located on golf course. Variation of rates reflects location. Maid service on request. Three pools. Cabana on nearby beachfront.

KAANAPALI ROYAL ★

2560 Kekaa Dr., Lahaina, Maui, HI 96761. (808-667-7200)
Agents: Hawaiiana Resorts 1-800-367-7040, Whaler's Realty 1-800-367-5632

1 BR (2,max 4)	g.v. $120/110	golf view $130/120	o.v. $140/130
2 BR (2,max 6)	g.v. 160/140	golf view 170/150	o.v. 190/170

3-night minimum. The 2-bedroom units offer washer/dryers. These very spacious condos, 1,600 – 2,000 sq.ft., offer air conditioning, lanais, and limited maid service. On golf course overlooking Kaanapali.

HONOKOWAI

INTRODUCTION

As you leave the Kaanapali Resort there is a stretch of yet undeveloped beachfront still planted with sugar cane. This was the site of the old Kaanapali Airport. Resorts will be stretched along this beach within the next few years. Ahead four large condo complexes signal the beginning of Honokowai, which stretches north along Lower Honoapiilani Highway. Accommodations are a mix of high and low rise, some new, however, most are older. The beachfront is narrow and many complexes have retaining walls. A close-in reef fronts the beach and comes into shore at Papakea and at the Honokowai Park. Between the reef and beach is generally shallow water unsuitable for swimming or other water activities. The only wide beach and break in the reef for swimming and snorkeling is at the Kaanapali Shores. In late 1987, several condominiums made a major investment in saving the beachfront by building a seawall beneath the sand to prevent winter erosion. A number of the condominiums are perched on rocky bluffs with no sandy beach. Many people return year after year to this quiet area, away from the bustle of Lahaina and Kaanapali and where prices are in the moderate range. A couple of small grocery stores can be found nearby, but the only restaurant is at the Kaanapali Shores. Other eating options will mean a short drive. (The Embassy Suites Hotel will offer a restaurant when it opens in 1989.) The condominiums are individually owned for the most part, and the quality and care of each (or lack of) is reflected by the owner. Perhaps it is the shape of the sloping ridges of Pu'u Kukui that cause this area to be slightly cooler and cloudier with more frequent rain showers in the afternoon than at neighboring Kaanapali.

BEST BETS: ***Kaanapali Shores*** - A high-rise surround by lovely grounds on the best beach in the area. ***Papakea*** - A low rise complex with attractive grounds and pool. ***Embassy Suites Hotel*** - Opening 1989.

ACCOMMODATIONS - HONOKOWAI

Mahana Resort	Makani Sands
Maui Kai	Kaleialoha
Embassy Suites Hotel	Hale Royale
Kaanapali Shores	Hono Koa
Papakea	Hale Ono Loa
Maui Sands	Lokelani
Paki Maui	Hale Mahina Beach Resort
Honokowai East	Hoyochi Nikko
Honokowai Resort Apts.	Kuleana
Hale Kai	Polynesian Shores
Pikake	Mahinahina Beach
Hale Maui Apt. Hotel	Mahina Surf
Nohonani	Noelani
Kulakane	

MAHANA
110 Kaanapali Shores Place, Lahaina, Maui, HI 96761. (808-661-8751) Agents: Aston 1-800-367-5124, Whaler's Realty 1-800-367-5632, Kumulani 1-800-367-2954

S BR 1 bath (1-2) $139/119	3-night minimum
1 BR 1 bath (1-4) 165/145	
1 BR 2 bath (1-4) 164/145	
2 BR 2 bath (1-6) 210/190	

All units oceanfront. Two tennis courts, heated pool, central air conditioning, saunas, elevators, small pool area. Located on narrow beachfront with offshore coral reef precluding swimming and snorkeling. A better swimming area is 100 yards up the beach.

MAUI KAI
106 Kaanapali Shores Place, Lahaina, Maui, Hi 96761. (808-661-0002) 1-800-367-5635. Agents: Maui 800 1-800-367-5224, Kumulani 1-800-367-2954

Studio (1-3) $110/75   1 BR (1-4) $135/90   2 BR (1-6) $185/165

79 Units. Weekly/monthly discounts available. Visa and Mastercard accepted. 2-night deposit, 2-night minimum. Units offer central air conditioning, lanais, therapy pool, ping pong, paddle tennis, and laundry facilities on each floor. 5th person in room $6 per night. No charge children under 2.

EMBASSY SUITES HOTEL ★
Anticipate 1989 opening. For information phone 1-800-EMBASSY (central office)

KAANAPALI SHORES ★
100 Kaanapali Shores Place, Lahaina, Maui, Hi 96761, (808-667-2211) Agents: Aston 1-800-367-5124, Condo Resorts 1-800-854-3823, Whaler's Realty 1-800-367-5632, Kumulani 1-800-367-2954

S BR g.v. $139/119,	o.v. $149/129		Extra person $10/night
1 BR g.v. 165/145,	o.v. 185/165		Weekly discounts
2 BR g.v. 200/180,	o.v. 215/195,	o.f.$300/280	

Under 18 free in existing beds. 3-night minimum, 7-night minimum over Christmas holiday. 463 units, all offer telephones, free tennis, daily maid service, and air conditioning. Nicely landscaped grounds and a wide beach with an area of coral reef cleared for swimming and snorkeling. This is the only resort on north Kaanapali Beach that offers a good swimming area. Putting green, jacuzzi and the Beach Club Restaurant are all located in the pool area.

PAPAKEA ★
3543 L. Honoapiilani, Lahaina, Maui, HI 96761. (808-669-4848) 1-800-367-5637
Agents: Whaler's Realty 1-800-367-5632, Condo Resorts 1-800-854-3823,
Rainbow Reservations 1-800-367-6092

S BR (2) partial o.v. $104,	o.f. $117		Weekly/monthly discounts
1 BR (4) partial o.v. 119,	o.f. 149		2-night deposit
2 BR (6) partial o.v. 159,	o.f. 189		7-day refund notice

Add $20 per night between 12/20 – 3/31 and 7/1 – 8/31

Crib or roll-away $6/day. Christmas holiday 14-day minimum with no refunds after October 1. 364 units, two pools, two jacuzzi's, two saunas, tennis court, putting green, washer/dryers, BBQ area. South end of complex has a sandy beach. The shallow water is great for children due to protective reef 10-30 yards offshore, but poor for swimming or snorkeling. Very attractive and spacious grounds and pool area.

MAUI SANDS
3559 L. Honoapiilani, Lahaina, Maui, HI 96761. (808-669-4811) 1-800-367-5037
Agent: Rainbow Reservations 1-800-367-6092

1 BR (2,max 4)	standard $65,	garden $ 81,	ocean $98
2 BR (2,max 6)	standard 91,	garden 105,	ocean 12

Extra persons $8 night, 15% monthly discounts. Some of the 76 units have air conditioning. One of the first complexes to be built along this section of beach. Large boulders along beachfront. Limited maid service.

PAKI MAUI
3615 L. Honoapiilani, Lahaina, Maui, HI 96761. (808-669-8235) Agents:
Aston 1-800-367-5124, Condo Resorts 1-800-854-3823, Kumulani 1-800-367-2954

S BR (1-2) o.f. $119/ 99		2-night deposit
1 BR (1-4) g.v. 119/ 99		Cribs $2/night
1 BR (1-4) o.f. 140/120		Children under 2 free
2 BR (1-6) o.f. 165–175 / 145–155		

This complex surrounds a garden and waterfall. No air conditioning.

HONOKOWAI EAST
3660 L. Honoapiilani Hwy., Lahaina, Maui, HI 96761 (808-669-8355)
51 units, mostly studios, in a 4-story building. Minimum three month stay.

HONOKOWAI PALMS RESORT
3666 Lower Honoapiilani, Lahaina, Maui, HI 96761. (808-669-6130)
1-800-843-1633

1 BR (2,max 4) non-oceanview $40,	oceanview $45	Extra person $6
2 BR (2,max 6) non-oceanview 55		

40 units across road from Honokowai Beachfront Park. Weekly and monthly discounts. Deposit $150 or 25% of first 28 days. For rentals of 28 days or longer, each 28 days is payable in advance. Cancellations must be made 30 days prior to arrival. Maid service available for extra fee. NO CREDIT CARDS.

HALE KAI
3691 L. Honoapiilani Hwy., Lahaina, Maui, HI 96761. (808-669-6333)

1 BR (2) $75,   2 BR (4) $100

40 units. 3-night minimum except Christmas. Deposit is $200 –$250, refundable with 45 day notice. NO CREDIT CARDS. Weekly and monthly discounts. The beach is rocky, but the units do have lanais, kitchens, and a pool.

PIKAKE
3701 L. Honoapiilani, Lahaina, Maui, HI 96761. (808-669-6086)

1 BR (2,max 4) $62 $100 deposit, 3-night minimum
2 BR (4,max 6) 93   Extra persons $10/night – NO CREDIT CARDS

Central laundry area, telephones, private lanais. Weekly maid service.

HALE MAUI APARTMENT HOTEL
P.O. Box 516, Lahaina, Maui, HI 96761. (808-669-6312)

1 BR suite (2) $50–80   Extra persons $6/night

Weekly and monthly discounts. 3-day minimum, 7-day during Christmas. All 1-bedroom units sleep 5. Lanais, limited maid service. Radios in all suites, TV's available. Coin-operated washer/dryer. BBQ.

NOHONANI
3723 L. Honoapiilani Hwy., Lahaina, Maui, HI 96761. (808-669-8208)
Office open 9 a.m. – 5 p.m. Mon. – Sat.

1 BR (1-2) $85/80   2 BR (1-4) $104/96   Weekly/monthly discounts

Extra persons $10/night. $200 deposit with 60-day refund notice, 4-day minimum stay. NO CREDIT CARDS. All units are oceanfront, no sandy beach. Complex has large pool, telephones, and is one block to grocery store. Maid service on checkout.

KULAKANE
3741 L. Honoapiilani (P.O. Box 5238), Lahaina, Maui, HI 96761
(808-669-6119) 1-800-367-6088

1 BR 1 bath (1-2) $75   2 BR 2 bath (1-4) $115   10% monthly discount

42 oceanfront units, lanais but no sandy beach. $10 extra person. 5-night minimum, $300 deposit. NO CREDIT CARDS. The first and second floor units are all 1-bedroom. The third floor are 2-bedroom townhouses that sleep up to six.

MAKANI SANDS
3765 L. Honoapiilani Hwy., Lahaina, Maui, HI 96761. (808-669-8223)

1 BR (2) $ 70	Deposit varies, weekly/monthly discounts
2 BR (4) 95	3-night minimum, extra persons $10/night
3 BR (6) 130	Penthouse (6) $160

Dishwashers, washer/dryers, elevator. All 30 units oceanfront with small sandy beach. Weekly maid service.

KALEIALOHA
3785 L. Honoapiilani, Lahaina, Maui, HI 96761. (808-669-8197) 1-800-222-8688

Studio (1-2) mtn.v. $59   1 BR (1-4) o.v. standard $69,   deluxe $79

67 units in a 4-story building. 3-night minimum. Deposit equal to three nights stay, $7.50 extra persons over age 2. Refundable if cancelled 45 days prior to arrival. NO CREDIT CARDS. Washer/dryers. Maid service extra charge. Discounts (10-15%) for off season.

HALE ROYALE
3788 L. Honoapiilani, Lahaina, Maui, HI 96761. (808-669-5230)

HONO KOA
3801 L. Honoapiilani, Lahaina, Maui, HI 96761. (808-669-0979) 1-800-225-7215

1 BR 2 bath (1-4) g.v. $ 80- 95
2 BR 2 bath (1-6) g.v. 115-130,   o.v. $130-160,   o.f. $165-195

Advance deposit of two nights, refunded with 7 day cancellation notice. $15 extra person. Limited maid service. 28 units with washer/dryer, dishwasher, microwave, and telephone. BBQs, pool area jacuzzi. Visa and Mastercard accepted.

HALE ONO LOA ★
3823 L. Honoapiilani, Lahaina, Maui, HI 96761. (808-669-6362)
Agent: Real Hawaii 1-800-367-5108

1 BR 1 bath (4,max 4) g.v. $100 ($560 week) partial o.v. 105 (600) o.v. 110 (640)
2 BR 2 bath (6,max 6) g.v. 150 ($840 week) o.v. 160 (920) o.f. 170 (1,000)

67 oceanfront and oceanview units. Phones. Maid service extra charge. Beachfront is rocky. The units we toured were roomy and nicely furnished. Grocery store nearby.

LOKELANI
3833 L. Honoapiilani Hwy., Lahaina, Maui, HI 96761. (808-669-8110)
1-800-367-2976. Agent: Rainbow Reservations 1-800-367-6092

1 BR (ground floor) (1-2) $ 85/75   2 BR (townhouses) (1-4) $115/100

71

Weekly discount, 3-night minimum low season, 7-night high season, extra persons $7.50, $10 cancellation fee. Three night deposit, balance due two weeks prior to arrival. NO CREDIT CARDS. 36 beachfront oceanview units with washer/dryers and dishwashers. The one bedroom units are on beach level with lanai, two bedroom units are townhouses with bedrooms upstairs, lanais on both levels.

HALE MAHINA BEACH RESORT
3875 L. Honoapiilani, Lahaina, Maui, HI 96761. (808-669-8441)
1-800-367-8047 ext. 441. Agents: Rainbow 1-800-367-6092

1 BR (1-2) $100/90   2 BR (1-4) $135/120   Extra persons $10/night

4-day minimum plus deposit, balance on arrival. 52 units with phones, lanais, ceiling fans, microwaves, washer/dryer. BBQ area, jacuzzi. NO CREDIT CARDS.

HOYOCHI NIKKO
3901 L. Honoapiilani, Lahaina, Maui, HI 96761. (808-669-8343)
Agents: Rainbow 1-800-357-6092, Kihei Maui Vacations 1-800-367-8047 ext. 116

18 one-bedroom oceanview units ($70–80) on rocky beachfront. Extra persons $7/night. $100 to $200 deposit with 30-day refund notice low season; 60-day high season. Prepayment required. NO CREDIT CARDS. Cars are available upon request with a minimum 14-day rental. Rooms have extra long twin beds and some have doubles. Maid service on check-out. Half size washer/dryers in units.

KULEANA
3959 L. Honoapiilani Hwy., Lahaina, Maui, HI 96761. (808-669-8080)
U.S. Mainland 1-800-367-5633, Canada 1-800-237-8256

1 BR o.v. $75/70,   o.f. 85/80   2 BR $125/110

Weekly/monthly discounts. 3 night minimum stay. Extra persons $5. Children under 2 free. Cribs $4/night. 3-night deposit refundable with 14 day notice, 1-bedroom units also have queen size sofa bed in living room. Large pool, tennis court, volleyball, and activity center. A short walk to sandy beaches.

POLYNESIAN SHORES
3975 L. Honoapiilani, Lahaina, Maui, HI 96761. (808-669-6065)
U.S. Mainland 1-800-433-MAUI, from Canada call collect.

1 BR 1 bath (1-2) $ 85/ 80	$10/night weekly discount
2 BR 2 bath (1-4) 125/120	$200 deposit
3 BR 3 bath (1-6) 150/145	3-day minimum

Discounts for stays of 21 nights or more. 52 units on a rocky shore but nice grounds with deck overlooking the ocean. Telephones.

MAHINAHINA BEACH
4007 L. Honoapiilani, Lahaina, Maui, HI 96761.
Units available only through owners.

MAHINA SURF
4057 L. Honoapiilani, Lahaina, Maui, HI 96761 (808-669-6068) 1-800-367-6086

1 BR 1 bath (2,max 4) $ 95/75	5% weekly, 15% monthly discounts
2 BR 1 bath (2,max 6) 110/90	Extra persons $8/night over age 2
2 BR 2 bath (2,max 6) 115/95	$150 deposit, 3-wk. refund notice

56 one-bedroom and one-bedroom with loft units. Dishwashers, telephones, maid service available at hourly charge. NO CREDIT CARDS. Located on rocky shore, the nearest sandy beach is a short drive to Kahana.

NOELANI
4095 Lower Honoapiilani Rd., Lahaina, Maui, HI 96761. (808-669-8375)
1-800-367-6030 Agent: Maui 800 1-800-367-5224

S BR 1 bath (1-2) $ 65	3-night deposit
1 BR 1 bath (1-2) 85	2-week refund notice
1 BR 2 bath (1-4) 110	10% weekly discount
3 BR 3 bath (1-6) 130	20% monthly discount

50 oceanfront units; kitchens with dishwashers and washer/dryers only in 1, 2, and 3-bedroom units. Complex has two pools and maid service every 4th day. Located on a rocky shore, nearest sandy beach is short drive to Kahana. Credit cards accepted.

KAHANA

INTRODUCTION

To the north of Honokowai, and about seven miles north of Lahaina is a prominent island of high rise condos with a handful of two story complexes strung along the coast in its lee. This is Kahana. The beach adjacent to these high rises is fairly wide, but tapers off quickly after this point. Several of the larger complexes offer very nice grounds and spacious living quarters with more resort type activities than in Honokowai. The prices are lower than Kaanapali, but higher than Honokowai. Several restaurants and quick-stop groceries are located nearby.

BEST BETS: *Sands of Kahana* - Spacious units on a nice white sand beach.
Kahana Sunset - Low rise condos surrounding a secluded and beautiful cove and beach.

WHERE TO SHOP

There are a few shops in the lower level of the Kahana Manor. A site adjacent to this has been proposed for a new bowling alley and theater but construction has not yet begun.

ACCOMMODATIONS - KAHANA

Kahana Beach Hotel   Pohailani Maui
Kahana Villa   Kahana Reef
Sands of Kahana   Kahana Outrigger
Valley Isle Resort   Kahana Village
Royal Kahana   Kahana Sunset
Hololani

KAHANA BEACH HOTEL
4221 L. Honoapiilani, Lahaina, Maui, HI 96761. (808-669-8611)
Agent: Pleasant Hawaiian Holidays (package tours) 1-800-242-9244

All units offer oceanview. The studios sleep up to four and have kitchenettes. The 1 BR units have kitchens, 2 balcony lanais, living room with queen-size sofa bed, bedroom with 2 queen beds, 2 full-size baths, dressing room, and will accommodate 7. Coin-op laundry on premises. Nice, white sandy beach fronting complex.

KAHANA VILLA
4242 L. Honoapiilani, Lahaina, Maui, HI 96761.   Agents: Colony Resorts 1-800-367-6046, Condo Resorts 1-800-854-3823, Whaler's Realty 1-800-367-5632

1 BR 1 bath g.v. $105/ 90, o.v. $125/105, o.v. superior $145/125
2 BR 1 bath g.v. 145/125, o.v. 165/145, o.v. superior 175/155

Across the road from the beach. Units have microwaves, washer/dryers, telephones. Daily maid service. Sauna, tennis courts, store, restaurants.

SANDS OF KAHANA ★
4299 L. Honoapiilani, Lahaina, Maui, HI 96761. (808-669-0400)
Agents: Aston 1-800-367-5124, Condo Resorts 1-800-854-3823,
Rainbow Reservations 1-800-367-6092

1 BR 1 bath o.v. $205/185, o.f. $195/175, mtn.v. $165/145
2 BR 1 bath o.v. 219/199, o.f. 260/240
3 BR 2 bath o.v. 330/310, o.f. 300/280

196 units on Kahana Beach. Extra persons $10. Under age 18 free in existing space. Very spacious units with dishwasher, microwave, large lanai and washer/dryer. Daily maid service. High rise structure with pool, 3 tennis courts, putting green, children's pool, and hydro-spa. Restaurant on property. Nearby grocery store.

VALLEY ISLE RESORT
4327 L. Honoapiilani, Lahaina, Maui, HI 96761. (808-669-5511)
Agent: Rainbow Reservations 1-800-367-6092

1 BR 1 bath (2) o.v. $128/118,   o.f. $138/128,   Studio $128/118
2 BR 2 bath (4) o.v. $170/160

Prices are for stays of 1 to 3 days. Substantial discounts for 5 or more days (i.e. 5 day stay, low season studio is $65) Additional persons $10 (under 3 free), Payment in full 30 days prior to arrival. Weekly maid service. Partial air conditioning. Telephones. Located on Kahana Beach. On site restaurant and grocery store.

ROYAL KAHANA
4365 L. Honoapiilani, Lahaina, Maui, HI 96761. (808-669-5911) Agents: Resort Mgmt. 1-800-524-3405, Jarvinen 1-800-421-0767, Kumulani 1-800-367-2954

S BR 1 bath (1-3) o.v. $ 86/ 72	2-night deposit
1 BR 1 bath (1-2) o.v. 112/ 88	15-day refund notice
2 BR 2 bath (1-6) o.v. 136/108	
2 BR 2 bath (1-6) o.f. 166/142	

High-rise complex with 236 oceanview units on Kahana Beach. Underground parking and air conditioning. A nice pool area with sauna, also tennis courts, and ping pong. Most units have microwaves. Studios have kitchenettes. Near grocery stores.

HOLOLANI
4401 L. Honoapiilani, Lahaina, Maui, HI 96761. (808-669-8021) 1-800-367-5032
Agents: Rainbow Reservations 1-800-367-6092, Maui 800 1-800-367-5224

2 BR 2 bath (2,max 6) $120/110   Extra persons $10/night

7-day/3-day minimum. $150 deposit, full payment 30 days prior to arrival. Children under 3 free. NO CREDIT CARDS. 63 oceanfront units on sandy, reef protected beach. Grocery store on premises. Weekly maid service.

POHAILANI
4435 L. Honoapiilani, Lahaina, Maui, HI 96761. (808-669-6125)
Agent: Rainbow 1-800-367-6092

Studio (1-2) o.f. $80–90 / $65–75   2 BR 1 bath (1-4) g.v. $90/80

Extra person $10/night. 5-night deposit, 5-night minimum except 14 days over Xmas holiday. Payment in full 30 days prior to arrival. 10% monthly discount. Weekly maid service. VISA & MASTERCARD ACCEPTED. 114 units in a low rise complex with 2-bedroom units of town-house design located across road from beach and the studio and 1-bedroom units oceanside. 2 pools, 2 tennis courts, 2 paddle tennis areas, an activity center, and 4 shuffleboard courts.

KAHANA REEF ★
4471 L. Honoapiilani, Lahaina, Maui, HI 96761. (808-669-6491)
Agent: Condo Resorts 1-800-854-3823, Kumulani 1-800-367-2954

1 BR 1 bath (2,max 5)   o.v. $90/80 $200 deposit, extra persons $6/night

Limited number of studios available. 15% monthly discounts. Maid service daily except Sunday. 88 well-kept units. NO CREDIT CARDS.

KAHANA OUTRIGGER
4521 L. Honoapiilani, Lahaina, Maui, HI 96761. (808-669-5544) Agents: Rainbow
1-800-367-6092, Maui Network 1-800-367-5221, Whaler's Realty 1-800-367-5632

3 BR 2 bath (6) $207/180   3 BR 3 bath (6) $218/190

12 3-bedroom oceanview condo suites in this low-rise complex. Located on a narrow sandy beachfront. Units are spacious and appointed with lots of Italian tile. On a recent inspection we noticed that these beautiful units have not been well maintained. All units have microwaves and washer/dryers.

KAHANA VILLAGE ★
4531 L. Honoapiilani, Lahaina, Maui, HI 96761. (808-669-5111) 1-800-824-3065
Agent: Maui 800 1-800-367-5224, Kumulani 1-800-367-2954

2 BR o.v. $155/125,   o.f. $215/180 $300 deposit, balance prior to arrival
3 BR o.v. 190/150,   o.f. 215/175   10% monthly discount

Additional person $10. 5-day minimum. Bi-weekly maid service. Second level units are 1,200 sq.ft.; ground level 3-bedroom units have 1,700 sq.ft. with a wet bar, sunken tub in master bath, phones, Jenn-aire ranges, lanais, and washer/dryers. Pool area jacuzzi. Nice but narrow beach offering good swimming. Attractive townhouse units, NO CREDIT CARDS

KAHANA SUNSET ★
P.O. Box 10219, Lahaina, Maui, HI 96761. (808-668-8011) 1-800-367-8047 ext.354
Agents: Parker Pacific 1-800-426-0494, Maui 800 1-800-367-5224

1 BR 1 bath (2) o.v. $110   Extra persons $6/night
2 BR 2 bath (2) o.v. 140   including infants
2 BR 2 bath (2) o.f. 180   10% monthly discounts

90 units on a beautiful and private white sand beach. Units have very large lanais, telephones, and washer/dryers. Each unit has its own lanai, but they adjoin one another, adding to the friendly atmosphere of this complex. One of the very few resorts with a heated pool so that it's near the same temperature as the ocean, also heated children's pool, BBQs. You can drive up right to your door on most of the two bedroom units making unloading easy (and with a family heavy into suitcases that can be) and a real back saver.

NAPILI

INTRODUCTION

This area's focal point is the beautiful Napili Bay, around which as many complexes have been fitted as possible. A number are located right on the beach, others a short walk away. The condominium units here are low-rise, with prices mostly in the moderate range. The quality of the units vary considerably, but generally a better location on the bay and better facilities demands a higher price. The complexes are small, most under 50 units, and all but one has a pool. A small grocery store or two is within walking distance and, depending on your location, a couple of restaurants could be reached on foot. A new shopping center is scheduled for development here soon.

BEST BETS: *Napili Sunset* – Centered right on the edge of Napili Bay, rooms are well kept. *Napili Kai Beach Club* – A quiet facility on the edge of Napili Bay. Large grounds and a restaurant are on site. Resort activities are offered.

ACCOMMODATIONS – NAPILI

Honokeana Cove	Napili Bay
Napili Sands	Napili Sunset
Coconut Inn	Hale Napili
Napili Point	Napili Village Hotel
Napili Shores	Mauian
Napili Surf	Napili Kai Beach Club

HONOKEANA COVE
5255 L. Honoapiilani,(RR 1 Box 200) Lahaina, Maui, HI 96761.
(808-669-6441) 1-800-237-4948

1 BR 1 bath (2,max 2) $ 85	5-night minimum, 3-night deposit
2 BR 1 bath (4,max 4) 113	Weekly 10% discount, monthly 20%
2 BR 2 bath (4,max 4) 125	Extra person $9/night
3 BR 2 bath (6,max 6) 143	NO CREDIT CARDS
Townhouse A (4) $195 Townhouse B (4) $150	

38 oceanview units on Honokeana Cove near Napili Bay. Direct-dial phones. Attractive grounds, pool area spa. Maid service weekly only if staying two or more weeks.

NAPILI SANDS
Hui F Rd., Lahaina, Maui, HI 96761

44 studios and 88 one-bedroom units in 11 two-story buildings. One block to small grocery store and walking distance to bus stop and beach. Long term stays only.

COCONUT INN
Hui Rd., P.O. Box 10517, Lahaina, Maui, HI 96761. (808-669-5712)
1-800-367-8006
Agent: Maui 800 1-800-367-5224, Condo Resorts 1-800-854-3823

Studio (2) $70   1 BR (2) $80   loft (2) $85

Extra persons $7.50/night. 41 units in two story retreat about 1/4 mile above
Napili Bay. No oceanviews. Pool, spa, daily maid service. Attractive tropical
grounds. Complimentary continental breakfast by pool. Direct-dial room
phones.

NAPILI POINT
5295 L. Honoapiilani, Lahaina, Maui, HI 96761. (808-669-5611)   Agents: Aston
1-800-367-5124, Condo Resorts 1-800-854-3823, Kumulani 1-800-367-2954

1 BR 1 bath (2,max 4)   o.v. $140/120,   o.f. $150/130,   o.f $200/180
2 BR 2 bath (2,max 6)   o.v. 175/155,   o.f. 170-180 / $190 -200

Located on rocky beach, but next door to beautiful Napili Bay. Units have
washer/dryer, direct dial phones, daily maid service. Two pools.

NAPILI SHORES
5315 L. Honoapiilani, Lahaina, Maui, HI 96761. (808-669-8061)   Agents:
Colony Resorts 1-800-367-6046, Rainbow 1-800-367-6092,
Condo Resorts 1-800-854-3823

S BR (2,max 3)   garden $115/100,   o.v. $125/110,   o.f. $135/120
1 BR (2,max 4)   garden 135/120,   o.v. 150/135

CREDIT CARDS ACCEPTED. Extra persons $15/night, 15% weekly discount,
no minimum stay, daily maid service. 152 units on Napili Bay. Rooms offer
lanais and the one-bedroom units have dishwashers. Laundry facilities on
premises as well as two pools, hot tub, croquet, and BBQ area. Restaurant,
cocktail lounge and grocery store on property.

NAPILI SURF
50 Napili Place, Lahaina, Maui, HI 96761. (808-669-8002)
Agent: Maui 800 1-800-367-5224

Studio (2,max 3) g.v. $72, o.v. $82   1 BR (2,max 5) $112

Extra persons $12/night, 10% monthly discount, $200 deposit, 14-day refund
notice, 4-night minimum except 10-day during Christmas. NO CREDIT
CARDS. 53 units on Napili Bay. Two pools, BBQs, shuffleboard, lanais, daily
maid service, telephones, and laundry facilities.

NAPILI BAY
33 Hui Drive, Lahaina Maui, HI 96761. (808-669-6044)
Agent: Maui 800 1-800-367-5224

Studio (2,max 4) on ocean $90,   off ocean $75

Extra persons $8/night. (No charge children under 12.) 3-night minimum, 2-night deposit, 7-day refund notice, weekly and monthly discounts. Studio apartments offer 1 queen & 2 single beds, lanais, kitchens, daily maid service. Coin-op laundromat with public phones. Major credit cards accepted. This older complex on Napili Bay is neat, clean and affordably priced.

NAPILI SUNSET ★
46 Hui Rd., Lahaina, Maui, HI 96761. (808-669-8083) 1-800-421-0680
Agent: Jarvinen 1-800-421-0767

S BR 1 bath (2)	g.v.	$ 70,	$230 deposit	10% monthly discount
1 BR 1 bath (2)	o.f.	120,	394 deposit	3-day minimum
2 BR 2 bath (4)	o.f.	180,	591 deposit	NO CREDIT CARDS

41 units located on Napili Bay. Daily maid service. Fifteen day notice of cancellation for full refund. Telephones. These units have great oceanviews and are well maintained. A very friendly atmosphere.

HALE NAPILI
65 Hui Rd., Napili, Maui, HI 96761. (808-669-6184)
Agent: Maui 800 1-800-367-5224

Studio (2) garden $66,   o.f. $76 1 BR (2)   o.f. $86 NO CREDIT CARDS

Three-night minimum. Extra persons $7/night, $150 deposit, 7-day refund notice, monthly discounts. 18 units ocean-front on Napili Bay. Daily maid service and lanai. Laundry facilities on property. No pool.

NAPILI VILLAGE
5425 Honoapiilani, Lahaina, Maui, HI 96761. (808-669-6228) 1-800-336-2185

Studio (2) $75/65   Extra persons $6/night, 3-night deposit

All rooms have king or queen size beds, daily maid service. Free laundry facilities on premises. Located a short walk from Napili Bay.

MAUIAN
5441 Honoapiilani, Lahaina, Maui, Hi 96761. (808-669-6205) 1-800-367-5034

Studio garden $70/65, o.v. $75/70, o.f. $90/85   Extra person $6/night

3-day minimum, 3-night deposit, 14-day refund notice. 5% two week and 12% monthly discounts. Rental crib $6/night. NO CREDIT CARDS. Studio apartments with kitchenettes, one queen and two twin day beds, on Napili Bay. BBQ area. Courtesy phone in office and television only in recreation center.

NAPILI KAI BEACH CLUB ★
5900 Honoapiilani, Lahaina, Maui, HI 96761. (808-669-6271) 1-800-367-5030,
Canada 1-800-263-8183. Agents: Maui 800 1-800-367-5224,
Condo Resorts 1-800-854-3823

S BR (2) std.o.v.	$130,	dlx.o.v.	$150, dlx.o.f.	$175	2-night deposit
1 BR (2) std.o.v.	160,	dlx.o.v.	175, dlx.o.f.	190	14-day refund notice
2 BR (4) std.o.v.	175,	dlx.o.v.	195, dlx.o.f.	225	NO CREDIT CARDS

Extra persons $15/night, children under 3 free. Cribs $15. Units feature lanais, kitchenettes, telephones, and washer/dryer facilities. Complimentary tennis equipment, beach equipment, croquet, putters, and snorkel gear. Daily coffee and tea party in Beach Club. Sea House Restaurant located on grounds. Two tennis courts, 4 pools, very large jacuzzi. The grounds are extensive and the area very quiet. A relaxed and friendly atmosphere, a great beach, and a wide variety of activities may tempt you to spend most of your time enjoying this very personable and complete resort. About 30 new luxury units are being added in what used to be the large lawn area.

KAPALUA

INTRODUCTION

Colin Cameron chose 750 oceanview acres of his family's 20,000-plus acre pineapple plantation for the development of this up-scale resort. The result is the Kapalua Bay Resort and Villas which opened in 1979. The mood reflected here is serene with their philosophy being quality of food and service in a resort setting offering the ultimate in privacy and luxury living. The grounds are spacious and sport an abundance of flowering poinsettias at holiday time. Recent renovations have meant a new butterfly-shaped pool located nearer the beachfront, and the landscaping has transformed some of the well-groomed lawn into a little oasis with pools and waterfalls. More than 500-condominium units are located in the Ridge, Golf and Bay Villas, of which about 140 are available for rent. There are two 18-hole championship golf courses, a tennis center, and a shopping area with assorted boutiques and a deli/restaurant.

There are several excellent restaurants to choose from ranging from the small eatery located at the Kapalua shops, to the posh and elegant Bay Club Restaurant located on a scenic promontory of the bay.

Kapalua Bay is a small cove of white sand, nestled at the edge of a coconut palm grove. The protected bay offers good snorkeling and safe swimming for all ages.

BEST BETS: The Kapalua Hotel & Villas – This resort offers quiet elegance, top service, great food and all the amenities. Any of the condominium units in this area would be excellent, however, they are not all located within easy walking distance of the beach. A shuttle service is available. The condominiums at Kapalua offer spacious living and kitchen facilities.

WHAT TO SEE AND DO

Kapalua, "arms embracing the sea", is the most north-western development on Maui. The logo for Kapalua is the butterfly, and with a close look you can see the body of the butterfly is a pineapple. One might enjoy a stop at the elegant Kapalua Bay Hotel. The lobby bar is ideally situated for an evening refreshment, music, and sunset viewing. The resort has a small shopping mall located just outside the hotel. The resort grounds are attractive and spacious. The road beyond Kapalua is paved and in excellent condition, and offers some magnificent shoreline views. However, it finally turns to a rough dirt road and rental car agencies are not responsible should you choose this route. (A wash out has closed this section of the road for some time, check with the county to see if it is accessible.) After several miles the road returns to pavement before you arrive at Wailuku. Slaughterhouse Beach is only a couple of miles beyond Kapalua and you may find it interesting to watch the body surfers challenge the winter waves. Just beyond is Honolua Bay where winter swells make excellent board surfing conditions. A good viewing point is along the roadside on the cliffs beyond the bay. Continuing on, you may notice small piles of rocks. This is graffiti Maui style. They began appearing a few years ago and these mini-monuments have been sprouting up ever since.

WHERE TO SHOP

The Kapalua Shops are a showcase of treasures. Here you will find *The Kapalua Shop* (669-4172) where everything from men's and women's resort wear to glassware display the Kapalua butterfly logo. *Auntie Nani Children's Boutique* (669-5282) features fashions for infants to teens. *The Market Cafe* (669-4888) has fresh pastries, wines, gourmet items to go, or enjoy breakfast, lunch, or dinner at their restaurant.

ACCOMMODATIONS - KAPALUA

Kapalua Bay Hotel & Villas
Kapalua Bay and Golf Villas
The Ridge

KAPALUA BAY HOTEL & VILLAS ★
One Bay Drive, Kapalua, Maui, HI 96761. (808-669-5656) 1-800-367-8000

g.v. $195–230/175–295,   o.v. $280–295/255–280,   o.f. $350/325
Parlor Suite $410–590/410–560,
1 BR suite $650–850,   2 BR suite $900–1,050

317 units. Children 14 or younger free if sharing room with parent. Extra person $35 high season, $25 low season. Cribs available at no charge. 3-nights deposit high season, one low season. 14-day refund notice. Modified American Plan is available at $60 per person. Rooms have service bars and refrigerators, no kitchens. All are air conditioned and newly renovated with warm neutral shades of taupe, rose and muted terra cotta. Four-star restaurants include the Bay Club, Plantation Veranda and the Garden. A cafe is available in the shopping mall. Lovely grounds and located on an excellent beach. The complex also offers the Bay Course and the Village Course, two 18-hole championship golf courses designed by Arnold Palmer, and a tennis garden with 10-plexipave courts with 4 lighted for night play. The new pool is butterfly shaped and has been relocated nearer to the ocean. The expanse of lawn has given way to a tropical jungle with waterfalls and pools.

KAPALUA BAY AND GOLF VILLAS ★
Agents: Kapalua Hotel 1-800-367-8000, Condo Resorts 1-800-854-3823, Whaler's Realty 1-800-367-5632

1 BR (4, max 6)	fairway v. $215/185,	o.v. $265/230,	o.f. $335/295
2 BR (4, max 6)	fairway v. 315/250,	o.v. 365/300,	o.f. 435/370

2-night deposit, extra persons $35/25 per night. There are over 300 units in these combined complexes and most are lavishly furnished. Units include kitchens, washer/dryers, and daily maid service. Several pools and tennis courts are available.

THE RIDGE ★
Agents: Ridge Rentals (808-667-2851) 1-800-367-8047 ext. 133, Kapalua Hotel 1-800-367-8000, Whaler's Realty 1-800-367-5632, Kumulani 1-800-367-2954

1 BR 2 bath oceanview $165/90   2 BR 2 bath oceanview $240/135

(The above prices quoted were through Ridge Rentals) 5-day minimum, $100 deposit, 14-day notice of cancellation between 12/15 and 4/15, other dates 48 hours. Maid service only on check in. NO CREDIT CARDS.

MAALAEA

INTRODUCTION

Maalaea is the most centrally located area of the island. A short 10 minutes from Kahului, 30 minutes from Lahaina and 15 minutes from Wailea. Many visitors have returned to this very quiet corner of the island each year, and it is a popular area for local residents to live. The condominium complexes are small and low-rise. Most are located on the harbor wall offering a scenic view of the boats and their activities rather than on the beach. The prices are moderate with no resort activities. Maalaea is in the valley between the two volcanic peaks which results in increased afternoon winds.

BEST BETS: ***Makani A Kai*** – A small, attractive complex, the only one with a sandy beachfront.

WHAT TO DO AND SEE

The Maalaea Harbor area is a scenic port from which a number of boats depart for snorkeling, fishing and whale watching. Also in this area is Buzz's Wharf Restaurant, open for dinner. Fresh Island Fish Company, a seafood market, open Monday thru Saturday 10 – 5.

ACCOMMODATIONS – MAALAEA

Maalaea Yacht Marina   Maalaea Banyans
Milowai   Kana'I A Nalu
Maalaea Kai   Hono Kai
Lauloa   Makana A Kai
Island Sands

MAALAEA YACHT MARINA
Hauoli St., (RR 1, Box 380) Maalaea, Maui, 96793.
Agent: Kihei Maui Vacations 1-800-367-8047 ext. 4000

1 BR (2) $95/70   2 BR (4) $115/95

All units oceanfront, washer/dryers. Some units air conditioned.

MILOWAI
Hauoli St., Maalaea, Att: Jody Jones, RR 1 Box 380, Wailuku, Maui, HI 96793.
1-808-242-6553 or 1-800-367-8047 ext. 421
Agents: Kihei Maui Vacations 1-800-367-8047 ext.4000

1 BR $65/55   2 BR $95/75   weekly/monthly discounts

Units on Maalaea Harbor, all oceanview. Washer/dryer.

MAALAEA KAI

Hauoli St., Maalaea, Att: Jody Jones, RR 1 Box 380, Wailuku, Maui, HI 96793.
1-808-242-6553 or 1-800-367-8047 ext. 421
Kihei Maui Vacations 1-800-367-8047 ext. 4000

1 BR (2) $65/55   2 BR (4) $95/75   weekly/monthly discounts

70 units all with view. 3-night minimum, $100 deposit with balance due on arrival. NO CREDIT CARDS. Complex has laundry facilities, putting green, BBQ, and elevator to upper levels. Short walk to beach.

LAULOA

Hauoli Street,(RR 1 Box 383) Maalaea, Maui, HI 96793.
Agent: Bonnie Stoneburner, (808) 242-6575

2 BR, 2 Bath (4) 1-6 nights $90/75   7-29 nights $85/70

47 2-bedroom, 2-bath units of 1,100 sq.ft. $200 deposit, 4-night minimum. Maid service extra charge. NO CREDIT CARDS.

ISLAND SANDS

Hauoli St.,(P.O. Box 391) Wailuku, Maui, HI 96793.
Agents: Maui Accommodations 1-800-252-6284

Studio (2) $60/50   1 BR 1 Bath (2) $75/60   2 BR 2 Bath (4) $90/75

Extra person $7.50/night. Weekly and monthly discounts. 4-night minimum, $200 deposit with 15-day refund notice. Children under 12 free. Washer/dryers, dishwashers. Complex offers a Maui shaped pool, BBQ, air conditioning and elevators.

MAALAEA BANYANS

Hauoli St., (RR 1 Box 384) Maalaea, Maui, HI 96793. (808-242-5668)
Agents: Oihana 1-800-367-5234, Maui 800 1-800-367-5224

1 BR 1 bath (2,max 4) $75/65   Extra persons $10/night
2 BR 2 bath (4,max 6) 90/80   7-night minimum, No Credit Cards

76 units, all with oceanview, lanai, washer/dryer. Weekly and monthly discounts. Oceanfront on rocky shore, short walk to beach. Pool area jacuzzi, BBQs.

KANA'I A NALU

Hauoli Street, Maalaea. Agents: Makani A Kai Rental (808-244-5627)
1-800-367-6084, Oihana 1-800-367-5234

2 BR (4) o.v. $90/75, o.f. $100/90   Extra persons $7.50/night
5-day minimum, $200 deposit, 30-day refund notice. Weekly and monthly discounts. 90 units with washer/dryers in four buildings with elevators. No maid service, no phones. Short walk to beach.

HONO KAI
Hauoli St., Maalaea. Agent: Makani A Kai Rentals (808-244-7012)
1-800-367-6084

1 BR $60–70 / 55–65   2 BR $82–88 / $72–78   3 BR $93/83

46 units located on the beach. Choice of garden view, oceanview or oceanfront. Prices are for 5–6 day stays, additional discounts for weekly stays or longer. $200 deposit, 30 day notice. Laundry facilities, no room phones.

MAKANI A KAI
Hauoli St., Maalaea. Agent: Makani A Kai Rentals (808-244-7012)
1-800-367-6084

1 BR $70–85 / 65–80   2 BR $90–100 / $75–85

5-day minimum stay. Prices are for 5–6 days, additional discounts for weekly stay or longer. Air-conditioned units in 3 buildings with sandy beachfront. Choice of oceanfront or oceanview. Maid service on request. 30-day notice for refund Laundry facilities available.

NORTH KIHEI

INTRODUCTION

North Kihei is 15 minutes from the Kahului Airport and located at the entrance to Kihei. The condominiums here stretch along a gentle sloping white sand beach. A small shopping center is located at the Kealia condominium complex and another at the Sugar Beach Condominiums. Several snack shop restaurants can be found along Kihei road in this area. A little to the south down Kihei Road are additional restaurants, grocery stores and large shopping areas. Due to its location so near the valley of the island, this area usually has brisk afternoon winds.

BEST BETS: Kealia, Maalaea Surf* and *Sugar Beach Condominiums

ACCOMMODATIONS – NORTH KIHEI

Kealia   Kihei Kai
Sugar Beach   Maalaea Surf
Kihei Sands   Kihei Beach Resort
Nani Kai Hale

KEALIA ★
191 N. Kihei Rd., Kihei, Maui, HI 96753. (808-879-9159) 1-800-367-5222
Agent: Kumulani 1-800-367-2954

Studio (2) $68/53   1 BR (2) $75/60   2 BR (4) $110/95

Extra person $5. 10% monthly discount. $100 deposit, $10 cancellation fee. 100% payment required 14 days prior to arrival. 7-day minimum winter, 4-day in summer. Children under 5 free. NO CREDIT CARDS. 51 air conditioned units with lanais, washer/dryers, and dishwashers. Maid service on request. Shops and a sandwich shop nearby. (Limited number of 2-BR for rent.) The one bedroom units are a little small, but overall a good value.

SUGAR BEACH RESORT ★
145 N. Kihei Rd. Kihei, Maui, HI 96753. (808-879-7765)
Agent: Condo Rental HI 1-800-367-5242

1 BR g.v. $90/55,   o.f. $95/65   2 BR o.v. $160/105

Extra persons $7.50/night, weekly discounts. 215 units in several six-story buildings with elevators. Air conditioning. Jacuzzi, putting green, gas BBQ grills. Sandwich shop and quick shop market on location.

KIHEI SANDS
115 N. Kihei Rd., Kihei, Maui, HI 96753. (808-879-2624)

1 BR (2) $80/65   2 BR (4) $95/80   Extra persons $6/night

30 oceanfront air-conditioned units. 3-day minimum, $100 deposit with $10 cancellation fee. Full payment on arrival. No maid service or room phone. Laundry area. NO CREDIT CARDS. Shops and restaurant nearby.

NANI KAI HALE ★
73 N. Kihei Rd., Kihei, Maui, HI 96753. (808-879-9120) 1-800-367-6032
Agent: Village Rentals 1-800-367-5634

Studio w/o kitchen (2) $ 40/30   with kitchen $70/45
1 BR 2 bath (2)   o.f. 100/70,   o.v. $85/60
2 BR 2 bath (2)   o.v. 120/90

The above prices are based on 7-day minimum stay/3-day minimum stay. Extra persons $10/$8 night, children under 5 free. $100 deposit, 10% monthly discount. 46 units in a six-story building. Under building parking, laundry on each floor, elevator. No maid service, no room phones. Patio and BBQs by beach. Lanais have ocean and mountain views.

KIHEI KAI
61 N. Kihei Rd., Kihei, Maui, HI 96753. (808-879-2357) 1-800-367-8047 ext. 248

1 BR (2,max 4) $55–65 / 50–60   Extra persons $5/night

24 units in a two-story beachfront building. Minimum 7-days winter, 4-days summer. $100 deposit ($200 deposit for 2 weeks or longer.) Full payment upon arrival. NO CREDIT CARDS. Recreation area and laundry room. Units have air conditioning or ceiling fans. BBQ. On seven-mile stretch of sandy beach, near windsurfing, grocery stores. A very good value.

KIHEI BEACH RESORT
36 S. Kihei Rd., Kihei, Maui, HI 96753. (808-879-2477) 1-800-367-6034
Agents: Maui Network 1-800-367-5221, Jarvinen 1-800-421-0767

1 BR (2,max 4) $96/82   2 BR (4,max 6) $133/113

Extra person $9/night. 3-day deposit with 3-day refund notice low season, 30-day high season. Balance must be prepaid in full. Weekly and monthly discounts. NO CREDIT CARDS. 54 beachfront units with oceanview, phones. Resort offers central air conditioning, recreation area, elevator, maid service.

MAALAEA SURF ★
12 S. Kihei Rd., Kihei, Maui, HI 96753. (808-879-1267) 1-800-423-7953

1 BR 1 bath (2,max 4) $130/110 $200 deposit   Extra persons $8/night
2 BR 2 bath (4,max 6)   190/160   300 deposit   NO CREDIT CARDS

59 oceanview units in 8 two-story oceanfront buildings. Units have air conditioning and private phones. High season balance due 30 days prior to arrival, low season on arrival. 60-day refund notice with $10 cancellation fee during high season, 30-day notice low season. Microwaves. Daily maid service. Two pools, two tennis courts, shuffleboard. Laundry facilities in each building. Very attractive complex.

SOUTH KIHEI

INTRODUCTION

South Kihei began its growth after that of West Maui, but unfortunately with no planned system of development. The result is a six-mile stretch of coastline littered with more than 50 properties, nearly all condominiums, with some 2,400 units in rental programs. Few complexes are actually on a good beach, however, many are across Kihei Road from one of the Kamaole Beach Parks. A variety of beautiful beaches are just a few minutes drive away.

This section of East Maui has a much different feel than West Maui or Lahaina. There are no large resorts with exotically landscaped grounds, very few units on prime beachfront, and more competition among the complexes making this area a good value for your vacation dollar. (A good location for extended stays.)

Kihei always seemed to operate at a quieter and more leisurely pace than that of Kaanapali and Lahaina, but the last year or two has seen a significant upsurge of development, not of condos, but of small shopping complexes. Even parts of South Kihei Rd. have been repaved and regular curbs installed. These changes indicate the increasing tourist activity along with a corresponding loss of Kihei's once laid-back charm.

Restaurant selections remain more limited and many vacationers staying in condominiums utilize their kitchens. Most needs can be filled locally at one of several large grocery stores or the growing number of small shopping centers. Kahului, Wailuku, Wailea and Lahaina remain an easy drive for additional shopping and dining out.

BEST BETS: Laule'a – One of the newer complexes, these units are superbly furnished and well equipped (including microwaves). While not beachfront, they have a pool and jacuzzi and are located on a large grassy park that offers tennis courts. The ocean is on the other side of the park. Better beaches are a short drive away. ***Maui Hill*** – Situated on a hillside across the road from the ocean, some units have excellent ocean views. The three-bedroom units here are especially roomy and a good value for large families. ***Maui Vista*** – Across the road from the Kamaole I Beach, this four-story facility has two pools and tennis courts. A newer complex and an overall good value. ***Haleakala Shores*** – Across from Kamaole III Beach Park. ***Mana Kai Maui*** – One of Kihei's larger resorts, and the only on a very good beach.

WHAT TO DO AND SEE

The only historical landmark is a totem pole near the Maui Lu Resort which commemorates the site where Captain Vancouver landed. A few shops are sprinkled along the way, but no noteworthy points of interest.

WHERE TO SHOP

Every corner of Kihei is sprouting a new shopping mall. The complexes all seem to have quick markets, video stores and a T-shirt shop. The following are now complete. Several others are in various stages of construction.

The Rainbow Mall is a small center on the Mauka side (towards the mountain) of South Kihei Road offering an ice cream shop, restaurant, and a limited number of assorted small clothing and souvenir shops.

The Kihei Town Center offers a selection of shops including sporting goods, (rental equipment), novelty shops, grocery, and clothing. Located on South Kihei Road by McDonald's.

Kamaole Shopping Center is one of the larger new malls offering several restaurant selections, including Denny's (open 24 hours), the Canton Chef and Erik's Seafood Broiler.

Dolphin Shopping Center is another of the new small shopping malls, across from Kamaole I Beach.

Paradise Fruits ★ is a small but very popular open air produce market with a health food snack bar. They also carry some grocery and sundry items. Located next to Kihei Town Center and open 24 hours.

Azeka's Place Shopping Center is where you can pick up Azeka's famous ribs at the market to cook yourself. The International House of Pancakes and Luigi's are the restaurants here. The best source of books on this side of the island is located here at the Silversword Book Store.

ACCOMMODATIONS – SOUTH KIHEI

Nona Lani	Maui Sunset	Kihei Alii Kai
Kihei Holiday	Leilani Kai	Royal Mauian
Wailana Sands	Kihei Garden	Kamaole Nalu
Pualani	Hale Kai O Kihei	Hale Pau Hana
Sunseeker Resort	Waiohuli Beach	Kihei Kai Nani
Maui Lu Resort	Kihei Beachfront	Kihei Akahi
Kihei Bay Surf	Kapulanikai	Haleakala Shores
Menehune Shores	Island Surf	Maui Parkshore
Kihei Resort	Shores of Maui	Kamaole Sands
Koa Lagoon	Puuahoa	Hale Kamaole
Koa Resort	Kalama Terrace	Maui Hill
Kau Hale Makai	Lihi Kai	Kihei Surfside
Leinaala	Maui Vista	Mana Kai Maui
Luana Kai	Kamaole One	Surf and Sand
Laule'a	Kamaole Beach Royal	Hale Hui Kai

NONA LANI
455 S. Kihei Rd.,(P.O. Box 655) Kihei, Maui, HI 96753. (808-879-2497)

1 BR (2) $65 (7-night minimum) / $49 (3-night minimum)

Extra person $10/$7 night. 4-night deposit, 1-night non-refundable. No personal checks or credit cards. 8 cottages with kitchens, queen bed plus a day bed, full bath with tub and shower, and lanais. Large grounds, public phone, two BBQs., and laundry facilities. Located across the road from beach.

KIHEI HOLIDAY
483 S. Kihei Rd., Kihei, Maui, HI 96753. (808-879-9228)
Agent: Kihei Maui Vacations 1-800-367-8047 ext. 4000

2 BR (4) $80/65   Extra person $5 night under age 12, $10 over age 12

Units are across the street from the beach and have lanais with garden views. Pool area jacuzzi and BBQs. $100 deposit with full payment 30 days prior to arrival. Maid service on request. NO CREDIT CARDS.

WAILANA SANDS
25 Wailana Place, Kihei, Maui, HI 96753. (808-879-2026) 1-808-879-3661

Studio $40/30   1 BR $40-50 / 50-55   2 BR $85/65

Two-story structure. 3-day minimum, $100 deposit. NO CREDIT CARDS.

PUALANI TOWNHOUSES
15 Wailana Place, Kihei. Agents: Maui Accommodations 1-800-252-MAUI

1 BR 1½ bath townhouses $75/55

SUNSEEKER RESORT
551 S. Kihei Rd. (P.O. Box 276) Kihei, Maui, HI 96753. (808-879-1261)

6 units include studios with kitchenettes, one and two bedrooms. Weekly and monthly discounts available. No room phones, no pool. Across street from beach.

MAUI LU RESORT
575 S. Kihei Rd., Kihei, Maui, HI 96753. (808-879-5881)
Agent: Aston 1-800-367-5124

Hotel rooms: std. (2) $78/68,   superior (2) $88/78,   dlx. (2) $98/88
Cottages: 1 & 2 BR (1-3) $98/88

Extra persons $10, under 18 no charge. 180 units on 26 acres. Weekly and monthly discounts. Cottages have full kitchens, fans, but no air conditioning. Hotel rooms have air conditioning, small refrigerator and hot water maker. Pool is shaped like the island of Maui.

KIHEI BAY SURF

715 S. Kihei Rd. (Manager Apt. 110), Kihei, Maui, HI 96753. (808-879-7650
Agents: Kihei Maui Vac. 1-800-367-8047 ext. 4000, Kumulani 1-800-367-2954

118 studio units ($65/55, weekly discounts) in 7 two-story buildings. Pool area
jacuzzi, recreation area, gas BBQs, laundry area, tennis. Across road from
beach. Phones.

MENEHUNE SHORES

760 Kihei Rd., Kihei, Maui, HI 96753. (808-879-1508)   Agents: Gladys
Williams 1-808-879-5828, Kihei Maui Vacations 1-800-367-8047, ext. 4000

1 BR 1 bath (2) $ 65/ 52   Extra persons $5/night
2 BR 2 bath (2) 105/ 80 $100 deposit
3 BR 2 bath (5) 115/100

Rates quoted are for a seven-night stay. Slightly higher for 4 –6 day stay. 4-day
minimum. 115 units with dishwashers, washer/dryers and lanais in a 6-story
building. Recreation room, roof gardens with whale-watching platform, and
shuffleboard.

KIHEI RESORT

777 S. Kihei Rd., Kihei, Maui, HI 96753. (808-879-7441) 1-800-367-6006
Agents: Village Rentals 1-800-367-5634, Maui Accommodations 1-800-252-6284

1 BR (2) $75/55   2 BR (4) $95/75   Extra persons $7/night

64 units. 10% monthly discount. 7-night minimum, $100 deposit with 10-day re-
fund notice. BBQs, pool area jacuzzi. NO CREDIT CARDS.

KOA LAGOON

800 S. Kihei Rd., Kihei, Maui, HI 96753. (808-879-3002) 1-800-367-8030

1 BR 1 bath (2,max 4) $90/70   2 BR 2 bath (4,max 6) $120/90

Supreme units $10 per night more. Extra person $10 additional. $30 charged for 5
days or less. 10% discount for 30 days or longer. $100 deposit, full payment 30
days prior to arrival. 60-day cancellation notice. 14-day minimum stay during
Christmas holiday. 42 oceanview units with bar and ice-maker, washer/dryer.
Pool area pavilion, BBQ's.

KOA RESORT

811 S. Kihei Rd., Kihei, Maui, HI 96753. (808-879-1161) 1-800-367-8047 ext.407
Canada 1-800-423-8733 ext 407. Agent: Village Rentals 1-800-367-5634

1 BR 1 bath (2,max 4) $ 90/ 70   Extra persons $10/day
2 BR 1 bath (4,max 4) 105/ 70   Children under 2 free
2 BR 2 bath (4,max 6) 115/ 95   10% monthly discount
3 BR 2 bath (6,max 8) 140/120 $100 deposit
3 BR 3 bath (6,max 8) 165/145   NO CREDIT CARDS

5-night minimum stay. 54 units (2,030 sq.ft.) located on spacious 5 1/2-acre grounds in 2 five-story buildings across road from beach. Two tennis courts, spa, jacuzzi, putting green. Units have washer/dryers.

KAUHALE MAKAI (Village by the Sea)
930-938 S. Kihei Rd. Kihei, Maui, HI 96753. (808-879-8888)
Agents: Oihana 1-800-367-5234, Village Rentals 1-800-367-5634, Maui Accommodations 1-800-252-6284, Kihei Maui Vac. 1-800-367-8047 ext.4000 Kumulani 1-800-367-2954

Studio (2) $55/45   1 BR (2) $70/50   2 BR (4) $95–100 / $70 –75

$5 additional person. 5-night minimum. 169 air-conditioned units in 2 six-floor buildings with phones. Complex features putting green, gas BBQs, children's pool, sauna, laundry center. The beach here is usually strewn with coral rubble and seaweed.

LUANA KAI ★
940 S. Kihei Rd., Kihei, Maui, HI 96753. (808-879-1268)
Agents: Hawaiian Island Resorts 1-800-367-7042, Maui 800 1-800-367-5224, Kihei Maui Vacations 1-800-367-8047 ext.4000

1 BR (2)	g.v. $105/ 80,	o.v. $115/ 90	2-night minimum high season
2 BR (4)	g.v. 125/ 95,	o.v. 140/110	No minimum stay low season
3 BR (6)	g.v. 175/135		

Weekly discounts. Children under 12 free. Extra person $8. Towel service midweek, linen service weekly. 113 newer units with washer/dryers are located adjacent to a large oceanfront park with public tennis courts. The beach, however, is almost always covered with coral rubble and seaweed. The grounds are nicely landscaped and include a putting green, BBQ area, pool area sauna and jacuzzi.

LAULE'A ★
980 S Kihei Rd, Kihei, Maui HI 96753. (808-879-5247)
Agents: Hawaiiana Resorts 1-800-367-7040

1 BR (4) garden $ 95/ 75,	o.v. $110/ 90	7-night minimum high season
2 BR (6) garden 120/100,	o.v. 130/110	2-night minimum low season
3 BR (8) garden 160/140		

2-night deposit high season,1-night deposit low season, 7-day refund notice, under 18 free. Completed in 1984, these 58 units have been tastefully decorated in mauves and blues and have washer/dryer, microwave, phones and maid service every other day. Full prepayment. Only one building has an elevator to the upper floors. Fronting these condos is a public park with 4 tennis courts and a beach that is usually strewn with coral rubble. On-site are a nice pool area, separate men's and women's saunas, wet bar area, and hot tub.

LANAKILA
992 S. Kihei Rd., Kihei, Maui, HI 96753. (808-879-5629)
No vacation rentals, long term only

LEINAALA
998 S Kihei Rd, Kihei, Maui, HI 96753. (808-879-2235)
Agent: Oihana 1-800-367-5234

1 BR (2) $75/65   2 BR (4) $90/80   Extra persons $10 night

Monthly discounts. $100 deposit with 30-day refund notice. Tennis courts, all oceanview. NO CREDIT CARDS.

WAIPUILANI
1002 S. Kihei Rd., Kihei, Maui, HI 96753. (808-879-1458)

1 BR (2) $60/55   2 BR (4) $90/85

No charge for children under age 3, others $7 per night. Monthly discounts available. $100 deposit with full payment 30 days in advance of arrival. NO CREDIT CARDS.

MAUI SUNSET
1032 S. Kihei, Rd., Kihei, Maui, HI 96753. (808-879-1971)   Agents:
Village Rentals 1-800-367-5634, Kihei Maui Vacations 1-800-367-8047 ext.4000
Kumulani 1-800-367-2954, Island Dreamscape (808-779-5783) 1-800-367-8047

1 BR $85–90/70–75   2 BR $107–115/80–85   3 BR $150/125

Extra persons $7/night. 225 air-conditioned units in two buildings. Complex has tennis courts, sandbox, wading pool, pitch and putt golf green, sauna, and roof-top observation deck. Located on beach that appeared corally upon our inspection.

LEILANI KAI
1226 Uluniu St.,(P.O. Box 296) Kihei, Maui, HI 96753. (808-879-2606)

Studio(2) $55/40   1 BR(2) $70/50   1 BR dlx(4) $85/50   2 BR(4) $85/60

8 garden apartments with lanais. $200 deposit. Extra person $7.50. Full payment prior to arrival. $10 monthly discount. 4-day minimum stay. NO CREDIT CARDS.

KIHEI GARDEN ESTATES
1299 Uluniu St., Kihei, Maui, HI 96753. (808-879-6123)
Agent: Kihei Maui Vacations 1-800-367-8047 ext.4000

1 BR (2,max 4) $95/75   1 BR loft (4) $140/110   2 BR (4,max 6) $95/75

Weekly and monthly discounts. $100 deposit, full payment prior to arrival. NO CREDIT CARDS. Across road from beach. Jacuzzi, BBQ's.

HALE KAI O KIHEI
1310 Uluniu Rd., Kihei, Maui, HI 96753. (808-879-2757)

1 BR (2) $475/345 weekly   2 BR 2 bath (4) $625/495 weekly

Daily rates upon request. Extra person $8.50/night. 10% monthly discount. $100 deposit. 90-day cancellation notice high season, 30-day low season (less $20 handling fee). 59-oceanfront units with lanais in 3-story building. Sandy beachfront. Shuffleboard, putting green, BBQs, laundry, recreation area. Maid service on request for extra charge. NO CREDIT CARDS.

WAIOHULI BEACH HALE
49 Lipoa St., Kihei, Maui, HI 96753. (808-879-5396)

1 BR (2) $70/60 day,	$450/375 wk	Monthly discounts
2 BR (4) 90/80 day,	600/500 wk	Extra person $8/night

52 units in four 2-story buildings. Olympic-size lap pool, BBQ area, shuffleboard, near shopping center. Located on beachfront that is poor for swimming or snorkeling, often covered with coral or seaweed. Spacious lawn area around pool.

KIHEI BEACHFRONT RESORT
Located at end of Lipoa St.   AGENT: Maui Accommodations 1-800-252-6284

2 BR standard $100/75   2 BR deluxe $115/90

Extra person $7.50/night, $200 deposit, 4-night minimum. 8 oceanview 2-bedroom units with washer/dryers, microwaves, dishwashers, and air conditioning in a single 2-story building. Large lawn area fronting units. Lanais on upper level. Beach here is well protected. No elevator. Pool area jacuzzi.

KAPULANIKAI APTS
73 Kapu Place, PO Box 716, Kihei, Maui, HI 96753. (808-879-1607)

Units are oceanview 1 BR, 1 bath ($60/45) with private lanais or open terraces. Grassy lawn area in front. BBQ's, laundry facilities, pay phone on property.

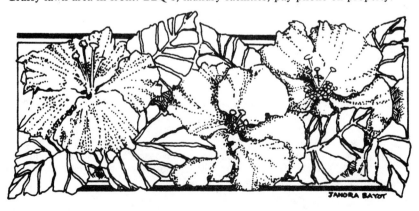

ISLAND SURF
1993 S. Kihei Rd., Kihei, Maui, Hi 96753.   AGENT: Kumulani 1-800-367-2954

This property is turning many of its units into commercial offices and shops on the first three floors. 82 1 BR ($60/50) and 2 BR ($85/65) units located across the road from the Kamaole I Beach Park. $100 deposit.

SHORES OF MAUI
2075 S. Kihei Rd., Kihei, Maui, HI 96753. (808-879-9140) 1-800-367-8002

1 BR $70/45 day, $490/270 wk   2 BR $90/60 day, $450/360 wk

$100 deposit, refundable with 30-day cancellation notice, full payment 30 days prior to arrival. Extra persons $5/night, monthly discounts. 3-day minimum (Christmas holiday 1-week minimum). NO CREDIT CARDS. 50-unit complex offers BBQs, tennis courts, spa, maid service on request. No room phones.

KALAMA TERRACE
35 Walaka, Kihei, Maui, HI 96753. No rental information available.

PUNAHOA
2142 Iliili Rd., Kihei, Maui, HI 96753. (808-879-2720)

Studio (2) $67/50   1 BR (2,max 4) $90–95/66–73   2 BR (2,max 6) $95/73

$200/100 deposit, 60-day refund notice. Extra persons $9/night. 10% discount for 14-day stay low season, or 28-day stay high season. 5-day minimum. 15-oceanview units with large lanais, telephones. No pool. Elevator, laundry facilities, beaches nearby. NO CREDIT CARDS.

LIHI KAI
2121 Iliili Rd., Kihei, Maui, HI 96753. (808-879-2335)

9 beach cottages, 16 apartments ($46 daily, $231 weekly) in two 2-story buildings. $100 deposit, 3-day minimum, 60/30 day refund notice. All units are 1 BR 1 bath with kitchen and lanai. Self-service laundromat. Next to Kamaole I Beach.

MAUI VISTA ★
2191 S. Kihei Rd., Kihei, Maui, HI 96753. (808-879-7966) 1-800-367-8047 ext.330   Agents: Oihana 1-800-367-5234, Kihei Maui Vacations 1-800-367-8047 ext.4000 Maui Accommodations 1-800-252-6284

1 BR (2,max 4) $90/69   2 BR (2,max 6) $110/89

5-night minimum stay low season, 7-night high season. Full payment prior to arrival. Monthly rates available. Credit cards accepted. 280 units in three 4-story buildings. Some units have air conditioning, some have washer/dryers. All have kitchens with dishwashers. The 2-bedroom units are on the fourth floor and are townhouses. The complex across road from nice beach. Some oceanview units. 6 tennis courts, 3 pools, BBQ's. We had some problem with sound carrying from a neighboring unit, but overall, a good value.

KAMAOLE ONE
2230 S. Kihei Rd., Kihei, Maui, HI 96753. (808-879-4811)
AGENT: Kumulani 1-800-367-2954

2 BR ground floor $130/110 , upper floors $120/100

$10 extra person charge. Two-story building. No elevators. Telephones. No pool. Beachfront. Washer/dryers in units. Compactors. Air conditioning and ceiling fans. Cable TV. Some have microwaves. NO CREDIT CARDS. Covered parking.

KAMAOLE BEACH ROYALE
2385 S. Kihei Rd.,(P.O. Box 370) Kihei, Maui, HI 96753. (808-879-3131)

1 BR 1 bath (2) $75/50   2 BR 2 bath (2) $90/65   3 BR 3 bath (2) $95/70

Extra person $10/$8 per night, 10% monthly discount, 4-day minimum, $200 deposit, balance due 30 days prior to arrival. $25 service charge. NO CREDIT CARDS. 64 units with washer/dryers and lanais in a single 7-story building across from Kamaole I Beach. Recreation area, elevator, roof garden.

KIHEI ALII KAI
2387 S. Kihei Rd., Kihei, Maui, HI 96753. (808-879-6770)
Agent: Kihei Maui Vacations 1-800-367-8047 ext.4000

1 BR (2) $75/60   2 BR (4) $90/70

Extra persons $5/night under age 12, over age 12 $10. $100 deposit, 7-day minimum winter, 5 summer. Full payment 30 days prior to arrival. NO CREDIT CARDS. All units have washer/dryers. No maid service. Complex features jacuzzi, sauna, two tennis courts, two BBQ areas, and shuffleboard. Across road and up street from beach.

ROYAL MAUIAN
2430 S. Kihei Rd., Kihei, Maui, HI 96753. (808-879-1262) 1-800-367-8009
Agent: Maui 800 1-800-367-5224

1 BR o.v. (2) $105/ 74,   sidewing (2) $ 95/68
2 BR o.v. (2) 120/ 79,   deluxe   (2) 130/88
3 BR o.v. (4) 175/130

$10 extra person (no charge children under age 6), 5-night minimum, $200/100 deposit with $25 cancellation fee. 14-day discounts summer/ 28-day winter. Maid service every 5 days. 107 units with lanai, washer/dryer, and phone in a 6-story building. Complex has shuffleboard, carpeted roof garden, and is next to Kamaole II Beach Park.

KAMAOLE NALU
2450 S. Kihei Rd.,(PO Box 157) Kihei, Maui, HI 96753 (808-879-1006)
U.S. Mainland toll free 1-800-367-8047 ext.435

2 BR 2 bath (2) o.v. $95/75, o.f. $105/85

$12 extra person. 3-day minimum. NO CREDIT CARDS. $200/100 deposit with
$25 cancellation fee. 36 2-bedroom 2-bath units with large lanai, dishwasher, and
washer/dryer in a 6-story building. Located on Kamaole II Beach with all units
offering oceanview. Weekly maid service provided during high season.

HALE PAU HANA
2480 S. Kihei Rd., Kihei, Maui, HI 96753. (808-879-2715) 1-800-367-6036
Agent: Condo Rental Hawaii 1-800-367-6036

1 BR 1 bath (2,max 4) $100   1 BR 2 bath (2,max 5) $100

25% discount daily rate for summer. Weekly and monthly discounts. $15 each
additional person. 78 oceanview units in four buildings. Limited maid service.
NO CREDIT CARDS. Laundry area, elevator. Located on Kamaole II Beach.

KIHEI KAI NANI
2495 S. Kihei Rd., Kihei, Maui, HI 96753. (808-879-9088) 1-800-367-8047 ext.332
Agents: Rainbow 1-800-367-6092, Kihei Maui Vacations 1-800-367-8047 ext.4000

180 1-BR (2) ($65/55) condo units with lanai or balcony in a 2 and 3-story struc-
ture. $7 extra person. 4-night minimum, $100 deposit with balance due 30 days
prior to arrival. This complex is one of the older ones along Kihei Rd. but it
boasts having the second largest pool on Maui. Laundry room and recreation
center. Across from Kamaole II Beach.

KIHEI AKAHI
2531 S. Kihei Rd., Kihei, Maui, HI 96753. (808-879-1881) 1-800-367-5242,
CANADA 1-800-663-2101   Agents: Kihei Maui Vac. 1-800-367-8047 ext.4000

Studio (2) $70/50   1 BR 1 bath (2) $82/55   2 BR 2 bath (4) $110/75

$5 per night discount after 6 nights. 10% monthly discount. $9 extra person
charge. 4-day minimum, $125 deposit, full payment 30 days prior to arrival. NO
CREDIT CARDS. 240 units with washer/dryers. Complex has two pools, tennis
court, BBQ's. Across from Kamaole II Beach Park.

HALEAKALA SHORES ★
2619 S. Kihei Rd., Kihei, Maui, HI 96753. (808-879-1218) 1-800-367-8047 ext.119

2 BR (1-4) $100/60 $6 extra person charge

Monthly discounts. 5-day minimum stay low season, 7-days high season. $100
deposit refundable with 30 day cancellation, $25 cancellation fee charged.
(Special restrictions during Christmas holiday) Maid service available for addi-

tional charge. Telephone available upon request. Located across the road from very nice Kamaole III Beach. NO CREDIT CARDS. Washer/dryers. Recreation room, putting green, covered parking, and shuffleboard. They also have a very thoughtful policy where returning guests receive an extra discount. A very good value, especially during summer season!

MAUI PARKSHORE
2653 S. Kihei Rd., Kihei, Maui, HI 96753. (808-879-1600)

2 BR 2 bath (4) $100/80   Extra person $7.50/5 per night

10% monthly discount. $100 deposit, payment in full upon arrival. NO CREDIT CARDS. 64 2-bedroom 2-bath oceanview condos with washer/dryers, and lanais in a 4-story building (elevator) across from Kamaole III Beach. Pool area sauna.

KAMAOLE SANDS
2695 S. Kihei Rd., Kihei, Maui, HI 96753. (808-879-0666)   Agents: Colony 1-800-879-6046, Maui Accomm. 1-800-252-6284, Condo Resorts 1-800-854-3823, Kihei Maui Vacations 1-800-367-8047 ext.4000, Kumulani 1-800-367-2954

1 BR 2 bath (2) $115–160/105–150   Weekly and monthly discounts
2 BR 2 bath (4) 150–190/140–180 $15 extra persons
3 BR 3 bath (6) 194–200/200–225

440 units in 10 four-story buildings. There are standard, superior and deluxe units with prices lower and higher than the average prices above. Includes daily maid service. 4 tennis courts, wading pool, 2 jacuzzi's and BBQs. Located on 15 acres across the road from Kamaole III Beach.

HALE KAMAOLE
2737 S. Kihei Rd., Kihei, Maui, HI 96753. (808-879-2698) 1-800-367-2970 Agents: Condo Rental Hawaii 1-800-367-5242, Kumulani 1-800-367-2954

188 units in 5 buildings (2 & 3-story, no elevator). Laundry building, BBQs, two pools, tennis courts. Some units have washer/dryers. Courtesy phone at office. Maid service only on check out. Located across road from Kamaole III Beach.

MAUI HILL ★
2881 S. Kihei Rd., Kihei, Maui, HI 96753. (808-879-6321)   Agents: Aston Hotels 1-800-367-5124, Maui 800 1-800-367-5224, Kumulani 1-800-367-2954

1 BR (1-4) $145/110   2 BR (1-6) $160/135   3 BR (1-8) $180/150

One night deposit. Refund 22 days prior to arrival during high season minus $10 handling fee. Full payment due 7 days prior to arrival. Limited maid service. 140 attractively furnished units with washer/dryers, air conditioning, microwaves, dishwashers, and large lanais. There are 12 buildings with a Spanish flair clustered on a hillside just above the Keawakapu Beach area. Upper units have oceanviews. The 3-bedroom units are very spacious. Large pool and tennis courts.

99

KIHEI SURFSIDE
2936 S. Kihei Rd., Kihei, Maui, HI 96753. (808-879-1488) 1-800-367-5240

1 BR 1 bath (2) $ 92/ 63   1 BR 1(1/2) bath (2) $102/70
2 BR 2 bath (4)   155/118

83 units. Extra persons $6. 3-night minimum, 3-day deposit, 14-day cancellation notice. 10% monthly discount. MAJOR CREDIT CARDS ACCEPTED. Maid service every fourth day. Short walk to Keawakapu Beach. Rocky shore with tide pools. Large grassy area and good view. Recreation area.

MANA KAI★
2960 S. Kihei Rd., Kihei, Maui, HI 96753. (808-879-1561) 1-800-525-2025

S BR 1 bath (2) $ 85/ 77,   includes car & breakfast (no kitchen)
1 BR 1 bath (2)   138/124,   includes car
2 BR 1 bath (2)   163/147,   includes car

1-night deposit. Full balance due 30 days in advance of arrival summer season, 60 days winter season. 14-day cancellation notice. Daily maid service. 8-story building with 92 units. The studio units are a room with an adjoining bath. The 1-bedroom units have a kitchen and the 2-bedroom units are actually the hotel unit and a 1-bedroom combined, with each having separate entry doors. Complex has laundry facilities on each floor, an oceanfront pool, and a restaurant off the lobby. This is the only major complex in South Kihei that is actually located on prime beachfront property. Keawakapu Beach is not only very nice but generally very underused.

SURF AND SAND HOTEL
2980 S. Kihei Rd., Kihei, Maui, HI 96753. (808-879-7744) 1-800-367-2958

Hotel unit $50–65   2 room suite $98–128 (kitchenettes extra charge)
Room and car special $64.90 for 2 people. 1-night deposit, 3-day refund notice

100 units with direct-dial phones, air conditioning, and daily maid service in several 2-story buildings. The exterior of these units is an Oriental brown and orange. The room we viewed was very small and, while ocean front, there was only one small window from which to view the surf, and no lanais. There was a small refrigerator, toaster, and hot plate. A shower, but no bathtub. The room appeared very clean, but the furnishings had seen a better day. Located on Keawakapu Beach and next door to the Outrigger Restaurant.

HALE HUI KAI
2994 S. Kihei Rd., Kihei, Maui, HI 96753. (808-879-1219)

2 BR 2 bath oceanview $120/100,   side oceanview $100/80

5-night minimum, $100 deposit, $5/day for over double occupancy. Oceanfront location, laundry facilities. Located on Keawakapu Beach.

WAILEA

INTRODUCTION

Wailea is a well planned and well manicured resort on 1,500 acres just south of Kihei. Developed by Alexander and Baldwin, Wailea encompasses two resort hotels and three condominium complexes which offer high quality accommodations. Included are two 18-hole championship golf courses, a large tennis center and a shopping center. The spacious and uncluttered layout is impressive, as are its series of lovely beaches.

The two resort hotels are the 600-room Maui Inter-Continental Hotel which opened in 1976, and the 350-room Stouffer Wailea Beach Resort (formerly the Westin Wailea) which opened in 1978. The Wailea condominium villages are divided into three locations, two are beachfront, while one is in the golf course. The Polo Beach condominiums are located a little beyond the Wailea resorts on Makena Road. The recently completed Wailea Point complex, located south of the Maui Inter-Continental, has 136 condos that are luxurious, expensive, and already sold out. The units are arranged in four-plexes which are laid out in a residential plan on 26-oceanfront acres. Privacy is maintained by a gate guard at the entrance.

Construction begun in late 1987 near Wailea's tennis club on Grand Champion Villas, another condominium project of 188 luxury units. Several new resorts are in the plans for the remaining undeveloped beachfront at Wailea.

BEST BETS: Stouffer Wailea Beach Resort - This complex happens to be our personal favorite with its tropical paradise grounds, Raffles' and Palm Court restaurants, and it fronts one of the island's finest beaches. ***Maui Inter-Continental Wailea*** - Also a topnotch resort hotel featuring a tropical flavor with lovely grounds, excellent restaurants, and two great beaches. ***Wailea Villas*** - Our choice among the three villages would be the Elua Village. These are more expensive, but beach aficionados will love having Ulua Beach at their front door. ***Polo Beach*** - Luxury units in a very secluded location with two small but good beaches.

WHAT TO SEE AND DO

The lovely Wailea beaches are actually well planned and nicely maintained public parks with excellent access, off-street parking and all but one have restrooms and rinse-off showers. Ulua Beach is our personal favorite. The Stouffer Wailea Beach Resort also offers lovely grounds you might want to enjoy.

WHERE TO SHOP

Wailea Shopping Center is located at the southern end of Wailea. It offers a small pantry market, a mall of shops, and a restaurant. The Stouffer Wailea Beach Resort and the Maui Inter-Continental Wailea both offer shopping areas.

ACCOMMODATIONS – WAILEA

Wailea Villas
  Ekolu
  Ekahi
  Elua

Stouffer Wailea Beach Resort
Maui Inter-Continental Wailea
Grand Champion Villas
Polo Beach Club

WAILEA VILLAS
3750 Wailea Alanui, Wailea Maui, HI 96753. (808-879-1595) 1-800-367-5246
Agents: Gerry Howell (Elua Condos only) (808-879-4726), Destination Resorts
(808-367-1595) 1-800-367-5246, Kihei Maui Vac. 1-800-367-8047 ext.4000,
Village Rentals 1-800-367-5634, Kumulani (only Ekahi condos) 1-800-367-2954

Some agents may have a limited number of units for slightly better prices than
those quoted above. The price range reflects location in the complex. Children
under 16 free in parent's room. Extra persons $20/night. 3-night minimum,
3-night deposit, 30-day refund notice, $25 cancellation fee. NO CREDIT
CARDS.

EKOLU VILLAGE	EKAHI VILLAGE	ELUA VILLAGE	
S BR (2)	$110/ 95		
1 BR (2) $150/130	165/135	garden-o.v. $180/150, o.f.	$225/195
2 BR (4) 200/160	225/175	garden-o.v. 260/230, o.f.	350/300
3 BR (6)		garden-o.v. 375/300, o.f.	450/400

Elua Village is located on Ulua Beach, one of the best in the area, we'd recommend these units. Ekahi Village is on the hillside above the south end of
Keawakapu beach, some units are right above the beach. Ekolu Village is a bit
farther away near the tennis center and the Wailea golf course.

STOUFFER WAILEA BEACH RESORT ★ (Hotel)
3550 Wailea Alanui, Wailea, Maui, HI 96753. (808-879-4900) 1-800-9-WAILEA

Mountainside and oceanside rooms $185–255, Mokapu Beach Club $350
One and two bedroom suites $475–1,200

347 units including 12 suites. A terrific value is the Entertainment Book (a
coupon type book purchased around the country) which offers a 50% discount
for mountain or oceanview rooms, for a maximum of 7 nights. Only available
low season, beginning April 15 on space available. This luxury resort covers 15
acres on beautiful Mokapu Beach. Each guest room is 500 sq.ft. and offers a
refrigerator, individual air conditioner, a stocked mini-bar, and lanai. The rooms
have been recently redecorated in soothing rose, ash and blue tones. An assortment of daily guest activities are available as well as summer and holiday programs for children. The Mokapu Beach Club is a separate beachfront building
with 26 units that features open beamed ceilings and rich koa wood furnishings,
plus a small swimming pool. The resort's restaurants are the Maui Onion, a poolside gazebo; Palm Court, serving international buffets in an open air at-

mosphere; Raffles', an award-winning gourmet restaurant; and a weekly Hawaiian luau. The Sunset Terrace, located in the lobby area, offers an excellent vantage point for a beautiful sunset and evening entertainment Monday – Friday, 5:30 – 8:30. The beach is excellent for both swimming and snorkeling. The grounds are a beautiful tropical jungle with a very attractive pool area which was recently expanded to include additional lounging areas and more jacuzzi pools.

MAUI INTER-CONTINENTAL WAILEA ★ (Hotel)
P.O. Box 779, Wailea, Maui, HI 96753. (808-879-1922) 1-800-367-2960
Honolulu 1-800-537-5589, Canada 1-800-268-3785

Minimum $175/145, Moderate $195/165, Maximum $215/185, Deluxe $275/225
Suites run $225–750. Full American Plan or Modified American Plan available
Golf, tennis and honeymoon package plans also available

The Maui Inter-Continental is situated on a low rocky promontory with a beautiful white sandy beach on either side. The restaurants in this lovely resort include the gourmet La Perouse, poolside Wet Spot, the Kiawe Broiler, and Lanai Terrace. There is also a Sunday brunch in the Makani Room. There are three pools, a seven-story tower and six low-rise buildings. The wonderful layout of this resort allows 80% of all guest rooms to have an ocean view. The pools are located in different areas of the property so that none are overly crowded. The units located nearest the beach afford wonderful private ocean views. Many complimentary daily activities and a weekly luau are available.

GRAND CHAMPION VILLAS
Located adjacent to the Wailea Tennis Center. 188 luxury condominium units on 12 oceanview acres. Construction began in late 1987, no rental information at time of publication. Units are on the market for $180,000 – $299,000.

WAILEA POINT VILLAGE
4000 Wailea Alanui, Wailea, Maui, HI 96753
Agent: The Vacation Co. 3750 Wailea Alanui, 808-879-0625

136 luxurious oceanview and oceanfront condominiums arranged in four-plexes which are laid out in a residential plan on 26-oceanfront acres. Privacy is maintained by a gate guard at the entrance.

POLO BEACH CLUB ★
20 Makena Rd., Wailea, Maui, HI 96753. (808-879-8847) Agents: Whaler's 1-800-367-5632, Colony Resorts 1-800-367-6046, Condo Resorts 1-800-854-3823

2 BR 2 bath (max 6) o.f.$260/215, o.v.$235/185 10% wkly, 25% mthly. discount

71 apartments in a single 8-story building located on Polo Beach. The units are luxurious and spacious. Underground parking, pool area jacuzzi. Very secluded area, although this end of the island is under further development.

MAKENA

INTRODUCTION

The area just south of Wailea is Makena, and the newest resort development on Maui. The project began with the completion of an 18-hole golf course in 1981. The Makena Surf condominium project opened in 1984. The Japanese conglomerate, Seibu, has a magnificent new resort, the Maui Prince Hotel, located at Maluaka Beach. Also in this area are several beaches with public access along dirt roads. They include Oneloa, Puuolai, Poolenalena and Palauea beaches. Since the area is not fully developed the end results remain to be seen. Shops are available at the Maui Prince Hotel.

BEST BETS: *The Maui Prince Hotel* and ***Makena Surf*** – Both are first class, luxury accommodations on very nice beaches.

WHAT TO DO AND SEE

Here are the last really gorgeous and undeveloped recreational beaches on Maui. Consequently, development in this area has met with a great deal of ongoing controversy. The new paved road (Makena Alanui) runs from Wailea past the Makena Surf and Maui Prince Hotel, exiting onto the Old Makena Rd. near the entrances to Oneuli (Black Sand) Beach and Oneloa (Big Makena)–Puuolai (Little Makena) Beaches. Past Ahihi Kinau Natural Reserve on Old Makena Rd. you will traverse the last major lava flow on Maui, which still looks pretty fresh after some 250 years. The road is very rough but passable and ends at La Perouse. (See BEACHES for more information).

ACCOMMODATIONS - MAKENA

Makena Surf   Maui Prince Hotel

MAKENA SURF ★
96 Makena Alanui Rd., Makena 96753 (808-879-1331) (1-800-367-8047 ext.510
U.S. or Canada 1-800-423-8733 ext.510.), Destination Resorts 1-800-367-5146

1 BR (2) $240–265 / $180–205	Prices listed are 2 or 3 nights
2 BR (2) 285–310 / 210–235	Discounts for 4 nights or longer
3 BR (4) 375–405 / 300–330	Extra person $15/night

Located 2 miles past Wailea. All units are oceanfront and more or less surround Chang's Beach. These very spacious and attractive condos feature central air conditioning, fully equipped kitchens, washers and dryers, wet bar, whirlpool spa in the master bath, telephones and daily maid service. Two pools, and four tennis courts are set in landscaped grounds. Three historic sites found on location have been preserved.

MAUI PRINCE ★ **(Hotel)**
6400 Makena Alanui, Makena 96753 (808-874-1111), Reservations: 1-800-321-6284

Partial o.v. $170, o.v. $200, o.v. prime $230, o.f. $250,
O.f. prime $270, mtn.v. suites $350, o.f. suites $600–700

In sharp contrast to the sophistication of some of the Kaanapali resorts, the Maui Prince radiates understated elegance in traditional Japanese fashion. Its simplicity in color and design, with an Oriental theme, provides a tranquil setting and allows the beauty of Maui to be reflected. The central courtyard is the focal point of the resort with a lovely traditional water garden complete with a cool cascading waterfall and ponds filled with gleaming fish. The rooms are tastefully appointed in cool neutral hues and equipped with the comfort of the guests in mind. The units have two telephones and a small refrigerator which is stocked with complimentary fresh fruit and sparkling water. Fresh flowers are provided in each and a yukata (summer kimono) is available for use during the guest's stay. A morning paper and 24-hour full room service add to the conveniences. There is plenty of room for lounging around two circular swimming pools, one with a three-foot depth, the other five-feet deep. Maluaka Beach (called Nau Paka by some locals) is the sandy crescent which fronts the hotel, offering good snorkeling and swimming. The resort is comprised of 1,700 acres and currently has one eighteen hole golf course with plans for several more courses in the future. On site restaurants include The Prince Court, Hakone and Cafe Kiowai.

WAILUKU AND KAHULUI

INTRODUCTION

The twin towns of Wailuku and Kahului are located on the northern, windward side of the island. Wailuku is the county seat of Maui and Kahului houses not only the largest residential population on the island, but also the main airport terminal and deep-water harbor. There are four motel-type accommodations located around the Kahului Harbor. While the rates are economical and the location is somewhat central to all parts of the island, we cannot recommend staying in this area for other than a quick stopover that requires easy airport access. This side of the island is generally more windy, overcast and cooler with few good beaches. While we feel there is little reason to headquarter your stay in this area, there are a few good reasons to linger.

WHAT TO DO AND SEE

Kahului has a very colorful history, beginning with the arrival of King Kamehameha I in the 1790's from the big island of Hawaii. The meaning of Kahului is "winning" and may have had its origins in the battle which ensued between Kamehameha and the Maui chieftain. The shoreline of Kahului Bay began its development in 1863 with the construction of a warehouse by Thomas Hogan. By 1879 the sugar cane industry had grown and created the need for a landing at the bay, and in 1881, the Kahului Railroad Company was set up. The city of Kahului grew rapidly until 1900 when it was purposely burned down to destroy the spreading of a bubonic plague outbreak. The reconstruction of Kahului created a full-scale commercial harbor, which was bombed along with Pearl Harbor on December 7, 1941. After World War II, a housing boom began, with the development of reasonably priced homes to house the increasing number of people moving to the island. The expansion has continued ever since.

Wailuku is the county seat of Maui and is experiencing a rebirth. It is often overlooked by visitors who miss out on some wonderful local restaurants and limited, but interesting shopping.

A *"Walking Tour of Wailuku Town"* guidebook is available for $2 at the Wailuku Main Street office, 68 Market St., next door to the old Iao Theater. Phone 244-3888.

Don't limit your excursion to the few shops on the corner of Market and Main streets. Wandering farther down Market will take you to some interesting shops. *Traders of the Lost Art* at 158 Market is operated by Tye Hartall. If you're lucky, he will be in and the shop open. On such occasions a variety of native carvings and primitive ritual art, which he brings back regularly from the secluded Sepik River area of Papua in New Guinea, will be on display. Next door a big Hawaiian Santa will greet you in front of the antique shop *Things from the Past. Alii Antiques* is next door. (See RESTAURANTS – Wailuku for some wonderful eating options).

107

Kaahumanu Church, Maui's oldest remaining church was built in 1837 at High and Main Streets in Wailuku.

Hale Hoikeike in Wailuku houses the *Maui Historical Society* and is known as the *Bailey House* (circa 1834). To reach it, follow the signs to Iao Valley and you will see the historical landmark sign on the left side of the road. It's open daily from 9 a.m. to 3:30 p.m., and a small admission is charged. Here you will find the Bailey Gallery, (once a dining room for the female seminary that was located at this site), with paintings of Edward Bailey done during the 19th century. His work depicts many aspects of Hawaiian life during earlier days. Also on display are early Hawaiian artifacts and memorabilia from the missionary days. The staff is extremely knowledgeable and friendly. They also have for sale an array of Hawaiian history, art, craft and photographic books available at prices LESS than other Maui bookstores. Originally, the Royal Historical Society was established in 1841, but it was not reactivated as the Maui Historical Society until 1956. The museum was dedicated on July 6, 1957, then closed for restoration on December 31, 1973 and reopened on July 13, 1975. Of special interest are the impressive 20″ thick walls that are made of plaster using a special missionary recipe including goat hair. The thick walls provided the inhabitants with a natural means of air conditioning.

The *Maui Jinsha Mission* is located at 472, Lipo Street, Wailuku. One of the few remaining old Shinto Shrines in the state of Hawaii, this mission was placed on the National Register of Historic Places in 1978.

The *Halekii and Pihana State Monuments* are among Maui's most interesting early Hawaiian historical sites. Both are of considerable size and situated on the top of a sand dune. These temples were very important structures for the island's early Alii. Their exact age is unknown, although one resource reported that they were used from 1765 to 1895. The Halekii monument is in better condition as a result of some reconstruction done on it in 1958. Follow Waiehu Beach Road across a bridge, then turn left onto Kuhio Place and again on Hea Place. Look for and follow the Hawaii Visitors Bureau markers. Some say the Pihana Heiau was built by the menehunes (Hawaii's little people), others believe by the Maui chiefton, Kahekili.

The *Iao Valley* is a short drive beyond Hale Hoikeike. Within the valley is an awesome volcanic shaft that rises 2,250 feet and is known as the Iao Needle. Parking facilities are available and there are a number of hiking trails. A recent addition is the *Tropical Gardens of Maui*. This botanical garden features the largest selection of exotic orchids in the Hawaiian islands. Stroll the grounds where they grow, and visit their gift shop filled with tropical flowers and Maui made products. Plants can be shipped home. Snack bar and picnic tables available. Phone 244-3085.

The *Heritage Garden/Kepaniwai Park* (244-3656) is an exhibit of pavilions and gardens which pay tribute to the culture of the Hawaiians, Portuguese, Filipinos, Koreans, Japanese and Chinese. Picnic tables and BBQ's available for public use. Located on Iao Valley Rd. Free admission, open daily. Public swimming pool for children is open daily from 9 a.m. to noon and again from 1 until 4:30.

Pacific Brewing Company, which produces Maui Lager beer, invites individuals or groups to tour their brewery. They are located on Imi Kala St. at the Millyard in Wailuku and open for tours 9 a.m. to 4 p.m. Call 244-0396 to schedule groups or for more information.

Just outside Wailuku in Waikapu is the *Maui Plantation*. which opened in 1984. Fifty acres have been planted with sugar cane, bananas, guava and other island produce. A ten acre visitor center includes exhibits, a marketplace, nursery and restaurant. A steep $5 is charged for a ride through the plantation on a trackless train, but it is interesting to see how the various tropical plants grow.

Baldwin Beach – See the section on BEACHES for Baldwin Beach and others in the area.

The Maui Zoological and Botanical Gardens are open 9-4 daily with FREE admission. Go up Kaahumanu to Kanaloa Street and turn by the Wailuku War Memorial Center. The zoo is on the right hand side. This is a zoo Maui style, with a few pygmy donkeys, sheep, goats, monkeys, Galapogos turtles, birds and picnic tables.

The Kanaha Wildlife Sanctuary is off Route 32, near the Kahului Airport, and was once a royal fish pond. Now a lookout is located here for those interested in viewing the stilt and other birds which inhabit the area.

A popular Saturday morning stop for local residents and visitors alike is *The Swap Meet* ★ held at the Kahului Fairgrounds (located off Pu'unene Hwy 35). For a fifty-cent admission (children free) you will find an assortment of vendors selling local fruits and vegetables, new and used clothing and household items and many of the same souvenir type items found at higher prices in gift shops. This is also the only place to get true spoonmeat coconuts. These are fairly immature coconuts with delicious mild and soft (to very soft) meat. We stock up on a weeks supply at a time. Free parking. Hours are 8 a.m. to noon. NOTE: The fairgrounds may be changing locations in mid-1988, for information call 877-3100.

The *Alexander and Baldwin Sugar Museum* ★, is located at 3957 Hansen Rd., in Puuene. Puuene is on Highway 35 between Kahului and Kihei, the tall stacks of the working mill are easily spotted. The museum is in a home that had been used since 1902 to house superintendents of the sugar mill. Memorabilia include the strong-box of Samuel Thomas Alexander and an actual working scale model of a sugar mill. The displays are well done and are very informative. Monday thru Friday 9:30 – 4 Admission charge: $2 adult visitors, $1 adult Maui residents. Visiting students 6-17 years $1. Maui students 6-17, 50 cents. Children under 6 are free. Call 871-8058.

WHERE TO SHOP

There are three large shopping centers in Kahului, all on Kaahumanu Street. The relatively new *Maui Mall* is only a two-minute drive from the airport. It offers two large grocery stores, Star and Safeway, and a large Long's Drugs which is great for picking up sundry items. They also have a variety of small shops and restaurants. The older *Kahului Shopping Center* is lined with Monkey pod trees and is filled with local residents playing cards. This mall did not appear to be as well kept up, but you will find an interesting drug store (TODA) that has a very reasonable luncheonette and some assorted shops. The largest shopping center is *Kaahumanu* with 47 shops and restaurants. It offers the largest selection of clothing, gift and department stores (Sears and Liberty House included). If you don't have accommodations with a kitchen, you might want to pick up a styrofoam type ice chest at one of these centers and stock it with juices, lunch meats and what not to enjoy in your hotel room. Hopefully, your accommodations will offer complimentary ice. Wailuku has no large shopping centers, but a cluster of shops down their Main Street makes for interesting strolling.

ACCOMMODATIONS - KAHULUI

Maui Hukilau   Maui Beach
Maui Palms   Maui Seaside

One advantage to choosing this area for headquarters is its proximity to Kahului Airport and its somewhat central location to all other parts of the island. Room rates are very economical and all run $40–60 a night. The motels are clustered together on the Kahului Harbor. The beach in this area is not suitable for swimming. In Wailuku there are no short-term places to stay.

MAUI HUKILAU (808-877-3311)

MAUI PALMS (808-877-0051)   Agent: Hawaiian Pacific 1-800-367-7040. They offer free airport pickup, in-room phones.

MAUI BEACH (808-877-0051)   Agent: Hawaiian Pacific 1-800-367-7040. They feature air-conditioned rooms, free airport service.

MAUI SEASIDE 1-800-367-7000, Our preference is this newer complex which has spacious rooms with refrigerators.

111

UPCOUNTRY and onward to HALEAKALA

INTRODUCTION

The Western slopes of Haleakala are generally known as upcountry and consist of several communities including Makawao and Pukalani. The higher altitude, cooler temperatures and increased rainfall make it an ideal location for produce farming. A few fireplace chimneys can be spotted in this region where the nights can get rather chilly. Accommodations are limited to two small lodges in Kula and a few cabins which are available with the park service for overnight use while hiking in the Haleakala Crater.

WHAT TO DO AND SEE

Enroute to upcountry is Pukalani, and the last stop for gas. There are also several places to enjoy a hearty meal. (See RESTAURANTS).

Haleakala means "house of the sun" and is claimed to be the largest dormant volcano in the world. The crater is truly awesome and it is easy to see why the old Hawaiians considered it sacred and the center of the earth's spiritual power. While free to visitors for many years, there is currently a $3-per car charge for admission to the crater, U.S. residents age 62 and older remain free. The most direct route is to follow Hwy. 37 from Kahului then left onto Hwy. 377 above Pukalani and then left again onto Hwy. 378 for the last 10 miles. While only about 40 miles from Kahului, the last part of the trip is very slow, with numerous switchbacks and bicycle tours doing the 38 mile downhill coast. Two hours should be allowed to reach the summit. Sunrise at the crater is a popular and memorable experience, but plan your arrival accordingly. Many visitors have missed this spectacular event by only minutes. The Maui News, the local daily publication, prints daily sunrise and sunset times. The park offers a recording of weather and viewing conditions which can be reached by calling 877-5124. The ranger's number is 572-7749. Be sure you have packed a sweater as the summit temperature can be 30 degrees cooler than the coast and snow is a winter possibility. Mid-morning from May to October generally offers the clearest viewing. However, fog can cause very limited visibility and a call to that recorded number may save you a trip.

At the park headquarters, you can obtain hiking and camping information and permits. Day-hike permits are not required, however, they do request you complete a registration form at the trail head and deposit it in the box provided. The first stop beyond the headquarters is Kalahaku Overlook. Here you can see the rare silversword which takes up to 20 years to mature, then blooms once in July or August, only to wither and die in the fall. Keep your eye out for the many animals which inhabit the volcano. Wild pig, goats, as well as the Nene goose are among the local residents. Hunting is permitted on a limited basis (seasonal) in the crater. Check with the ranger for information.

At an elevation of 9,745 feet is the visitors' center which provides an assortment of information on the crater. It is open daily from about 9 a.m. to 3 p.m. (hours may vary subject to staff availability). The ranger gives an hourly talk which is well worth the wait. A short distance by trail will bring you to the Puu Ulaula outlook. This glassed-in vantage point is the best for sunrise and is the highest point on Maui. The view on a good day, is nothing short of awesome. The crater is seven miles long, two miles wide, and 3,000 feet deep. A closer look is available by foot or horseback (see RECREATION AND TOURS – Horseback riding.) A unique excursion begun by Cruiser Bob's is a 33-mile downhill ride on a specially designed bike. (See RECREATION & TOURS – Biking).

The park service maintains 30 miles of well-marked trails, three cabins and two campgrounds. The closest cabin is about seven miles away from the observatory. Arrangements for these cabins need to be made 90 days in advance and selection is made 60 days prior to the dates requested by a lottery-type drawing. For more information, write: Superintendent, Haleakala National Park, P.O. Box 369, Makawao, Maui, HI 96768.

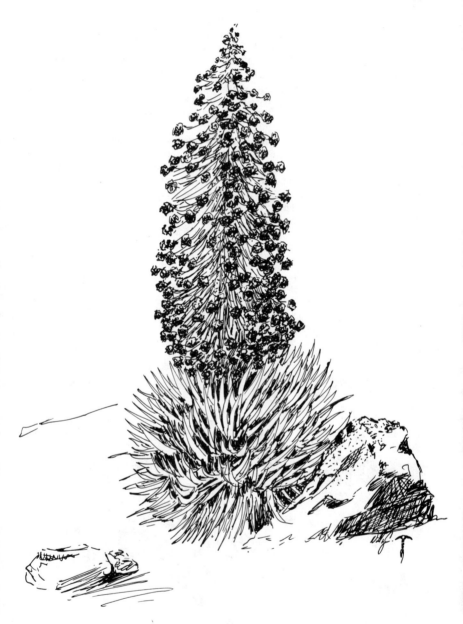

Silversword

Short walks might include the three-fourth mile Halemauu Trail to the crater rim, one-tenth mile to Leleiwi Overlook, or two-tenth mile on the White Hill Trail to the top of White Hill. Caution, the thin air and steep inclines may be especially tiring. (See RECREATION AND TOURS –Hiking.)

Science City can be seen beyond the visitor center, but it is not open to the public. It houses a solar and lunar observatory, operated by the University of Hawaii, television relay stations, and a Department of Defense satellite station.

IF TIME ALLOWS, THERE IS MORE OF UPCOUNTRY TO BE SEEN.

The Kula area offers rich volcanic soil and commercial farmers harvest a variety of fruits and vegetables. Grapes, apples, pineapples, lettuce, artichokes, tomatoes and, of course, Maui onions are only a few. It can be reached by retracking Hwy. 378 to the Upper Kula Road where you turn left. The protea, a recent floral immigrant from South Africa, has created a profitable business. *The Botanical Gardens* (878-1715) offers close-hand views with admission charged, adults $2.50, children 50 cents, 9 a.m. – 4 p.m.

Poli Poli State Park is high on the slopes of Haleakala, above Kula at an elevation of 6,200 feet. Continue on Hwy. 377 past Kula and turn left on Waipoli Rd. If you end up on Hwy. 37, you've gone too far. Look for the road sign indicating Poli Poli, it's another 10 miles to the park over a road which deteriorates to deep ruts and is often muddy. A 4-WHEEL DRIVE IS REALLY A NECESSITY FOR THIS ROAD. The park offers miles of trails, a picnic area, restrooms, running water, a small redwood forest and great views. A cabin, which sleeps up to 10, is available through the Division of Parks, P.O. Box 537, Makawao, Maui, HI 96768.

Wine making is reappearing after an absence of nearly 40 years. Approximately 9 miles past the Kula Botanical Gardens on Hwy. 37, is the Ulupalakua Ranch. *The Tedeschi Vineyards* (879-6058), part of the 30,000 acre ranch, made its debut in 1974. The tasting room is located at the Ranch (not at the vineyards themselves) in the old jail and provides samples of their pineapple, champagne and red table wines.

If you continue on past the ranch on Hwy. 37 it's another very long 35 miles to Hana with nothing but beautiful scenery. Don't let the distance fool you. It is a good 3-hour trip, at least, over some fairly rough sections of road, which are not approved for standard rental cars. During recent years this road has been closed often to through traffic due to severe washouts. Check with the county to see if it is currently passable. If you're not continuing on, we suggest you turn around and head back to Pukalani and Makawao. Unfortunately, the Ulupalakua Road down to Wailea has been closed due to a dispute between the Ranch and the county. It is hoped that this or some other access between upcountry and the Kihei/Wailea area will soon be developed. On the way down you can go by way of Makawao, the colorful "cowboy" town, and then on to Paia. Both have several good restaurants. (See RESTAURANTS – Upcountry).

WHERE TO SHOP

The town of Makawao offers a western flavor with a scattering of shops down its main street, a few restaurants and numerous grocery stores. We recommend the **Komoda Store** for its popular bakery.

The Pukalani Shopping Center is a new mall with a grocery store and small shops.

WHAT TO SEE AND DO

The **Hui Noeau Visual Arts Center** may at first seem a little out of place, located at 2841 Baldwin Avenue, down the road from Makawao. However, there could not be a more beautiful and tranquil setting than at this estate, built in 1917, by Harry and Ethel Baldwin. In addition to a gift shop, which is open year round, classes and workshops are also offered. Ethel Baldwin was one of the founders of Hui Noeau some 50 years ago, and the society has been located at this site for about 10 years. Call for current class schedule and, if you are on Maui during the first part of December, you will delight in the Country Christmas House held each year. Daily 9 a.m. – 1 p.m. 572-6560.

Fourth of July weekend is wild and wonderful in Makawao. Festivities include a morning parade through town and several days of rodeo events.

ACCOMMODATIONS – UPCOUNTRY

Accommodations are limited in upcountry. Five and one-half miles past Pukalani is the Kula Lodge, and just beyond, the Silversword Inn. Both offer rustic cabins and restaurants.

KULA LODGE
RR 1, Box 475, Kula, Maui, HI 96790 (808-878-1535). Rates run $65 (2) a night for Chalets 1 & 2 which feature a queen bed, Swedish fireplace and loft with twin beds. Chalets 3 & 4 run $56 (2) with queen bed and loft with two twin beds. Chalet 5 has a double and one twin with fireplace for $56. Additional persons $10. Full payment with reservation and one week refund notice.

SILVERSWORD INN
RR 1, Box 469, Kula, Maui, HI 96790 (808-878-1232)
Rustic cabins available for rent.

HANA

INTRODUCTION

If you do not plan staying a few days in Hana, you might consider an overnight stop at one of the facilities to break up the long drive to this isolated east coast of Maui. Here is a different Maui from the sunny, dry resort areas on the leeward coast. The windward coast here is turbulent with magnificent coastal views, rain forests, and mountain waterfalls creating wonderful pools for swimming. The trip to Hana by car from Kahului will take at least three hours, or the alternative is a very short flight from the Kahului Airport.

Accommodations vary from hotel/condo to campgrounds and homes at a variety of price ranges. The 7,000 acre Hotel Hana Ranch has been involved in some major renovations. Creating an "elegant ranch atmosphere" is the resorts goal. Several moderately priced condominiums are available. Waianapanapa State Park, just outside Hana, has camping facilities and cabins. Ohe'o also has a tent camping area.

Hana offers a quiet retreat and an atmosphere of peace (undisturbed by the constant flow of tourist cars and vans) that has lured many a prominent personality to these quiet shores. Restaurant choices are extremely limited and shopping is restricted to the Hasegawa General Store, the Hana Ranch Store or a few shops at the Hana Hotel.

WHAT TO SEE AND DO

PAIA - ALONG THE ROAD TO HANA

A little beyond Wailuku, and along the highway which leads to Hana, is the small town of Paia. The name Paia translated means "noisy", however, the origin of this name is unclear. This quaint town is reminiscent of the early sugar cane era when Henry Baldwin located his first sugar plantation in this area. The wooden buildings are now filled with antique and other gift shops to attract the passing tourist. (See RESTAURANTS for more information) The advent of windsurfing is giving a rebirth to this small charming town. A number of new restaurants have recently appeared and a new hotel is being considered.

The Maui Crafts Guild, a group of local artisans owns and operates this store. Pottery, koa furniture, weaving, wall sculptures, woods serving pieces, prints and basketry are featured. Very lovely, but expensive, hand-crafted items.

HANA

Anyone who endures the three-hour (at least) drive to Hana deserves to sport the "I survived the Road to Hana" T-shirts which are sold locally. While it may be true that it is easy to fall in love with Hana, getting there is quite a different story. The drive to Hana is not for everyone, although many guide books claim otherwise. It is not for people who are prone to motion sickness, those who don't like a lot of scenery, those who are in a hurry to get somewhere or those who don't love long drives. However, it is a trip filled with waterfalls and lush tropical jungles (which flourish in the 340-inch average annual rainfall). Maps are deceiving. It appears you could make the 53-mile journey much faster than three hours but there are 617 (usually hairpin) curves and 56 miniature bridges along this narrow road. Even with recent repaving, most cars travel in the middle of the road, making each turn a possibly exciting experience, especially at night.

The Hana Hwy. was originally built in 1927 with pick and shovel, which may account for its narrowness, to provide a link between Hana and Kahului. There can also be delays on the road of up to two hours if the road is being worked on. In days gone by when heavy rains caused washouts, it is said that people would literally climb the mud barricades and swap cars, then resume their journey. Despite all this, 300–500 people traverse this road daily, and it is the supply route for all deliveries to Hana and the small settlements along the way.

Now, if we haven't dissuaded you and you still want to see spectacular undeveloped scenery, plan to spend the whole day (or even better, stop overnight in Hana). Get a very early start, take a picnic lunch and a warm sweater. We also might recommend that if you drive, select a car with an automatic transmission (or else be prepared for constant shifting). Another choice is to try one of the small van tours which go to Hana and leave the driving to them. These vans will take you around the other side of the island, a road not recommended for rental cars, if the road is open. Good tour guides will also be able to point out the sights of interest along the way that are easy to miss! The other alternative is to fly into Hana's small airport.

Two miles from the point where Hana Highway intersects Route 400 look for a small roadside trail marker by the Hoolawa Bridge. This area, known as Twin Falls, offers a pleasant spot for swimming. The first pool has two waterfalls, but hiking a little beyond is another pool with a taller single waterfall. Mosquitos can be prolific so pack bug spray. There are no safe beaches along this route for swimming, so for a cool dip, take advantage of one of the swimming holes provided.

Waikamoi Ridge - A picnic area and nature trail.

Puohkamoa Falls - This is sort of the half-way point and is near roadside marker #11. The pools are larger than at Waikamoi. A nice area with tables for picnics.

Kaumahina State Park - Overlooks the Honomanu Gulch and Peninsula and is a little past roadside marker #12. Toilets and a picnic area are provided here.

Keanae and Wailua - This agricultural area has an abundance of taro fields. *The Miracle Church* in Wailua has an interesting background. At the time of construction there was no building material. Then a huge storm hit and, by some miracle, deposited a load of coral onto the beach, thus providing the means for building the crushed coral walls of the church.

The Shell Shop - Turn left at the Coral Miracle Church sign. The shop is located across the street from the church. Since 1974 five local divers have been creating original shell jewelry from the limpet shell. The jewelry is sold exclusively at this location.

The YMCA's Camp Keanae - Offers overnight accommodations for men and women (housed separately). The rate is $5 a night. Arrival is requested between 4 p.m. and 6 p.m. Bring your own food and sleeping bag. (Phone 808-248-8355 for more information.)

Wailua Lookout - Located just past Wailua on the roadside, look for a turnoff. Park and follow the tunnel through a tangle of huge tree roots that lead you up the steps to the Lookout. The trek up is worth the excellent view.

Puaa Kaa State Park - 14 miles before Hana. The park has two waterfalls and pools that are roadside. This is a favorite stop for a picnic lunch. The waterfalls and large pool have combined with this lush tropical locale to make you feel sure a menehune must be lurking nearby. There are new restrooms here.

With a little effort a sharp observer can spot the open ditches and dams along the roadside. These are the **Spreckles Ditches** built over 100 years ago to supply water for the young sugar cane industry. These ditches continue to provide the island with an important part of its supply of water.

Waianapanapa (pronounced WHY-A-NAHPA-NAHPA) **State Park** is four miles before Hana, and offers a black sand beach (not safe for swimming), a number of caves, a blow hole, and many old Hawaiian legends. Camping is allowed and there are rustic cabins available for rent (See ACCOMMODATIONS - Hana).

The Helani Gardens (248-8274) is a self-guided botanical tour by foot or car through some very dense vegetation. Its five acres seem like hundreds as you drive up, down, and around on a maze of one-lane dirt roads through a jungle of amazing flowering trees and shrubs. This is really quite an enjoyable adventure, and one usually overlooked by those in a hurry to or from Hana and the Seven Pools (Ohe'o). Take your time and explore this unusual attraction. Admission $2 for adults, $1 children 6–16. Located about one mile before Hana. Picnic areas, fish ponds and restrooms available.

The last curve of the road will put you at **Hana's Gardenland**. Its free to browse and they thoughtfully provide picnic tables and a restroom. The plants sold here include the rare and beautiful and available for shipping anywhere.

Now, back in the car for a drive into downtown Hana, but don't blink, or you might miss it.

As we prepared for this edition we learned of a new project called **The Hana Hawaiian Village**. Henry Noa and his family are undertaking this endeavor and plan to create an authentic Hawaiian village with all Hawaiian speaking employees. Crafts demonstrations as well as examples of the Hawaiian way of life are planned. The village is open for a limited number of hours each week and a great deal more work needs to be done before its completion. We were unable to get directions or a phone number. As additional information becomes available it will be released in THE MAUI UPDATE newsletter.

Hana Cultural Center (248-8622) opened in August of 1983. It contains a collection of relics of Hana's past in the old court house building and a small new museum. Open Monday through Saturday 11 a.m. – 4 p.m. Located near Hana Bay, watch for signs.

Hana Bay has been the site of many historical events. It was a retreat for Hawaiian royalty as well as an important military point from which Maui warriors attacked the island of Hawaii, and then were in turn attacked. This is also the birthplace of Ka'ahumanu (1768), Kamehameha's favorite wife.

The climate on this end of Maui is cooler and wetter, creating an ideal environment for agricultural development. The Ka'eleku Sugar Company established itself in Hana in 1860. Cattle, also a prominent industry during the 20th century, continues today. You can still view the paniolos (Hawaiian cowboys) work at nearby Hana Ranch. There are 5,000 head of cattle which run on 4,500 acres of land. Every three days the cattle are moved to fresh pastures. (Our family was thrilled when a paniola flagged us to stop on the road outside Hana, while a herd of cattle surrounded our car enroute to fresher pastures.)

Hana has little to offer in the way of shopping, however, the Hasegawa General Store offers a little bit of everything. You may even run into one of the celebrities who come to the area for vacation. The Hana Ranch Store is open daily and the Hana Resort has a gift shop and boutique.

SOME LOCAL HANA INFORMATION:

St. Mary's Church: Sat. Mass 6 p.m., Sun. 8 a.m., Puuiki Mass at 9:30 a.m.
Wananalua Protestant Church: (1832) Services Sunday 10 a.m.
Hana Ranch Store: 7:30 a.m. to 6:30 p.m. daily.
Hasegawa General Store: 7:30 a.m. to 6 p.m. Mon. to Sat., until 3 on Sun.
Hana Medical Center: Mon. to Fri. 8 a.m.–5 p.m., Sat. 9 a.m.–noon.
Bank of Hawaii: Mon. to Thur. 3–4:30 p.m. and Fri. 3–6 p.m.
Library: Tues. to Fri. 8–5 p.m., Mon. 8–8 p.m.
Post Office: 8 a.m.–4:30 p.m. Mon. through Fri.

The oldest building in town, built in 1830, currently houses the laundry facility for the Hana Hotel, but will be adapted for a new use. The current site of the Hana Store will become the laundry, while a small new town center is planned near the Post Office, and will be lined with monkey pod trees.

On Lyon's Hill stands a large stone cross in memory of Paul Fagan. It was built by two Japanese brothers from Kahului in 1960. Although the access road is chained, the front desk of the Hotel Hana will provide a key. The short trip to the top will reward the visitor with a spectacular panoramic view of Hana Bay and open pasture of the Hana Ranch.

Kaihalulu Beach (Red Sand Beach) is located in a small cove on the other side of Kauiki Hill from Hana Bay and is accessible by a narrow, crumbly trail more suited to mountain goats than people. The trail descends into a lovely cove bordered by high cliffs and is almost enclosed by a natural lava barrier seaward. For more details see BEACHES.

Hamoa Beach – This gorgeous beach has been very attractively landscaped and developed by the Hotel Hana Maui in a way that adds to the surrounding lushness. The long white sand beach is in a very tropical setting and surrounded by a low sea cliff. As you leave Hana toward Ohe'o Gulch look for the sign 1-1/2 miles past Hasegawa store that says "Koki Park - Hamoa Beach - Hamoa Village." Follow the road, you can't miss it.

You quickly pass fields of grazing world-famous Maui beef and reenter the tropical jungle once more. Numerous waterfalls cascade along the roadside. After ten curvy, bumpy miles on a very narrow two-lane road, and a 45–60 minute drive, you arrive at one of the reasons for this trip, *Ohe'o Gulch.* Popularily known in the past as the Seven Sacred Pools as a tool for attracting tourists, the original and proper name is trying to be reclaimed by the Park Service. The blue-grey lava flow here has created many incredible pools beneath magnificent waterfalls. The water then flows over a small black sand beach into the ocean. The pools are safe for swimming so pack your suit, however, swimming off the black sand beach is very dangerous and many drownings and near drownings have occurred here. The bluff above the beach offers a magnificent view of the ocean and cliffs, so have your camera ready. This area is also of historical significance and signs warn visitors not to remove any rocks. A pleasant hike will take you to the upper falls. Check with the park service to see if the free Saturday morning, ranger-guided hikes are available.

Two miles further on is the Charles Lindbergh grave, located in the small cemetery of the 1850 Kipahulu Hawaiian Church. He chose this site only a year prior to his death in 1974, after living in the area for a number of years.

It is sometimes possible to travel the back road from Hana thru Upcountry and back to Kahului. This is Maui's desert region and it is a vivid contrast to the lush windward environs. While very parched, this route presents a hazard which can take visitors unaware. Flash floods in the mountains above, which are most likely November to March, can send walls of water down the mountain, quickly washing out a bridge or overflowing the road. The road is sometimes closed for months due to serious washouts. Check with the county to see the current status of this route. Car rental agencies post warnings that travel is not advised on this route for standard cars and that renters are responsible for all damage.

If this route is passable (which at the time of printing was not) consider stopping at **The Kaupo General Store**. It has been operating for years and is open based upon the whim of the management.

Take note of the many rock walls. This area supported a large native Hawaiian population and these walls served as boundaries as well as retaining walls for livestock, primarily pigs. The walls are centuries old and unfortunately have suffered from visitor vandalism. Cattle are now the principle area residents.

As you enter Upcountry and civilization once more, look for the **Tedeschi Winery**. Located at the Ulupalakua Ranch it offers tasting daily from 9 - 4. They began in 1974 and produced only a pineapple wine until 1983 when they harvested their first grapes. They also offer a champagne and a red table wine.

On the way back down you might stop at **The Botanical Gardens** which feature a close up look at the unusual protea flowers. Admission is charged. (See Upcountry for more information)

ACCOMMODATIONS - HANA

Hana Bay Vacation Rentals	YMCA Camp Keanae
Hotel Hana Maui	Hana Kai Resort Apartments
Waianapanapa State Park	Heavenly Hana Inn

HANA BAY VACATION RENTALS ★
Stan and Suzanne Collins, PO Box 318, Hana, Maui, HI 96713 (808-248-7727)

As an alternative to condominium and hotel living you might be interested in one of eight private homes available in and around Hana. They offer fully equipped one, two or three bedrooms homes with ocean or bay views. Prices range from $60 for the Kauiki Cabin to $150/night for a newly constructed pole home with jacuzzi. They require a 50% deposit with reservation and payment in full upon arrival. For stays of 3 days or less, full payment in advance is required. There is a 10% cancellation fee. Rates are $20 higher November to January and June to August.

HOTEL HANA MAUI ★
P.O. Box 8, Hana, Maui, Hi 96713 (808-248-8211) 1-800-321-HANA
Agent: Maui 800 1-800-367-5224

Garden Lanai Rooms	single $338	double $416	
Junior Suites	single 363	double 441	
1-Bdrm. Suites	single 408	double 486	
Hanahou Jr. Suites	single 408	double 486	
Noe Noe Suites	single 408–428	double 486–506	
Kauiki Jr. Suites	single 408–453	double 486–531	
Waikaloa Suites	single 453–478	double 531–556	
Sea Ranch Cottages	single 460–568	double 538–646	

Prices include all meals. Third adult in room $130/night and includes breakfast, lunch and dinner. Children under age 7 when occupying room with two adults runs $65/night for all meals. No charge for infants under age of two. Extra rollaway and crib available upon request.

This is the most secluded Maui resort and a Hana landmark. It has been called an island on an island. Five plantations were consolidated when Paul Fagan saw that the end of the sugar industry in Hana was close at hand. There had been 5,000 residents in Hana in 1941, and only 500 remained when he began the hotel and cattle ranch which rejuvenated Hana. Approximately 1/3 of Hana's population of 900 are employed in some fashion by the hotel, ranch or "Zen" flower nursery. Hotel Hana Ranch was opened for public use in 1947 and renamed Hotel Hana Maui the following year.

The 60-room hotel resembles a small neighborhood with the single story units scattered about the grounds. The rooms are simple, but elegant with hardwood floors, and tiled bathrooms with deep tubs. The resort prides itself on the fact that it has no televisions or room air conditioning. Newer additions are the 46 sea ranch cottages located oceanfront at Kaihalulu Bay. These resemble the early plantation style houses. These cottages include oceanview, oceanfront, one bedroom suites and some offer spas.

Numerous hotel activities include a weekly luau, cocktails at the old plantation house, (now the residence of the hotel's general manager), many trails for hiking or horseback riding, or cookouts at Lehoula beach. A shuttle provides convenient transportation for the three mile trip to beautiful Hamoa Beach with private facilities for hotel guests. Shuttles are also available to tour the Ohe'o Gulch, or the botanical gardens where the hotel raises mature indoor plants and flowers for use at the resort and to send to the mainland. An outdoor pool is located on the hotel grounds. They also offer a dining room as well as a coffee shop. (Restaurant dining and the weekly luau is available to non-hotel guests on a space available basis. Call for reservations.) Children's activities and overnight sitters are available.

Recent renovations include a bar with a large fireplace and an open deck with a quiet lounge adjoining to provide a peaceful atmosphere for conversation or reading. The new restaurant has a 35-foot ceiling with skylight, hardwood floors and a deck opening to a magnificent oceanview and excellent food. The new library contains rare volumes of early Hawaiiana, some so valuable that they will be under lock and key and require white gloves to handle. There is also a small boutique with resort fashions and jewelry in addition to a beauty salon. The "golf adventure" is three holes in the midst of the resort. The new Club Room has a television, and evening lectures are given here. A more peaceful and beautiful setting is difficult to imagine.

WAIANAPANAPA STATE PARK
P.O. Box 1049, Wailuku, Maui, HI 96753. (808-244-4354)

1 adult–$10/day   2 adults–$14   4 adults–$24   6 adults –$30;
1 adult 1 child–$10.50   2 adults 2 children–$18   2 adults 4 children–$20

This must be the cheapest place to stay on all of Maui unless you can stay with friends or relatives for free!! The State Park Department offers cabins that sleep up to six people. The units have electric lights and hot water, showers and toilet facilities. The kitchen is equipped with a range, but no oven, and a refrigerator. Bedding is provided and clean linens and towels are refreshed every three days. No pets are allowed and bring your own soap! A five-day maximum stay is the rule and guests are required to clean their units before departure, leaving soiled linens. A 50% deposit is required for reservations and they are booked way ahead. A prorated list of rates will be sent to you by the Parks Department on request. Included here are a few sample prices. The beach is unsafe for swimming, however, there are some interesting trails, pools, and lava tubes. The beach is not of sand, but actually very small, smooth black pebbles. Mosquito repellent is recommended, even for a short walk through the pool area.

YMCA CAMP KEANAE
In Keanae. (808-248-8355) Beds run $6 a night. Bring your own sleeping bag and food. No separate facilities for men and women. Accommodations are dormitory style.

HANA KAI RESORT APARTMENTS
P.O. Box 38, Hana, Maui, HI 96713 (808-248-8426) or (808-248-7742)
Studio (1-3) single $50, double $53   1 BR (1-4) single $60, double $63

Extra persons $6/night. 19 oceanfront units on Hana Bay, fully furnished including kitchens. Maid service is daily and there are laundry facilities available. They feature a lava rock pool and attractive, well kept grounds. Hana Kai can also arrange a rental car for you while in the area.

HEAVENLY HANA INN
P.O. Box 146, Hana, Maui, HI 96713. (808-248-8442)

Four modern units in a single Japanese-style inn. Each unit has a two-bedroom, bath, and lanai arrangement that sleeps two to six people. Units begin at $60 for a studio for two and up to $90 for a unit for four. Two cottages in town are also available and sleep up to 8, priced $55–90. NO CREDIT CARDS. Payment in full is requested in advance to hold reservations.

BOOKING AGENTS

AMFAC HOTELS
Amfac Resorts Hawaii
PO Box 8520
Honolulu, Hi 96830-0520
1-808-945-6121   1-800-227-4700

Royal Lahaina Resort
Kaanapali Beach Hotel

ASTON HOTELS & RESORTS
2255 Kuhio Avenue
Honolulu, Hi 96815
1-808-922-3368   1-800-367-5124

Kaanapali Villas	Napili Point
Paki Maui	Sands of Kahana
The Mahana	Kaanapali Shores
Maui Hill	Maui Lu Resort

COLONY RESORTS
32 Merchant St.
Honolulu, HI 96813
1-808-523-0411   1-800-367-6046

Kahana Villas	Napili Shores
Kamaole Sands	Polo Beach

CONDOMINIUM RENTAL HAWAII
2439 S. Kihei Rd.
Kihei, Maui, Hi 96753
1-808-879-2778   1-800-367-5242

Hale Kamaole	Sugar Beach
Hale Pau Hana	Wailea Ekahi
Kihei Akahi	

GENTLE ISLAND HOLIDAYS
PO Box 1441
Kihei, Maui, HI 96753
1-808-879-0629
1-800-367-8047 ext. 303

Bookings for the majority of condos with a broad selection of units. We found them very congenial and helpful with some units below standard front desk prices.

CONDO RESORTS INTERNATIONAL
3303 Harbor Blvd. Suite K-8
Costa Mesa, CA 92626
1-800-854-3823

Coconut Inn	Napili Kai Club
Kahana Reef	Napili Point
Kaanapali Alii	Napili Shores
Kaanapali Shores	Papakea
Kahana Villas	Paki Maui
Kamaole Sands	Polo Beach Club
Kapalua Villas	Puunoa Estates
Laule'a	Sands of Kahana
Mahana	The Whaler

Bookings are for package plans which include rental car.

DESTINATION RESORTS
3750 Wailea Alanui
Wailea, Maui, HI 96753
1-800-367-5246   1-808-879-1595

Wailea Condominiums

HANA BAY VACATION RENTALS ★
PO Box 318
Hana, Maui, HI 96713
1-808-248-7727

Stan and Suzanne Collins have a great alternative to condo vacationing. Choose one of their Hana cottages or homes.

HAWAIIAN PACIFIC RESORTS
1150 South King St.
Honolulu, HI 96882
1-800-367-5004
1-800-663-1118 Canada

Maui Beach
Maui Palms

HAWAIIANA RESORTS INC.
1100 Ward Ave. Suite 1100
Honolulu, HI 96814
1-800-367-7040
1-800-663-1118 Canada

Kaanapali Royal
Kaanapali Villas
Laule'a

JARVINEN
1-800-421-0767

Kihei Beach	Napili Sunset
Maui Eldorado	Puamana
Maui Islander	Royal Kahana

KIHEI MAUI VACATIONS
P.O. Box 1055
Kihei, Maui, HI 96753
1-808-879-7581
1-800-367-8047 ext. 4000
1-800-423-8733 Canada

Kamaole Sands	Maalaea Yacht
Kauhale Makai	Marina
Kihei Akahi	Makena Surf
Kihei Alii Kai	Menehune Shores
Kihei Bay Surf	Milowai
Kihei Garden Estates	
Kihei Holiday	Maui Sunset
Kihei Kai Nani	Maui Vista
Luana Kai	Wailea Condos
Maalaea Kai	Homes-Cottages

MAALAEA RENTALS
RR 1 Box 380
Wailuku, Maui, HI
1-800-367-8047 ext. 421
1-808-242-6553

Milowai	Maalaea Kai

MAKANI A KAI RENTAL
RR 1 Box 389
Wailuku, Maui, HI 96793
1-808-244-5627   1-800-367-6084

Hono Kai	Makani A Kai
Kanai A Nalu	

KUMULANI
1-800-367-2954

Haleakala Shores	Kihei Akahi
Hale Kamaole	Lahaina Shores
Hololani	Luana Kai
Island Sands	Maalaea Banyans
Island Surf	Mahana
Kaanapali Shores	Mana Kai
Kaanapali Villas	Maui Hill
Kahana Reef	Maui Kai
Kahana Villa	Maui Sunset
Kahana Village	Maui Vista
Kamaole One	Napili Point
Kamaole Sands	Paki Maui
Kapalua Ridge	Royal Kahana
Kauhale Maki	Sands of Kahana
Kealia	Valley Isle Resort
Kihei Bay Surf	Wailea Ekahi

MAUI 800
Tom Morrow & Assoc. Inc.
P.O. Box 1506
Kahului, Maui, HI 96732
1-808-244-5627 (244-7012)
1-800-367-5224

Coconut Inn	Maui Eldorado
Hale Napili	Maui Hill
Hololani Maui	Maui Islander
Hotel Hana Maui	Maui Kai
Kahana Sunset	Napili Bay
Kahana Village	Napili Kai
Lahaina Shores	Napili Surf
Laule'a	Noelani
Luana Kai	Pioneer Inn
Maalaea Banyans	Royal Mauian

Plus 60 other hotels and condos on
Maui. Bookings for the other islands
also.

MAUI NETWORK LTD.
PO Box 1077
Makawao, Maui, HI 96768
1-800-367-5221
1-800-423-8733 ext. 260 (Canada)

Kahana Outrigger	Kuleana
Kihei Beach Resort	Whaler

MAUI ACCOMMODATIONS
48 Market St.
Wailuku, Maui, HI 96793
1-808-244-0848   1-800-252-MAUI
1-800-423-8733 ext. sun (Canada)

Island Sands   Kihei Resort
Kamaole Sands   Maui Vista
Kauhale Makai   Pualani

OIHANA PROPERTY
MANAGEMENT
840 Alua
Wailuku, Maui, HI 96793
1-808-244-7684   1-800-367-5234

Kana'I A Nalu   Leinaala
Kauhale Makai   Maui Vista
Maalaea Banyans

PLEASANT HAWAIIAN
HOLIDAYS
P.O. Box 5020
Westlake Village, Ca. 91359-5020
1-800-242-9244

Hyatt Regency   Maui Marriott
Kaanapali Beach   Napili Point
Kaanapali Shores   Napili Shores
Kaanapali Villas   Royal Kahana
Kahana Beach   Royal Lahaina
Kamaole Sands   Sands of Kahana
Intercontinental   Sheraton Maui
Mahana   Stouffer's Wailea
Maui Islander

Bookings are for package plans of 7
to 14 nights on one or more islands
and includes airfare and rental car.

PREMIER CONNECTIONS
33 Market St., Suite 200
Wailuku, Maui, HI 96793
1-808-244-4877

Office hours 7 a.m.–noon Mon.–Fri.
Luxury homes and estates, the finest
suites and penthouses

RAINBOW RESERVATIONS INC.
PO Box 11453
Lahaina, Maui, HI 96761-6453
1-808-667-7858   1-800-367-6092

Hale Mahina   Papakea
Hololani Resort   Pohailani
Kahana Outrigger   Royal Kahana
Kihei Kai Nani   Valley Isle Resort
Maui Sands   The Whaler
Napili Shores

RIDGE REALTY RENTALS
888 Wainee St. #207
Lahaina, Maui, HI 96761
1-808-667-2851
1-800-367-8047 ext. 133

The Ridge (Kapalua)

VILLAGE RENTALS
Azeka's Place
P.O. Box 1471
Kihei, Maui, HI 96753
1-800-367-5634   1-808-879-5504

Kalama Terrace   Nani Kai Hale
Kauhale Makai   Sugar Beach
Kihei Garden Estates
Kihei Resort   Wailana Sands
Maui Sunset   Wailea Condos

WHALER'S REALTY ★
Whaler's Village, Suite A-3
2435 Kaanapali Parkway
Lahaina, Maui, HI 96761
1-808-661-8777   1-800-367-5632

Bay Villas   Kahana Villa
Golf Villas   Lahaina Shores
Ironwoods   Mahana
Kaanapali Alii   Maui Eldorado
Kaanapali Royale   Papakea
Kaanapali Shores   Polo Beach
Kaanapali Villas   Ridge Villas
Kahana Outrigger   The Whaler
Kaanapali Plantation

They offer high quality
condos at fair prices.

Restaurants

INTRODUCTION

This section continues to be the most enjoyable to investigate! We have included the majority of restaurants in the Maalaea to Makena, and Lahaina to the Kapalua areas. For the adventurer or budget conscious traveler, take special note of the wonderful local dining opportunities in Kahului and Wailuku.

Needless to say, we haven't been able to eat every meal served at every restaurant on Maui, but we do discuss with a great many people their experiences in order to get varied opinions. We also welcome your comments. (See READER RESPONSE.)

Whether it is a teriburger at a local cafe or a romantic evening spent dining next to a swan lagoon, Maui offers something for everyone.

Following this introduction, the restaurants are first indexed alphabetically and then also by food type. The restaurants are then divided by geographical area, separated by price range, and listed alphabetically in those price ranges. These are: "INEXPENSIVE" under $10, "MODERATE" $10 to $17, and "EXPEN-SIVE" $17 and above. As a means of comparison, we have taken an average meal (usually dinner), excluding tax, alcoholic beverages and desserts, for one person at that restaurant. The prices listed were accurate at time of publication, but we cannot be responsible for any price increases.

We hope that the sample offerings from their menus will also be helpful to you. An important post-script here is the rapidity with which some island restaurants open and close, change names and raise prices. Our quarterly newsletter, THE MAUI UPDATE, will keep you abreast of these changes. (See ORDER INFORMATION).

One of our favorite meals out is fresh island fish that has been properly prepared. To help you make a selection from these fish with their unusual Hawaiian names, we have included "A Word or Two about Fish." This section gives a brief description of the most popular varieties and is included in GENERAL INFORMATION.

If you prefer to enjoy gourmet meals at home, check into Have Cooks Will Travel. They can come in and fix a single meal or prepare meals for the entire week. They also provide catering services. Phone 871-7127.

RESTAURANTS
Introduction

Our favorite restaurants are generally either a real bargain for the price, or serve up a very quality meal, and are indicated by a ★.

BEST BETS

TOP RESTAURANTS
Our criteria for a top restaurant is excellence of food preparation and presentation, a pleasing atmosphere, and service that anticipates or responds promptly to one's needs. While the following exemplify these criteria they are also "deep pocket" restaurants, so expect to spend $70 - $100 or more for your meal, wine and gratuity for two. Generally, anything you have will be excellent. Remember, even the best restaurants may have an "off" night, but these are seldom. Also, chefs and management do change, rendering what you may have found to be excellent on one occasion quite different the next. However, the following have proven to be consistent through the years. Enjoy your meal, enjoy being a little bit spoiled, and remember those muu-muus are great for covering up all those calories!!

✓Hakone, Maui Prince Hotel
Bay Club, Kapalua
La Perouse, Hotel Inter-Continental in Wailea
Plantation Veranda, Kapalua Resort Hotel
Raffles', Stouffer Wailea Beach Resort
Prince Court, Maui Prince Hotel
Sound of the Falls, Westin Maui Resort
Spats II, Hyatt Regency at Kaanapali
Swan Court, Hyatt Regency at Kaanapali

TOP RESTAURANTS IN A MORE CASUAL ATMOSPHERE
While these restaurants are less expensive, it is still easy to spend $50 or more for dinner for two. They serve a superior meal in a less formal atmosphere.

Avalon in Lahaina
El Crab Catcher, Whaler's Village at Kaanapali
✓Island Fish House, Kihei and (Kahului, now Mickeys)
Kapalua's Garden Restaurant, Kapalua Resort Hotel
Kapalua Grill and Bar, Kapalua
★Longhi's, Lahaina
Palm Court, Stouffer Wailea Beach Resort
★ Makawao Steak House, Makawao
★★Mama's Fish House, Paia — *lunch*
The Villa, Westin Maui at Kaanapali

LA CUISINE FRANCAIS
Maui's French restaurants all fall in the "champagne" price range. Personally, we find that each has its own special merits that make for an enjoyable evening and dinner and that one cannot be singled out as "the best."

Chez Paul, Olowalu
Gerard's, Lahaina
La Bretagne, Lahaina

BEST BUFFETS

These buffets are a good way to enjoy a great meal with a wide selection of food at a moderate price. You also may not have to eat for the next two days. The best of the best are Raffles', Prince Court, and Sounds of the Falls for their Sunday champagne brunches, and Swan Court or Sound of the Falls for their daily breakfast buffet. The others are all excellent, just not quite as extravagant.

Prince Court (Maui Prince Hotel, Makena) spectacular displays of over 160 food choices, each arranged as a work of art.

Raffles' (Stouffer Wailea Beach Resort, Wailea) has a true taste extravaganza for their champagne Sunday brunch.

Makani Room (Maui Inter-Continental Hotel, Wailea) has a fine Sunday brunch that is a little more casual.

Sounds of the Falls (Westin Maui, Kaanapali) serves a marvelous Sunday champagne brunch.

Royal Ocean Terrace (Royal Lahaina Resort, Kaanapali) offers a nice, less expensive Sunday champagne brunch.

Swan Court (Hyatt Regency, Kaanapali) features a lovely breakfast buffet daily in an elegant atmosphere.

The Mayfair luncheon (Kapalua Bay Resort, Kapalua) is served daily.

Palm Court (Stouffer Wailea Beach Resort) serves an international dinner buffet nightly.

TOP "LOCAL" RESTAURANTS (Kahului/Wailuku)

We have delighted in exploring the many small, family-owned "local" restaurants in Kahului and especially in Wailuku. The food in these establishments is not only plentiful and well prepared, but also very inexpensive. The service is often better and friendlier than at many of the resort establishments. If the thought of vinyl seats (sometimes with rips or patches) and chipped dinnerware is not offensive, then you just may be in for a fun culinary experience.

Fujiya's (Japanese)   Tokyo Tei (Japanese)
Sam Sato's (Japanese/noodles)   Wailuku Grill (mainland gourmet)
Siam Thai (Thai)   Yori's (Hawaiian)
Tasty Crust (home style)

BEST PIZZA

Pizza Circus, phone 871-1133, in Kahului, has limited seating and pizza to go. The crust is the secret ingredient in making this pizza an outstanding choice. Our recommendation for the best pizza in West Maui goes to Longhi's Deli (661-8128), Lahaina. You'll need lots of napkins as they really load on the goodies! (Postscript: The new owners have promised to maintain the high quality.)

BEST SANDWICHES

Longhi's Deli offers an array of very good sandwiches, limited seating and not much atmosphere. Paradise Fruits in Kihei, also with limited seating and a "health food" menu.

RESTAURANTS
Introduction

GOOD AND CHEAP
One of the best meals for the price may be an Early Bird Special at one of Maui's better restaurants. The restaurants sometimes offer these only during low season, so check to see if it is currently available and the current price. Hours vary with the restaurant, but usually begin between 5 and 5:30 and end between 6 and 6:30. The following are our personal favorites and offer quality meals. Generally, the meals are the same ones that you would pay more for an hour later, but you are limited in your selections.

Idini's in Kihei (Italian/seafood)
Island Fish House in Kihei
Moana Terrace at Marriott Hotel, Kaanapali (buffet)
Kihei Prime Rib and Seafood House ·
Sam's Beachside Grill in Lahaina

BEST HAWAIIAN
Yori's located on Market Street in Wailuku is small, quaint, and very inexpensive. A couple new contenders are the Lahaina Luau Cafe at 505 Front St. and Maui Boy in Wailuku.

BEST FAST FOODS
Azeka's Market and Paradise Fruits in Kihei offer good food at good prices.

BEST RIBS
Chris's Smokehouse features great ribs at their Lahaina restaurant. In Kihei, stop at Azeka's market for their specially marinated ribs that you can cook.

FAVORITE BREAKFASTS
Pioneer Inn has it hands down as our favorite breakfast stop. The French toast, made of Portuguese Sweet Bread, is fabulous. The rustic atmosphere is reminiscent of by-gone days and the prices reasonable. All of the waitresses are terrific, but if you're lucky enough to have Ma serve you, you'll get an especially warm aloha along with your meal. In an atmosphere of tropical delight a breakfast buffet is served daily at Swan Court. The macadamia nut pancakes are light and fluffy, and cooked to order. On the other side of the island in Wailuku is Tasty Crust, an inexpensive local restaurant where unusual crusty pancakes are their specialty.

MOST OUTRAGEOUS DESSERT
The Lahaina Provision Company's Chocoholic Bar at the Hyatt Regency is a chocolate lover's dream come true. This dessert buffet features soft, self-serve ice cream and an array of splendors. Hot caramel sauce, hot fudge, hot coffee-chocolate sauce, strawberries, shaved chocolate, chipped chocolate, chocolate kisses, grated chocolate, chocolate mousse, and the list continues. You can make the trip through as many times as you or your waistline can tolerate.

BEST BAKERY
Our favorite is located in the industrial area of Lahaina. Turn at the Pizza Hut sign off Honoapiilani Hwy. Cleverly named, THE BAKERY, an early stop will ensure you the best selection of their wonderful French pastries. Cheese and luncheon meats are also available.

ALPHABETICAL INDEX

FOOD TYPE INDEX

AMERICAN

BRUNCH

CHINESE
PHILIPPINE AND THAI

CONTINENTAL

DESSERTS

FAMILY DINING

LUAUS AND DINNER SHOWS

★ For a local luau, check the Maui News. You may be fortunate to find one of the area churches sponsoring a fund raising luau. The public is welcome and the prices are usually half that of the commercial ventures. You'll see spontaneous, local entertainment.

Most of the luaus are large, with an average of 400 - 600 guests, with the smallest being the Old Lahaina Luau with only 200. Many still serve the traditional foods, while others have switched to the all-American prime rib. The entertainment ranges from splashy broadway-style productions to a country barbecue, or a more authentic Hawaiian dance and song. It is very difficult to judge these luaus due to their diversity. While one reader raves about a particular show, another reader will announce their disappointment with the same event. Tastes vary, so read carefully the information provided and make your own choice.

HANA RANCH
"Hana Ranch Luau" at Lehoula Beach. Fridays at 6 p.m. Open to non-hotel guests based on availability for $50. Guests are transported via hay wagon or van to the beachfront luau location. Phone 248-8211.

HYATT REGENCY
Presents "Drums of the Pacific" in their outdoor dining room Monday through Saturday. The dinner show, seating at 5:30 p.m., includes mai tais, soup, salad, and a choice of fish, steak, or chicken. The price for adults is $36, junior (ages 6-12 years) $30, children ages 6 and under free. Cocktail show seating at 6:15. Adults $22, juniors $19. The show begins at 7:30. Phone 667-7474.

JESSE'S LUAU GARDENS
Jesse Nakooka performs three nights a week at this Polynesian buffet in Kihei at 1945 S. Kihei Rd. Jesse has been involved with luaus for many years. The food for this luau is provided by Island Fish House. Prices for adults $37, children 3-12 $20, under age three are free. Phone 879-7227.

KAPA ROOM
A contemporary dinner show, "Maui, My Enchantment" combines the beauty of Polynesian men and women with the beauty of Hawaiian song and dance. This production is done more in the style of a broadway show. Nightly except Sundays at the Maui Westin in Kaanapali. Dinner seating 6 p.m., cocktail seating 7:30 p.m. The menu features seasonal island specialties, such as broiled island chicken marinated in saffron and lime juice, Hawaiian sea prawns, and baked Maui onions with yams. Dinner show $45 per person, cocktail show $25. Phone 667-2525.

MAUI INTER-CONTINENTAL WAILEA

"Maui's Merriest Luau" takes place every Thursday at 5:45 p.m. on the hotel's oceanfront luau gardens. Adults are $37, children age six to ten are $20. Tax and gratuity included. The festivities include authentic poi pounding and coconut husking demonstrations with the imu ceremony at sunset. The buffet features island favorites such as kalua pig, lomi lomi salmon, and oriental short ribs. A Polynesian revue follows. Phone 879-1922.

MAUI LU

"Remember the good times of old Hawaii?" queries the Maui Lu. Well if you don't, they suggest you try their traditional luau on Saturday night. $32 for adults and $19 for children. Phone 879-5858.

OLD LAHAINA LUAU

Located on the beach in front of 505 Front Street in Lahaina, they invite guests to join them for a "celebration of aloha in the traditional Hawaiian style", Monday, Tuesday, Thursday and Saturday evenings at 5:30. $37 adults, $16 children. This luau is smaller and more personal, with a maximum of 200 people. The entertainers and help are dressed in are real Hawaiians and wear traditional island garb. Phone 667-1998.

ROYAL LAHAINA RESORT

A Polynesian luau is offered in their luau gardens nightly at 5:30. A buffet dinner includes Kalua pig, teriyaki ribs and other exotic taste treats. Adults $36, $18 for children age 12 and under. Phone 661-3611.

SHERATON MAUI HOTEL

The Discovery Room offers a dinner show, "Maui, Moonlight, Magic", nightly. Dinner selections from the menu beginning at 6:30, show at 8:30 with $4 cover charge for non-diners. Phone 661-0031.

The Sheraton Maui Luau "Aloha Luau" is nightly at 5 p.m. Children under 12 – $19, adults – $36. Phone 661-0031.

STOUFFER WAILEA BEACH RESORT

"Hawaiian Hula Review" begins with an open bar each Monday and Wednesday at 6 p.m. Dinner and entertainment follow until 9 p.m. Adults – $38, Children – $21. Phone 879-4900.

TROPICAL PLANTATION BAR-B-QUE, SUNSET HAYRIDE & COUNTRY PARTY

Each Monday and Wednesday the charcoals are fired up for an all-you-can-eat BBQ feast. Grilled steaks, BBQ chicken, chili, corn on the cob, corn bread, fresh fruits, and a dessert table which includes a variety of pies. Tropical drinks, fruit punch, or iced tea. Entertainment includes plantation cowboys and cowgirls who sing and dance to some Hawaiian and country favorites, as well as a tour of the plantation. Adults – $38, children – $28, small fee for roundtrip transportation from Lahaina, Kaanapali, Kihei, Wailea and Kahului. Phone 244-7643.

LAHAINA

INEXPENSIVE

AMILIO'S DELICATESSEN
Lahaina Square (above Lahaina Shopping Center – north end of town) (661-8551). TYPE OF FOOD: Sandwiches and pizza. COMMENTS: Take out or eat in.

ARBY'S
At the corner of Limahana and Honoapiilani Hwy. HOURS: Daily for breakfast, lunch and dinner. TYPE OF FOOD: Roast beef is their specialty in a fast food format.

THE BAKERY ★
911 Limahana (turn off Honoapiilani Hwy. by Pizza Hut) (667-9062). HOURS: Monday through Saturday 7 a.m–5 p.m., Sunday 7 a.m.–noon. TYPE OF FOOD: Pastries, sandwiches. SAMPLING: Whole wheat cream cheese croissants for 85 cents, also ham, or turkey stuffed croissants, or small sandwiches such as turkey dijon. Huge fresh fruit tortes, fudge, and fresh breads are made here daily. COMMENTS: There is no seating area. Arrive early in the day to insure getting the best selections. It's well worth the stop if you are a lover of pastries. The selection is magnificent and tasty too!

BLACKIE'S BAR
On Hwy. 30 between Lahaina and Kaanapali (667-7979). Look for the tree house structure with the orange roof. HOURS: Daily, 10 a.m.–10 p.m. TYPE OF FOOD: Burritos, enchiladas, tacos, nachos, smoked hot dogs, good burgers and Louisiana hot links. COMMENTS: Jazz on Fridays and Sundays, 5-8 p.m.

BURGER KING
South end of Lahaina by the Banyan Tree. HOURS: 6:30 a.m. – 11 p.m. serving breakfast, lunch, and dinner. TYPE OF FOOD: Breakfast sandwiches, salad bar, and the usual burgers at prices slightly higher than the mainland. COMMENTS: Open air with seating available.

CHRIS'S SMOKEHOUSE
At Lahaina Square Shopping Center, north end of Lahaina by Foodland (667-2111). HOURS: Lunch 11:30 a.m.–2:30 p.m.; dinner 5:30–11 p.m. TYPE OF FOOD: BBQ ribs, steak, fish, and chicken. Also take-out. SAMPLING: Ribs $9.95, chicken dishes $10.95 – $12.95, N.Y. steak $13.50, charbroiled fish priced daily.

CHRISTINE'S FAMILY RESTAURANT
At Lahaina Square (661-4156). HOURS: Tuesday thru Saturday 6 a.m.–9:30 p.m. Sunday and Monday 7 a.m.–3 p.m. Breakfast served anytime, lunch and dinner menus are the same. TYPE OF FOOD: "Homestyle" sandwiches, plate lunches. SAMPLING: Plate lunches $4.95-$6.85, burgers from $4, dinners $9-$10. COMMENTS: Very popular spot for local residents.

COLONEL SANDERS' CHICKEN
Lahaina Shopping Center (661-3422).

DENNY'S
Lahaina Shopping Center (667-9878). HOURS: 24 hours a day. TYPE OF FOOD: Mainland, burgers, some local style dishes. SAMPLING: Breakfast served anytime. Dinners include steak, seafood and chicken $6.79-$10.79.

FISHERMAN'S WHARF
Upper level of Wharf Shopping Center (667-9535). HOURS: Lunch 11 -3, dinner 5-9:30 p.m. TYPE OF FOOD: seafood specialty. SAMPLING: Spaghetti, seafood, and steak $6.75- $16.95. Dinner entrees are served with fruit cup, salad or chowder, vegetable, rice or fries, rolls, coffee or tea. COMMENTS: They feature entertainment 6 p.m.-10 p.m., Tuesday through Saturday.

GOLDEN PALACE
Lahaina Shopping Center (661-3126). HOURS: Lunch and dinner, 11 a.m.-9 p.m. Also take out. TYPE OF FOOD: Chinese. SAMPLING: A large variety of selections with Chinese and some Szechuan dishes. Affordably priced from $4-$8. COMMENTS: Beer, cocktails, and Chinese wine are also available.

GREAT JANE'S EATERY
888 Wainee St., Lahaina (661-5733). HOURS: Monday thru Friday 7 -4, Saturday 7-3, closed on Sunday. TYPE OF FOOD: Sandwiches. SAMPLING: All sandwiches are served by the inch and range from 4 to 24 inches. Ham and cheese, roast beef, American and Italian sub, shrimp, or BBQ beef. Also hot dogs. 4" sandwiches begins at $1.95, top price for a 24" is $17. Breakfast omelets $3.95 -$4.50. Located across from McDonald's in the old Travel Lodge. COMMENTS: 4 tables outside, 2 inside. Food to go. Free delivery Lahaina area 11-2.

GREENTHUMB'S
839 Front Street (667-6126). HOURS: Daily 10 a.m.-10 p.m. TYPE OF FOOD: Salads, sandwiches, and assorted entrees. SAMPLING: Garden salad at $6.50, a chef salad at $8.50, or a Tuna salad at $7.50. Sandwiches run $4.25 for avocado and cheese, to their extravaganza with ham, turkey, salami, and cheese at $6.50. COMMENTS: Nice oceanside view and very casual atmosphere. Orders available to go.

HAMBURGER MARY'S ORGANIC GRILL
608 Front St., a little off-the-beaten-track, down at the south end of Lahaina across from Kam 3 School (667-6989). HOURS: 7 a.m.-11 p.m. for breakfast, lunch, and dinner. Cocktails served. TYPE OF FOOD: Hamburgers and more! SAMPLING: Salads $2.50-$6.95. Burgers $3.95-$6.95. Salads include papaya, avocado, or tomato stuffed with your choice of chicken salad, tuna salad, seafood, cottage cheese, cream cheese, or raw milk cheese. They have a large variety of hamburgers, which are among the biggest we've found on Maui. COMMENT: Outdoor eating under a canopy. You might try splitting a hamburger if you aren't *really* hungry.

HAPPY DAYS ★
Lahainaluna Street a block up from Front St. (667-6994). HOURS: Breakfast 7-11, lunch/dinner 11-9 p.m. TYPE OF FOOD: Sandwiches, burgers, and soups. SAMPLING: 1/4 or 1/3 pound burgers and sandwiches from $3.95. Homemade soup. COMMENTS: As its name implies, this place takes one back to the 1950's. Their fountain serves up favorites such as "real flavored" cokes, egg creams, hand-dipped milkshakes and malts. Yum!

HARPOONER'S LANAI ★
On Front St., wharfside at the Pioneer Inn, (661-3636). HOURS: Daily, breakfast 7-11 a.m. and lunch from 11:30 a.m. TYPE OF FOOD: Varied. SAMPLING: Eggs with ham, links, Portuguese sausage, or bacon for $4.25. Coconut, banana, macadamia nut, or blueberry pancakes at $4.50. French toast runs $3.25. Lunches might include Portuguese bean soup at $2.25, or a hamburger at $4.25. COMMENTS: Our usual order is their French toast which is four half-slices of Portuguese Sweet Bread that are thick and custardy. The atmosphere is rustic, casual, and makes one feel almost as if the clock had been turned back.

LAHAINA BROILER
Under renovations, no information available.

LAHAINA TREEHOUSE AND SEAFOOD BAR RESTAURANT
Lahaina Marketplace on Front St. (667-9224). HOURS: Lunch 11:30 –2:30. SAMPLING: Salads, sandwiches, entrees $6.95-$8.95. COMMENTS: No credit cards.

LANI'S PANCAKE COTTAGE ★
Wharf Shopping Center, across from the Banyan Tree (661-0955). HOURS: Breakfast and lunch 6:30 a.m.-3:30 p.m. TYPE OF FOOD: Breakfast items and sandwiches. COMMENTS: Very busy during breakfast hours, offering seating indoors or on the patio.

LEI CAFE
819 Front St., (667-2233). HOURS: 7:30 a.m.-10:30 p.m. TYPE OF FOOD: Varied. SAMPLING: Sandwiches, pizza slices, stuffed potatoes, nachos, hot dogs, chili, quiche, salads, fruit smoothies, desserts, pastries.

LONGHI'S DELI AND PIZZA ★
930 Wainee Street, Lahaina (661-8128). HOURS: 8 a.m.-11 p.m. TYPE OF FOOD: Pizza and sandwiches. SAMPLING: Hot and cold sandwiches are offered including Peking duck along with more usual selections and are priced $5.50-$7. Cheese and tomato pizzas available in $8, $10, $12, and $16 sizes. Additional items extra. Thick crust optional. They also offer daily specialty items and salads. COMMENTS: On our visit they had whole roasted chickens basted with lemon and basil that smelled divine. A few tables for eating, but mostly a take-out location. This place gets our award for the best pizza in West Maui! They deliver too!! Although this popular deli has just changed ownership, the new owners intend to keep the same name and menu items.

MAMA'S PIZZA
658 Front Street at the Wharf Shopping Center (667-2531). HOURS: Daily 11 a.m.-midnight. TYPE OF FOOD: Filipino and Italian. COMMENTS: This restaurant has changed ownership and did some remodeling. While they have kept the name, they have added some Filipino entrees to their menu.

MARIE CALLENDAR
Located at the Cannery Shopping Center, Kaanapali side of Lahaina (667-7437). HOURS: 7 a.m.-10 p.m. Monday thru Thursday and Sunday. Until 11 p.m. on Friday and Saturday. TYPE OF FOOD: Mainland style, pies their specialty! SAMPLING: Breakfast omelets from $5.25 and a selection of fresh fruit waffles. Lunches include pasta, hamburgers, salads, and sandwiches. Dinner begins daily at 4 p.m., priced $8.95-$12.95. Daily specials vary, but might include the very popular prime rib sandwich. COMMENTS: The atmosphere is cozy with an old time saloon look. Good family dining. Entertainment in the evenings.

MAUI BUNS
Lower level and back corner of the Wharf Shopping Center, 844 Front St. (667-7666). HOURS: 7-5 daily. TYPE OF FOOD: 20 types of buns and bunwiches. SAMPLING: Buns come in an assortment for breakfast, lunch, snacks or dinner and include tuna, ham, spinach, cheese, turkey, chocolate, cinnamon or berry. Prices run $1.40-$3.25 COMMENTS: A few tables in common area.

MCDONALD'S
Located at Lahaina Shopping Center. HOURS: Open for breakfast, lunch, and dinner. TYPE OF FOOD: The usual for McDonald's with a few added items such as Saimin. COMMENTS: Indoor eating and also a drive-through.

MOOSE McGILLYCUDDY'S
844 Front St., upper level of Mariner's Alley, a small shopping alley at the north end of town (667-7758). HOURS: Breakfast from 7:30 a.m., also lunch and dinner. TYPE OF FOOD: Lots of burgers. SAMPLING: Their early bird breakfast special is $2.49. The real big eater may want to tackle a moose omelette consisting of 12 eggs with two types of cheese, bacon, sausage, mushrooms, sprouts, spinach, and onion for $12.95. Twenty or more burgers are offered including the bareburger, a plain patty with a cottage cheese, fruit, and tossed salad, an Egg McMoose which is a burger with fried egg and cheese on it, or an Air Burger, a veggie burger with no meat, no cheese, and no mayo. Priced $4.75 and up. Pizza available to go, it'll fill you up but won't win any awards. COMMENTS: Early bird dinner specials, evening music on the wild side.

ORGAN GRINDER
811 Front St., by the seawall (661-4593). HOURS: Open for breakfast lunch and dinner TYPE OF FOOD: Sandwiches and burgers. SAMPLING: Turkey & avocado or Maui burger $5.25. COMMENTS: Family-owned and operated with the emphasis on food, not decor. One of the best bargains for a real waterfront view. No credit cards.

PANCHO & LEFTY'S
658 Front Street at the Wharf Shopping Center on the courtyard level in the rear (661-3956). HOURS: Daily 11 a.m.–11 p.m. TYPE OF FOOD: Mexican. SAMPLING: Their house specialty is frajitas served with chicken, beef or seafood. Prices run $6.95–$12.95. Cocktails.

PIZZA HUT
127 Hinau, Lahaina, (661-3696).

SEASIDE INN ★
Front Street across from the Cannery Shopping Center (661-7195). HOURS: Bentos available from 6:30 a.m., hot lunches and okazuya service from 10 a.m.–2 p.m. TYPE OF FOOD: Local, Hawaiian, oriental. SAMPLING: Hot lunches from $4 with items changing daily. (Okazuya is a buffet style where you pay for each serving you choose). Bentos (plate lunches) run $4–$4.75. COMMENTS: Formerly Naokee's Too, Jane Nagasako, of the Lahaina Supermarket, has refurbished and refreshed this lovely oceanview location. It now seems apparent that you can get a good plate lunch in Lahaina as they frequently sell out! They hope to be opening for dinner in the near future.

SIR WILFRED'S ESPRESSO CAFE
The Cannery Shopping Center, Kaanapali side of Lahaina (667-1941). HOURS: Breakfast until 11 with a lunch/dinner menu served until 9:30 p.m. TYPE OF FOOD: Sandwiches. SAMPLING: Breakfasts include Eggs Sir Muffin, Eggs Florentine or Quiche priced $2.95 –$3.95. Daily lunch specials include sandwiches and salads from $3.55–$4.95. COMMENTS: A very small, pleasant eatery. Great coffee and espresso. Gourmet coffees available to purchase.

SKIPPER'S
658 Front Street, Wharf Shopping Center. TYPE OF FOOD: Seafood. COMMENTS: Usual fare at Skipper's with slightly higher than Mainland prices.

SONG'S
658 Front Street at the Wharf Shopping Center (667-1990). HOURS: Daily for lunch and dinner TYPE OF FOOD: Chinese/Hawaiian. SAMPLING: This is buffet style with selections varying daily. After viewing the selections in the display case, your plate is dished up for you. Only a single table near the door offers seating, or get yours to go. Saimin, lomi lomi, stuffed cabbage, prices $1.50–$5. COMMENTS: A little hard to find in a remote location in the rear.

SOUTH SEAS/SNUG HARBOR
At Pioneer Inn, harborside (661-3636). HOURS: Open only for dinner. TYPE OF FOOD: Seafood, beef, and chicken. SAMPLING: Broil-your-own ground beef, 1/2 chicken, beef stir fry, or pork chops $9.95–$12.95 served with salad bar, baked beans, rolls. COMMENTS: Seating at South Seas is poolside at the very rustic Pioneer Inn Hotel. The Snug Harbor has indoor seating at the same location, same menu. Very casual atmosphere and they do offer a children's menu.

SUNRISE CAFE
693A Front St.,(661-3326). HOURS: Breakfast and lunch. SAMPLING: Breakfasts around $5, sandwiches begin at $4.50. COMMENTS: Operated by owners of La Bretagne. This is a very small eatery, food available to go. Very limited menu.

TAKE HOME MAUI
143 Luakini (turn by the Baldwin House off Front Street) (661-7056). SAMPLING: Fresh fruit smoothies, toffuti, sandwiches ($3.95ish), ice cream and sodas in the freezer. Fruits and Hawaiian coffee are among the items to be shipped or taken home. COMMENTS: This is a fast food type stop, limited seating. Fruit smoothies are delicious!

THAI CHEF
Lahaina Shopping Center (667-2814). HOURS: Lunch 11-2:30, dinner 5-10 nightly. TYPE OF FOOD: Thai. SAMPLING: Entrees are $5-$10 and include chicken, pork and seafood. Seating for 40. Reservations suggested.

TIPANAN
Lahaina Square Shopping Center (661-5595). HOURS: 10:30-9 p.m. Mon. - Sat. TYPE OF FOOD: Filipino. SAMPLING: Entrees include bistek tagalog, daing na bangus, paksiw na pata. (These translate to filet of beef tenderloin with lemon juice and soy, milkfish fried to a savory taste, and tender pork stewed in sweet-sour sauce). Priced $3.00-$6.50 they are served with rice. COMMENTS: This little family-operated restaurant is new to Lahaina and we were not able to review it. However, as it is tucked around the corner at the Lahaina Shopping Center (where Foodland is located) they may have to be discovered by word of mouth. They also have a location in Wailuku (1276 Lower Main St.).

VILLAGE PIZZERIA
At 505 Front St. (661-8112). HOURS: Lunch and dinner daily TYPE OF FOOD: Pizza. SAMPLING: Pizza is available in Neapolitan style (thin crust) or Sicilian (thick crust). A 14″ plain pizza starts at $10, a combo of 4 items $14.25.

OLD LAHAINA CAFE AND LUAU
At 505 Front St. (661-3303). HOURS: Daily 11 a.m.-2 p.m.TYPE OF FOOD: Local Hawaii style. SAMPLING: Lau lau, and other authentic Hawaiian dishes as well as some interesting variation including scallops deep fried in poi, 11 - 2 COMMENTS: Renovations have created an open air Hawaiian style cafe. This operation is in conjunction with the luau held on the beach that fronts 505 Front St. Not open for review, but if it keeps up with the standards of their luau, it should be a great place for lunch!

MODERATE

ALEX'S HOLE IN THE WALL ★
834 Front St. (661-3197). HOURS: Dinner only, 6-10 p.m., daily except Sunday. TYPE OF FOOD: Italian. SAMPLING: A variety of seafood, veal or chicken dishes at $15. Pasta entrees $13.00. Veal and scampi priced $19. Spaghetti is $8.00 adult portions, also in children's portions. COMMENTS: They serve wonderful pasta that is made fresh locally. Visa and Mastercard accepted.

AVALON ★

844 Front St., (location formerly Marco's) (667-5559). HOURS: Daily 11-11. TYPE OF FOOD: Fresh local foods with the influence of Mexico to Indonesia, termed Pacific-Basin Cuisine. SAMPLING: They fresh island food served in creative new ways. Mexican specialties served with plantain include tacos and burritos made with chicken, fish or steak, and guacamole prepared tableside will be among the selections. Vietnamese Summer Rolls (similar to Spring rolls except that they are not deep fried) are served with a cucumber-chili sauce. Another unique menu item is Gado Gado salad from the island of Bali. This layered salad has brown rice on the bottom which is topped with shredded lettuce, lightly steamed vegetables, cubed tofu and cucumbers, and served with a peanut sauce. Other specialties include fresh whole Dungeness crab (from their live crab tank) served in a spicy black bean sauce or island chicken marinated and grilled with Indonesian spices. COMMENTS: The name Avalon, according to Celtic or Gaelic legend, is the West Pacific island paradise where King Arthur and other heroes went following death. The look here is 40's Hawaiian with big tropical prints and multi-colored oversized dishes. Some patio seating is available in this recently renovated shopping area.

BETTINO'S

At 505 Front St. (661-8810). HOURS: Breakfast begins at 7 a.m. Also open for lunch and dinner. Bar opens at 8 a.m. TYPE OF FOOD: Everything. SAMPLING: Lunches, including sandwiches and burgers are priced $4-$5.50. Dinners run $10-$20. Mahi Mahi, chicken Mediterranean or short ribs run $12.95, chicken parmesan $10.95. COMMENTS: This is a little off the tourist track, and a no frills type of place, but who needs them with a window table right next to the ocean. One of their specialties, Shrimp Bettino offered an abundance of huge shrimp and wonderful pasta at only $14.95. The ribs and chicken parmesan were equally good dinner values. Food quality seems to be a little inconsistent lately.

THE BOATHOUSE KEG

730 Front St. (661-3137), upstairs. HOURS: Lunch 11:30-3 p.m. and dinner 5:30-9:30 p.m. TYPE OF FOOD: Steak and seafood. SAMPLING: Kiawe broiled chicken, pasta, prime rib, steak or seafood run $9.95-$19.95. Keiki menu. Music nightly.

CHART HOUSE ★

1450 Front St. (661-0937). HOURS: Dinner daily 5:00-9:30 p.m. TYPE OF FOOD: Seafood and beef. SAMPLING: Fresh fish, chicken, top sirloin, scallops, teriyaki beef kabobs, $11.25-$19.95. COMMENTS: Entrees are served with an unusual, all you can eat salad bar. A large bowl filled with mixed greens, tomatoes, onions, eggs and cucumbers is served at your table along with smaller bowls filled with croutons, fresh pineapple and several kinds of homemade dressing. If it's not enough, ask for more. The bread is fresh and homemade with a choice of white sourdough or molasses "squaw" bread. There is a comfortable open air atmosphere with lots of wood and lava rock. The limited number of oceanview tables are a hot commodity and require that you arrive when they open. They also have a waitress who stops by to take orders from their seafood appetizer bar. Potatoes and rice are available at an extra charge. They provide one of the best keiki menus we've seen. The menu serves as a coloring book and a small pack of crayons are thoughtfully provided. The children's selections include four very reasonable dinners, $1.95 for ground sirloin, chicken teriyaki or beef kabobs at $3.95, and a small sirloin steak at $5.95. The entree portions were large. Included with the meal was salad, rice or potato and a soft drink. A paradise for parents! The adult entree prices may be slightly higher than other restaurants, but the cut of prime rib was enormous and the fresh fish portion very ample. They don't take reservations so there can be a long wait. They also offer another restaurant in Kahului.

HARBOR FRONT
Wharf Shopping Center, top level (667-7822). HOURS: Lunch 11:30-2 p.m. weekdays, dinner 5-10 p.m. daily. TYPE OF FOOD: Chicken, fish, and beef. SAMPLING: Fish and chips for lunch at $8.95 or seafood combo at $9.95. Dinner entrees from $9.95 for fish and chips, to bouillabaisse at $21.95. COMMENTS: No harbor view here, and the eating is inside. We have heard good things, but on the occasions we've visited, we were never too impressed. For a fun dessert they prepare bananas flambe and cherries jubilee at your table.

KIMO'S ★
845 Front St. (661-4811). HOURS: Dinner served daily. TYPE OF FOOD: Speciality is seafood, also beef and chicken dishes. SAMPLING: Their fresh fish varies daily as does its price. Baked scallops $10.95, shrimp Tahitian $11.95, top sirloin $9.95 and mahi or Kalua pork $8.95. Keiki dinners, or for less hungry adults, include hamburgers and chicken sandwiches priced $5.50-$5.95. COMMENTS: No reservations, so plan on a wait. Put in your name, have the hostess give you a time frame, and just enjoy prowling the Lahaina shops. They have a waterfront location and, if you're really lucky, you'll get a table with a view. Opinions vary greatly about Kimo's. Some really like it and others really don't. Our experience has been very good service and nicely prepared fresh fish. They also have a bar on the lower level that offers a young crowd and a ocean view for sunset.

KOBE'S STEAK HOUSE ★
136 Dickenson (667-5555). HOURS: Daily for lunch and dinner. SAMPLING: Teriyaki chicken $9.40, Teppan shrimp $15.50, lobster $21.50, sushi bar. Dinners include soup, shrimp appetizer, vegetables, rice, and green tea ice cream. COMMENTS: Kobe's opened in early 1986 in a beautifully decorated new building. A sister of the Palm Springs and Honolulu restaurants, they offer teppan cooking (food is prepared on the grill in front of you) and the show is as good as the meal. We were impressed with the generous portions and the quality, and appreciated the very affordable prices. They have a small parking lot adjacent to the building. Keiki menu. Reservations are recommended.

LAHAINA STEAK AND LOBSTER
1312 Front St. (667-5558). HOURS: 7 a.m.-10 p.m. TYPE OF FOOD: Steak, seafood and chicken. SAMPLING: New York steak, teriyaki chicken, stir fried beef, or pork ribs $10-$20. Dinners include soup, salad bar, rice, vegetable and rolls. COMMENTS: They have recently begun providing comedy entertainment.

LONGHI'S ★

888 Front St. (667-2288). HOURS: 7:30 a.m.–10 p.m.; dessert served until 11 p.m. TYPE OF FOOD: Varied. SAMPLING: The menu is given orally by waiter. A possible selection might include zucchini frittatta, shrimp Longhi, or prawns amaretto. They are famous for their desserts. COMMENTS: They have become a near legend in Lahaina and have recently done a little remodeling that offers more seating on the upper floor. The setting is casual, with lots of windows open to the bustling Lahaina streets. They offer capuccino and a good wine selection. Popular for breakfast. Valet parking.

MUSASHI

Lahaina Shopping Center (667-6207). HOURS: Lunch 11 a.m.–2 p.m., dinner 5–10 p.m. TYPE OF FOOD: Japanese. SAMPLING: Beef or chicken teriyaki, sukiyaki, nabe. Lunches run $5.25–$7 with an all you can eat Sushi Bar at lunch only. Dinners include a combination plate for $14.95 and Nabe (cooked at the table for two) $15.95 per person. COMMENTS: Formerly Fujiyamas.

OCEANHOUSE and SEAFOOD CAFE

831 Front St. (661-3359). HOURS: Daily for lunch and dinner. TYPE OF FOOD: Seafood, chicken, beef. SAMPLING: The Oceanhouse serves dinner only, $16.95–$26. COMMENTS: Gone is the rustic atmosphere, replaced with a more sophisticated one with higher prices. Upstairs is their Seafood Cafe open 11:30 a.m.–10:30 p.m. which offers casual style, and more reasonable prices. Pizzas from $5.95, dinners $9.25–$13.95.

SAM'S BEACHSIDE GRILL ★

505 Front Street (667-4341). HOURS: Lunch 11–4 p.m. Mon. –Sat., dinner daily 5–10 p.m., Sunday brunch 9–2 p.m. TYPE OF FOOD: Seafood, beef, or chicken. Kiawe broiling. SAMPLING: Lunch entrees include pork chops with pineapple chili relish or fettucini $6.50–$11.50, also fish and chips, salads, sandwiches or soup from $2.25–$10.00. Dinners include fresh vegetable, potato, rice or pasta served with local fresh fish, duckling, chicken or shellfish from $8.95–$20.95. Sunday brunch $4.95 –$9.95. COMMENTS: The upstairs dining location offers a pleasant oceanfront view. Downstairs they have pupu's and cocktail service. We took advantage of an early bird dinner offer and enjoyed well prepared meals, good portions and friendly service.

WHALE'S TALE

Across from the Pioneer Inn at 666 Front St., upstairs (661-3676). HOURS: Lunch served from 11:30–2:30 p.m., dinner from 5:30 p.m. TYPE OF FOOD: Seafood and beef. SAMPLING: Lunches run $4.95–$9.95 for an assortment of sandwiches, salads and fresh fish. Dinner selections include fish, ribs, chicken and steak priced $10.95–$15.95. COMMENTS: Entertainment daily from 4 p.m. until closing. Reservations accepted.

EXPENSIVE

CHEZ PAUL ★
Five miles south of Lahaina at Olowalu (661-3843). HOURS: Dinner 5:30–10:30 p.m. TYPE OF FOOD: French. SAMPLING: Dinners run $18.95 for a vegetarian fare to $24.95 for most selections. The menu includes veal, fish, duck, and beef in wonderful French sauces. Dinners include French bread, soup or salad and two vegetables. Pate, escargot, and shrimp are available as appetizers. Save room for some very special desserts. COMMENTS: This small restaurant has maintained a high popularity with excellent food and service. It's not surprising they have won numerous dining awards. The wine list is excellent, although expensive. Wines are also available by the glass. Two seatings for dinner are offered, 6:30 or 8:30. Reservations are a must. Visa and Mastercard are accepted.

GERARD'S ★
Now in its new location off the lobby of the Plantation Inn at 174 Lahainaluna Rd. (This is a major street which intersects Front Street near the center of Lahaina.) (661-8939). HOURS: Breakfast daily from 7:30. Lunch from 11 a.m. and dinner served Monday through Saturday from 6 p.m. TYPE OF FOOD: French. SAMPLING: Breakfast can be a simple fresh croissant or poached eggs with crab and smoked salmon. Cappucino, espresso and fresh juices are available. (Lunch and dinners remain the same delicious selections which vary daily.) For dinner you might choose roast beef au jus, duckling ala orange, braised leg of lamb, pepper steak, fresh chicken breast sauteed in raspberry vinegar sauce, or steak tartare. Desserts are made fresh daily. COMMENTS: The new location is lovely and offers patio seating as well as indoor seating and air conditioning. The sauces served with the meals here are outstanding.

LA BRETAGNE RESTAURANT FRANCAIS ★
Mokuhinia Place, off Front St. between Banyan Tree and 505 Front St. (661-8966). HOURS: Dinner only. TYPE OF FOOD: French. SAMPLING: Entrees $22–$25 include salad, vegetable, French bread. COMMENTS: Once the home of Sheriff Kaluakini, a lawman during Lahaina's heyday, it's a little tricky to find off Front Street. The flowered upholstery on the chairs and the brocade wall coverings all add to the wonderful atmosphere here. Combined with personable service at a relaxed pace, it feels like you are dining in the home of a friend. Our meals were all excellent. Reservations are highly recommended, and while dress is casual, shorts aren't advised. Visa and Mastercard accepted.

KAANAPALI

INEXPENSIVE

BEACH BAR
Westin Maui, located near the beach (661-8939). HOURS: 9-6 p.m. TYPE OF FOOD: Salads/sandwiches SAMPLING: Hot dog $4, sandwiches of ham or prime rib, or tropical fruit salad $6.75-$8. Ice cream too!

GARDEN BAR
Westin Maui. (667-2525) Located atop the center island of the pool complex. HOURS: 9 a.m.-11 p.m. TYPE OF FOOD: Light snacks and sandwiches.

KAANAPALI BEACH HOTEL COFFEE SHOP
Kaanapali Beach Hotel (661-0011). HOURS: Breakfast from 6 a.m.; lunch from 11 a.m., and dinner from 5 p.m. TYPE OF FOOD: American. COMMENTS: Cafeteria style with $5-$7 plate lunches. A good value, but lacking in atmosphere.

KAU KAU BAR
Poolside at the Maui Marriott. HOURS: Breakfast 7:30-10:30 a.m., lunch and snacks 10-4 p.m. TYPE OF FOOD: Breakfast items and hamburgers. SAMPLING: Continental breakfast $4.95, waffles $6.50, cheeseburger with fries $6.25.

RICCO'S
Whaler's Village Shopping Center (661-4433). HOURS: 10-10 p.m. daily. TYPE OF FOOD: Sandwiches, burgers, salads and pizza.

ROYAL OCEAN TERRACE ★
Royal Lahaina Hotel (661-3611). HOURS: Daily for breakfast lunch and dinner 6 a.m.-10 p.m. Sunday brunch served 9-2 p.m. TYPE OF FOOD: American and assorted. SAMPLING: A daily breakfast buffet is $9.50 or order off the menu. Champagne brunch on Sunday. Lunch choices include sandwiches and salads $5.95 -$8.50. The Royal Ocean Terrace Food Fare is a smorgasbord of at least 25 salads and is $8.75 a la carte or $2.75 with any dinner. (This is one of the islands best salad bars!) Dinners include steak, chicken, lamb and seafood from $10.50-$16.95. COMMENTS: This is a very attractive, airy restaurant. The night we dined their salad bar had 26 items and included lettuce or spinach salad, pasta salad, an excellent "new potato" salad, shrimp salad, fresh vegetable salad and more. To accompany your green salad, they offer the standard dressings as well as carafes of unusual oils and vinegars to combine on your own, i.e. grape seed oil, walnut oil, raspberry vinegar. The dessert bar tempts you on your arrival and you might want to save room for one of their special ice cream drinks! For the iighter eater they offer several sandwich selections as well.

YAMI YOGURT
Whaler's Village (661-8843). TYPE OF FOOD: Salads, sandwiches, and yogurt items. SAMPLING: Sandwiches such as cheese and egg salad in the $3-$4 range. COMMENTS: No seating in the restaurant, but a few tables outside. Call ahead and have them pack a picnic lunch for you.

MODERATE

BEACH CLUB

Maui Kaanapali Villas (667-7791). HOURS: Breakfast 7:30-11 a.m., Lunch 11:30-3:30 p.m., Dinner 6-9:30 p.m. TYPE OF FOOD: Seafood, beef, chicken. SAMPLING: Fresh fish, hamburgers or chicken dishes $6.95-$14.95. COMMENTS: Early bird dinner special offered 6-7 p.m. features a choice of prime rib, BBQ chicken, or mahi mahi for $8.95. A pleasant atmosphere in this eatery located near the pool of this resort.

BLACK ROCK TERRACE

Poolside at the Sheraton Hotel (661-0031). HOURS: Continental breakfast, lunch 11-3:30 p.m., and dinner 6-9:30 p.m. TYPE OF FOOD: American. SAMPLING: Early bird dinners 5:30-7:30 p.m. are prime rib with salad, fresh vegetables, potato, rolls, coffee or tea and burgundy wine for $13.95. Sandwiches begin at about $6. Other dinner items include fresh fish or N.Y. steak priced $13.95-$20. All dinners include salad bar. Children's portions available.

CAFE KAANAPALI

Whalers Village (661-4944). HOURS: Breakfast 7-11 a.m., lunch 11-4 p.m., and dinner 4-10 p.m. Appetizers available all day in the lounge. TYPE OF FOOD: varied. SAMPLING: Lunch menu available at dinner as well as a selection of complete dinners. Fresh fish specials nightly. Pasta, Mexican selections, steaks, sandwiches, salads and cafe burgers are complimented by a complete soda fountain. Sandwiches and burgers are in the $5-$6 range and no dinners are priced over $20 except specials. COMMENTS: A moderately priced restaurant with a variety of menu selections which is a welcomed addition to Whaler's Village. This location was previously Ming Court.

CHICO'S

Whalers Village Shopping Center (667-2777). HOURS: Daily for lunch 11:30-2:30 and for dinner. Taco bar open 11:30 a.m. to midnight. TYPE OF FOOD: Mexican. SAMPLING: Enchiladas $6.95 -$7.95, tostados $6.95. Keiki menu offers selections at $3.95.

CHOPSTICKS

Royal Lahaina Resort (661-3611). HOURS: Dinner nightly 6-9:30 p.m. TYPE OF FOOD: Chinese, Japanese, and Thai. SAMPLING: "The Place to Graze." Nutty chicken $5.95, sweet and sour pork $3.95, coconut shrimp, ginger beef, chicken wings or crispy almond duck for $6.95. COMMENTS: So what is grazing? Chopsticks is the first restaurant on Maui to introduce the concept of grazing and it really is a wonderful idea for the adventurous eater. Items from Mainland China, Micronesia, Hong Kong and Thailand are served in appetizer size portions. The menu is a la carte and in the style of a passport. Each item ordered is validated and with enough credits you can "earn" a complimentary selection. The light eater can be satisfied easily, while the more hearty appetite can pick and choose himself/herself a banquet. This provides a nice opportunity to try something new and unusual, without being committed to an entire meal of it.

COOK'S AT THE BEACH ★

Westin Maui, north side of the swimming pool (667-2525). HOURS: Breakfast 6:30–11, lunch and dinner 11–11 p.m. TYPE OF FOOD: Light fare, soups, salads and sandwiches. SAMPLING: Egg dishes from $8.25, sandwiches, salads and burgers $4.50–$11.75. You could select a Hawaiian field salad, ogo seaweed salad, or seafood salad with lemongrass dressing. Pasta and pizzas $8 –$9.50. Fresh seafood $12.75–$14.75. Meat and poultry items range from stir-fried chicken at $10.50, to noisettes of lamb with fresh rosemary at $16.25. COMMENTS: Keiki menu. An unusual opportunity to enjoy gourmet foods while dining in swimwear.

EL CRAB CATCHER ★

Whaler's Village Shopping Center (661-4423). It's a little hidden on the ocean side. HOURS: Lunch 11:30–3 p.m. and dinner 5:30 –10:30 p.m. TYPE OF FOOD: Seafood is their specialty. SAMPLING: Dinner entrees are served with soup or salad, vegetable and bread basket. Fresh island fish and its preparation varies daily and is priced at $17.95. Other selections include scampi saute, crab florentine, veal oscar, or prime rib all running between $14.95 –$21.95. Their bar menu has a wonderful selection of salads and sandwiches priced $4.95–$9.95. COMMENTS: This was once an athletic club and the pool remains beachside around which you can dine or enjoy a sunset and cool drink. Some have been known to even take a dip! They do a wonderful job with their fish preparation. Save room for one of their scrumptious desserts. This is a very popular place and reservations are a good idea unless you want to wait an hour or more for restaurant dining. However, their bar area offers some light meal selections and often times immediate seating. The prime rib sandwich we tried was dynamite. Visa, Mastercard, and American Express. Cocktails available.

H. S. BOUNTY

Whaler's Village Shopping Center (661-0946). HOURS: Breakfast, lunch and dinner are served. Early bird dinner specials nightly from 5–6:30 p.m. and available nightly. TYPE OF FOOD: Seafood, chicken, and beef. SAMPLING: Dinners include soup and salad bar, rice, fries or baked potato, and bread. Prime rib, shrimp scampi, fried shrimp, bouillabaisse, short ribs, or veal marsala are priced $12.95–$17.95. COMMENTS: No reservations taken here. Children's (Keiki) portions available. Cocktails served.

LEILANI'S ★

Whaler's Village Shopping Center, on the beach (661-4495). HOURS: Dinner from 5 p.m. TYPE OF FOOD: Seafood, pork, beef, and chicken. SAMPLING: Ginger chicken $9.95, half-pound cheeseburger $7.50, and Malaysian shrimp or double cut lamb chops $15.95. Fresh fish priced daily. COMMENTS: This restaurant is a branch of the Kimo's and the Kapalua Bar and Grill operations. A bar is located on the lower level and it's completely open to the beach. A seafood bar serves sandwiches and salads from $2.50–$9. Some tables offer good beach viewing. They also offer a limited children's menu, and some luscious desserts. They don't take reservations or personal checks, but do honor major credit cards. A reliable stop for a good meal.

LUIGI'S PASTA PIZZERIA
Kaanapali Resort, by the golf course (661-3160). HOURS: Daily 11:30 a.m. until midnight, bar until 2 a.m. TYPE OF FOOD: Italian. SAMPLING: Lunch selections include pasta or pizza as well as sandwiches such as submarines, French dip or club. Dinner selections $8-$17 include pizza, calzone, spaghetti, fettucini, scampi and steak. COMMENTS: Entertainment nightly in their lounge.

MOANA TERRACE ★
Maui Marriott Hotel (667-1200). HOURS: 6:30 a.m.-11 p.m. TYPE OF FOOD: Varied. SAMPLING: Mon. through Sat. their breakfast buffet runs $11.25, $5.25 children 12 and under, and is served from 6:30-11:00 a.m. Items off the menu also. Sunday brunch is from 8-1 p.m. and is $14.00. Lunch is 11:30-5 p.m. Mon. -Sat. with sandwiches and salads. They feature a nightly theme buffet served 5-9 p.m. with a discount "Sundowner Buffet Special" for early diners. Complete dinners from the menu include soup or salad with your entree, which may include pasta primavera $14.20, chicken teriyaki $15.90, or prime rib $17.90. A la carte dinners as well as salads or sandwiches are also available. The evening buffets run $17.50 adults, $13.50 for early bird diners, and $6.50 for children 12 and under. They feature a Hawaiian theme night twice weekly, seafood night twice weekly, and the remaining three nights are prime rib with a variety of different entree accompaniments. COMMENTS: Dinner and Sunday brunch reservations recommended. Their early bird buffet special is a great value, call to confirm the hours it is offered. Major credit cards accepted.

MOBY DICK'S
At the entrance to the Royal Lahaina Resort (661-3611). HOURS: Dinner nightly 6-9:30 p.m. TYPE OF FOOD: Seafood and steak. SAMPLING: Dinners are served with salad or homemade clam chowder and the "Chef's accompaniments." Entrees include chicken tarragon $16.50, island prawns $19.50, fresh fish $17.95, and New York steak $18.50.

NANATOMI
Kaanapali Golf Course Club House (667-7902). Lunch served 11-3, dinner 5-9:30. TYPE OF FOOD: Steak and seafood. SAMPLING: Lunches are "All American" with a variety of tuna, turkey, ham, or beef sandwiches from $4.99-$5.99. Dinners include vegetable, potato or rice, soup or salad and are priced $9.95-$13.95 for grilled ahi, chicken parmesan, or a variety of steaks. COMMENTS: Keiki menu available. Owners also operated Tai Koh Japanese Restaurant. Weekend entertainment. Check for early bird breakfast and dinner specials.

PAVILION
Hyatt Regency Hotel, lower level (661-1234). HOURS: Lunch daily 11:30-6 p.m. and dinner 6-11 p.m. TYPE OF FOOD: Varied. SAMPLING: Luncheon offerings include sandwiches $5-$7. Dinners run $8-$16. COMMENTS: Located near the pool. For the less hearty eater, you can order from their lunch menu at dinner. Keiki dinner menu also available.

THE RUSTY HARPOON ★

Whaler's Village (661-3123). HOURS: Daily for breakfast 8 -11a.m., lunch 11:30-3, and dinner 5-10 p.m., tavern menu served noon to midnight. TYPE OF FOOD: Beef, chicken, seafood, and burgers. SAMPLING: Dinner entrees include rice or pasta and vegetable. Kalbi ribs $11.50, stir-fry chicken $9.95. COMMENTS: Check for possible early bird dinner specials.

TIKI TERRACE

Kaanapali Beach Hotel (661-0011). HOURS: Breakfast 7-11 a.m., dinner 6-9:30 p.m., brunch served Sundays. TYPE OF FOOD: American, Polynesian. SAMPLING: Stir-fry chicken or shrimp $12.95, Chinese roast duck $15.95, or filet mignon $23. Soup and salad bar included with all entrees. Salad bar alone $7.95. Children's menu runs $5-$7.

VILLA RESTAURANT ★

Westin Maui, lobby level (667-2525). HOURS: Lunch 11:30-3 p.m., dinner 5:30-11 p.m. TYPE OF FOOD: Seafood specialty. SAMPLING: Lunch selections (a la carte) include sauteed grey snapper with tomato and caper concassee, broiled ono on a bed of snow peas, or stir-fried island chicken, all priced $10.50-$13.50. Dinners run $16-$21 a la carte with selections such as broiled filet of beef, grilled and glazed lamb chops, sea scallops with red pepper sauce, and stir-fried watercress or steamed onaga in romaine leaf with riesling sauce. COMMENTS: A beautiful setting for excellent seafood. All tables look out onto the lagoon where swans, and exotic ducks float along peacefully.

EXPENSIVE

DISCOVERY ROOM

Sheraton Hotel, atop picturesque Black Rock (661-0031). HOURS: Breakfast 6:30-11:00 a.m., dinner daily. TYPE OF FOOD: Continental and American. SAMPLING: Breakfast buffet served 6:30-10:30a.m., with a regular breakfast menu available until 11 a.m. Dinner menu priced $23-$32 with an international buffet and dinner show at $24.95 each Tuesday.

LAHAINA PROVISION ★

Hyatt Regency Hotel (661-1234). HOURS: Lunch 11:30-3 p.m. and dinner 6-10:30 p.m. The lounge is open from 11:30 a.m.-11:30 p.m. TYPE OF FOOD: Seafood and steak. SAMPLING: Luncheon items run $6-$12 for sandwiches or hot entrees. Dinner selections include fresh fish, T-bone steak or lamb chops $12-$28. COMMENTS: This restaurant is cleverly perched above the pool and on the edge of one of the Hyatt's waterfalls. This place may be a favorite if you're a chocolate lover. They have a CHOCOHOLIC BAR (served 6-11 p.m.) that features rich ice cream with an incredible choice of terrific temptations to top it with. If you have dinner, it's an additional $3.95, but you can come later for dessert only and indulge for $5.95. Reservations are recommended for dinner or dessert. Major credit cards are accepted.

LOKELANI ★
Maui Marriott Hotel (667-1200). HOURS: Dinner served 5:30-10 p.m. TYPE OF FOOD: Seafood. SAMPLING: Scampi, sauteed fresh fish, scallops, or crab legs share the menu here. Dinners include salad, cup of soup, and freshly baked bread. Prices run $15.95 -$19.95. COMMENTS: The food was nicely prepared. An after dinner delight was the coffee, which was accompanied by a tray of wonderful additions; raw sugar, cinnamon sticks, anise covered M & M's, chocolate chips, lemon peel, and fresh whipped cream. They are currently featuring an early bird dinner special, 6-7 p.m., $12.95-$14.95 for entrees which include fresh fish or prime rib. Reservations recommended. Major credit cards accepted.

NIKKO'S JAPANESE STEAK HOUSE ★
At the Maui Marriott Hotel (667-1200). HOURS: Dinner only. TYPE OF FOOD: Japanese. SAMPLING: Shrimp and chicken $19.75 (that's the cheapest), steak or shrimp at $23. Dinner includes an appetizer, Japanese broth, island salad, vegetables and rice. Meals cooked teppan style. COMMENTS: Part of the price is the "show." The chef works at your table and is adept at knife throwing and other dazzling cooking techniques. Children's menu includes a complete dinner for $11.75. Check for their sunset dinner special served from 6-6:30 p.m. Fewer selections but the complete dinners are more affordably priced between $11.95 and $15.95. Reservations recommended. Major credit cards accepted.

PEACOCK RESTAURANT
On Kekaa Drive above the major Kaanapali hotels, on the golf course (667-6847). HOURS: Lunch weekdays 11:30-2 p.m. and dinner nightly 5-10 p.m. TYPE OF FOOD: Continental, Polynesian. SAMPLING: All dinner entrees include soup or salad, choice of rice, potato or pasta, and fresh bread. Seafood and fish selections run $13.75-$23.50 and include Mahi Mahi, scampi, roast pork loin, and broiled chicken breast. COMMENTS: The decor here is tastefully done with an open air Oriental motif, although it could definitely use some freshening up. The service and food are both good. Hawaiian entertainment in their lounge, Thurs. -Sun. Courtesy pick-up may be available, call ahead. Men are requested to wear long pants at dinner. Check to see if they are offering their sunset dinner specials. Reservations are recommended. Major credit cards accepted.

Kaanapali/Expensive

SOUND OF THE FALLS ★

Westin Maui (667-2525). HOURS: Champagne brunch served Mon. -Sat. 9 a.m.-2 p.m. Sunday brunch 8:30 a.m.-2:30 p.m. Dinner 6-midnight. TYPE OF FOOD: Blend of French and Oriental influences. SAMPLING: A lovely brunch is served daily for $12.75, with a more elaborate Sunday champagne buffet for $19.75. The dinner menu features sauteed Hawaiian baby abalone and leeks in walnut vinaigrette, stuffed quails with a mousseline of goose liver and truffles served with port wine sauce, and Hawaiian snapper with lemon and caper sauce. Prices a la carte $20-$36. COMMENTS: A beautiful setting and impeccable service.

SPATS II ★

Hyatt Regency Hotel (661-1234). HOURS: Dinner only. TYPE OF FOOD: Italian pecialty. SAMPLING: Dinners generally run $14-$22. COMMENTS: The interior resembles more an elegant British pub than a restaurante italiano. The food and service were both spectacular. The a la carte pasta appetizers proved sufficient for a child's portion or would be adequate for a light eater. Dishes like Scallopine al Marsala or Petti di Pollo Milanese are worth the calories! Save room for dessert. Reservations recommended. "Top 40" music is played in their lounge from 10 p.m.-2 a.m. Sunday through Thursday, and until 4 a.m. on Friday and Saturday. Dress code requires slacks, shirts with collars and covered shoes.

SWAN COURT ★

Hyatt Regency Hotel (661-1234). HOURS: Open for breakfast 6:30 -11:30 a.m and for dinner. TYPE OF FOOD: Continental. SAMPLING: Their breakfast buffet is $12.95 and includes fresh-squeezed orange juice, macadamia pancakes with a variety of toppings, French toast, cereals, yogurt, fresh fruits, and a good choice of hot breakfast foods. The menu items run $6-$9. Dinners are a la carte $21-$38, salads $5-$6, and soups $4-$5. COMMENTS: The atmosphere and the view of the Swan Court are worth it for a special treat! The dinners are fabulous and many unusual preparations are offered. The service here makes one feel very pampered. Reservations, especially for dinner, are advised. Major credit cards accepted.

KAPALUA/NAPILI/KAHANA

BAR ONLY

KAPALUA BAY RESORT - BAY LOUNGE ★
Enjoy a fabulous sunset in this elegant setting. Pupus served are complimentary.
On one occasion we had a variety of fresh imported cheeses and small shish-kabobs to cook ourselves over a small BBQ. The tropical drinks run $4-$6 with some the size of small fishbowls. A pupu menu is available which offers sushi, sashimi or shrimp cocktails. Live soft background music is provided.

INEXPENSIVE

DOLLIE'S
4310 Honoapiilani Hwy. (667-2623). HOURS: Breakfast, lunch, and dinner. TYPE OF FOOD: Pizzas, sandwiches, and pasta. COMMENTS: Items delivered and food to go! It's located five miles north of Kaanapali at Kahana Manor.

HONOLUA GENERAL STORE
Above Kapalua as you drive through the golf course. HOURS: Daily for breakfast and lunch. TYPE OF FOOD: Sandwiches. COMMENTS: This was a quaint, little old market until the Kapalua Hotel recently refurbished it. The front portion is now an assortment of Kapalua clothing and some locally made food products. The old lunch counter is now a large meat department and deli section. Breakfast choices are limited to croissants and such. Sandwiches are available ready made or made to order.

MARKET CAFE
Kapalua Bay Hotel Shops (669-4888). HOURS: Daily for breakfast, lunch and dinner. Open 8 a.m.-9 p.m. TYPE OF FOOD: Pastries, continental. SAMPL-ING: Breakfasts $4.95-$8.95. Dinner (from 5 p.m.) $8.95-$13.95 includes spaghetti, liver and onions or scampi. Sandwiches, soups and salads $5-$7. Beer & wines. COMMENTS: This small restaurant is part of a market that carries some unusual imported foods.

MODERATE

BEACH CLUB
Kaanapali Shores Resort (667-2211). HOURS: Breakfast 7:30-11 a.m., lunch 11:30-3:00 and dinner from 5 p.m. TYPE OF FOOD: Varied. SAMPLING: Dinners range from seafood and chicken to steak. Bar service. COMMENTS: A recent change in the menu now offers complete dinners. Our food and service were good. Check for early bird dinner specials.

BEACH CLUB

Sands of Kahana Resort (669-0400). HOURS: Breakfast 7:30–11, lunch 11–3, and dinner 5:30–9. TYPE OF FOOD: Varied. SAMPLING: Pupu menu at bar. Cocktail lounge with T.V., sometimes live entertainment. Lunches are $5–$8 and include sandwiches, salads, tuna stuffed papaya, hamburgers, steak sandwiches, ice cream cakes, and fresh pastry. Dinners of N.Y. steak, Steak Diane, veal, lobster, chicken, and scampi run $12–$18. Complete dinners include soup or salad, rolls, vegetables, rice or potatoes. Fresh catch and chef's specials daily, plus theme nights – Chinese, Japanese. A $9.95 early bird special is served 5:30–6:30 p.m. and offers a choice of Mahi, chicken or top sirloin steak. COMMENTS: Oceanview dining.

CHINA BOAT

4474 L. Honoapiilani (669-5089). HOURS: Lunch daily 11–3 except Tuesday, dining nightly. TYPE OF FOOD: Cantonese, Szechuan, and Mandarin. SAMPLING: Shrimp with vegetables, beef with broccoli, and some hot and spicy dishes as well for $6.95–$9.95. COMMENTS: This location has had difficulty maintaining a restaurant business. This is the newest to open and, by the full dining room, it may have a better chance. The atmosphere is simple, very crisp and clean. The waitresses were all oriental (a nice change) and very pleasant. Our food was good with portions average in size. The shrimp with vegetables was a little disappointing considering the canned mushrooms and frozen peas and carrots, however, the sauce was pleasant enough to compensate.

ERIK'S SEAFOOD GROTTO

4242 Lower Honoapiilani Hwy., on the second floor of the Kahana Villa Condo (669-4806). HOURS: Dinner daily 5–10 p.m. TYPE OF FOOD: Seafood and limited beef and chicken selections. SAMPLING: Dinners include chowder or salad, potatoes or rice, and bread. Halibut steak, baked stuffed prawns, Louisiana catfish, rack of lamb, or lobster thermidor run $10.95–$16.95. COMMENTS: Check for early bird dinner specials. Visa, Mastercard, and American Express.

KAHANA KEYES

At the Royal Kahana on Kahana Beach (669-8071). HOURS: Dinner 5 –10:00 p.m. TYPE OF FOOD: Seafood and steak. SAMPLING: Beef brochette, prime rib, shellfish platter, crab legs, scallops, and chicken breast are among selections which are priced $9.95 –15.95. They offer an early bird dinner special daily from 5:30 –7:00 p.m. which currently runs $9.95–$11.95. This special includes salad bar, rice, potatoes or pasta. COMMENTS: A number of items in children's portions. Mediocrity and abundance are key words here. The early bird special is extensively advertised and packs in the people, but promptly at 7 p.m., the place clears out. Their regularly priced dinners are only slightly more expensive than the specials. The dinners we had lacked taste, and many are deep fried. All dinners include the salad bar which is advertised as the island's largest, but bigger isn't always better. While it is a large array, it is unimaginative, and some items seemed none too fresh. The indoor/outdoor carpeting and synthetic wood paneling add little to the ambience. You may leave full, but don't expect much quality for your money. A very limited number of tables offer an ocean view.

KAPALUA GRILL AND BAR ★

200 Kapalua Drive, just across the road from the Kapalua Hotel and a short drive up Kapalua Drive (669-5653). HOURS: Lunch 11:30 –3 p.m. and dinner 5:00–10 p.m. TYPE OF FOOD: Seafood, assorted others. SAMPLING: Lunches include burgers and hot sandwiches for $3.95–$9.95. The dinner menu offers seafood, veal, pasta and chicken dishes for $6.95–$19.95. Their wine list is very good, priced from $8.25–$15 a bottle. COMMENTS: Tank tops are okay daytime attire, but not appropriate for evening. This is a sister facility to Leilani's and Kimo's, but its menu is a little more gourmet. A golf course and ocean view adds to the pluses of this restaurant. Try one of their baked artichokes at $6.95 instead of dessert! It's a popular restaurant, so you might want to call ahead. Visa and Mastercard.

ORIENT EXPRESS

Napili Shores Resort, one mile before Kapalua (669-8077). HOURS: Dinner 5:30–10 p.m. TYPE OF FOOD: Thai and Chinese. SAMPLING: Ginger beef, garlic shrimp, seafood in clay pot, and spinach pork are priced $7.95–$14.95. COMMENTS: Our only experience has been a take-out meal that had very small portions and was uninspiring. Early bird specials from 5 p.m.–7 p.m.

PINEAPPLE HILL

Up past Napili on the "freeway to nowhere", turn left for Kapalua and you will see the entrance (661-0964 or 669-6129). HOURS: Dinner 5:30–10 p.m. with cocktails beginning at 4:30. TYPE OF FOOD: Continental. SAMPLING: Prime rib, steaks, lamb, chicken, and seafood. COMMENTS: This was once the home of a plantation manager, and has been converted into a restaurant with one of the loftiest settings for sunset viewing. We recommend enjoying cocktails out on the front lawn while watching the sun descend. Dinners and service have varied greatly the last few years. Visa, Mastercard, and American Express accepted.

POOL TERRACE RESTAURANT AND BAR ★

Kapalua Hotel, poolside (669-5656). HOURS: Breakfast 6:30–10 a.m., lunch and dinner 11 a.m.–10:30 p.m. TYPE OF FOOD: International. SAMPLING: The pizzas, $9–$10, are both interesting and unique. Maui Lager pizza features dough made with Maui Lager beer topped with onions, garlic and a special blend of cheeses. Pasta selections include fettucini and spaghetti. Salads are priced $6–$8. Sandwiches and burgers run $4–$10. These selections are available for lunch and dinner. Complete dinners are served from 5 p.m. and include chicken with artichoke, lemon duck, fresh catch, or prime rib and are reasonably priced at $16–22. A full wine list is available and an extensive selection of appetizers run $8. COMMENTS: The beautiful location of this casual poolside setting features an oceanview from every seat.

SEA HOUSE (Formerly Teahouse of the Maui Moon)

Beachfront at Napili Kai Beach Club (669-6271). HOURS: Breakfast 8–11, lunch 12–3, and dinner 6–9. TYPE OF FOOD: Varied. SAMPLING: Lunch includes sandwiches & salads that run $3–$8. Dinners, $8.95–$18.95, include scampi, lobster, roast duck, and rack of lamb. Rice or baked potatoes, and vegetable included. Hawaiian music performed Mon., Wed., Thurs., & Sat., 8–10 p.m.

EXPENSIVE

THE BAY CLUB ★

At Kapalua near the entrance to the resort (669-8008 after 5 p.m., 669-5656 before 5 p.m.). HOURS: Lunch 11:30–2 and dinner 6–9:30 p.m. TYPE OF FOOD: Seafood/Gourmet. SAMPLING: Dinners include lamb chops, veal, chicken, steak and a variety of seafoods. Dinners are a la carte and priced $19 and up. They include N.Y. Steak with shallot butter $22, lamp chops with apple coules $23, or chicken supreme with morels & cream $19. COMMENTS: Of special note is the wonderful service that we have received here. The restaurant is situated on a promontory overlooking the ocean, a perfect spot from which to enjoy the scenic panorama along with pupus and cocktails. Their wine list is extensive. The dress code requires swimsuit coverups for lunch and, in the evening, long sleeve dress shirts or jackets for men and no denim. With new management at Kapalua changes are taking place, including new black and white uniforms. A pianist serenades you through dinner adding a romantic touch. Reservations are strongly recommended. Major charge cards accepted.

THE GARDEN RESTAURANT ★

Kapalua Bay Resort Hotel (669-5656). HOURS: Breakfast 6:30–10 a.m., luncheon buffets 12–2:30 Mon.–Sat., 11:30–2:30 Sunday, and dinner nightly 6–9:30. TYPE OF FOOD: Continental. SAMPLING: Dinners are a la carte, priced $15–$23, and include Bombay curry chicken or beef, pasta with shrimp, or rack of lamp. Soup and salads from $2.50. The Mayfair buffet is a bargain at $15.50. COMMENTS: Enjoy continental dining in this semi-open tropical setting. Excellent food and service make this a pleasant dining experience. Reservations recommended and a must for Sunday brunch.

PLANTATION VERANDA ★

Kapalua Bay Hotel (669-5656). HOURS: Dinner only, days and hours vary seasonally, call for current hours. TYPE OF FOOD: Continental. SAMPLING: A la carte dinners. Soups and salads $2.50–$5.00. Entrees include fresh fish, poached with saffron, sauteed with lobster, or Kiawe broiled at $20, Long Island duck $18, and scampi and scallops $22. COMMENTS: This formal setting offers elegant dining. Fine wine by the glass is available from their cruvinet. Enjoy your dinner serenaded by harp music. Jackets are required and reservations are advised.

KIHEI

INEXPENSIVE

AZEKA'S SNACK SHOP ★
Azeka's Place Shopping Center on South Kihei Rd. HOURS: 9:30-4 p.m. Mon.-Sat. TYPE OF FOOD: Burgers and plate lunches. SAMPLING: Plate lunches $2.75-$3.85, tuna sandwiches 95 cents, teriburger $1.90, hamburger $1.25. COMMENTS: The teriburger contains marinated beef and is quite tasty. Among the plate lunch selections are teriyaki beef or meat loaf, served with rice and macaroni salad and packed in a styrofoam carton for convenience "to go." Several picnic tables offer limited outdoor seating.

DENNY'S
Kamaole Shopping Center. HOURS: 24 hours daily. TYPE OF FOOD: Mainland, burgers, some local style dishes. SAMPLING: Dinners include steak, seafood and chicken $6.79-$10.79. Breakfast served anytime.

INTERNATIONAL HOUSE OF PANCAKES
Azeka's Place Shopping Center on South Kihei Rd. HOURS: Sun. -Thurs. 6 a.m.-midnight, Fri. and Sat. 6 a.m.-2 a.m. TYPE OF FOOD: Breakfast, lunch, and dinner choices served anytime. SAMPLING: Omelettes from $4.95, waffles from $2.95, sandwiches include grilled cheese at $3.95, or a steak sandwich at $6.45. Dinners run $5.95-$10.95 and include soup or salad, roll and butter. COMMENTS: A children's menu is available. Very crowded on weekends.

ISLAND SURF PIZZA AND GRILL
1995 South Kihei Rd., Island Surf Building (879-8881). HOURS: Daily for breakfast, lunch and dinner. TYPE OF FOOD: Mainland style, burgers, pizza, steaks, stuffed potatoes, sandwiches, children's portions. COMMENTS: Delivery service.

McDONALD'S
1900 area of South Kihei Rd. at the Kihei Shopping Center. HOURS: Breakfast, lunch, and dinner. Breakfast served only from 6 a.m. -10 a.m. TYPE OF FOOD: Fast. SAMPLING: There are a few unusual island items added to the menu. For breakfast, you can have Portuguese sausage with rice, and chase it down with chilled guava juice. COMMENTS: Indoor seating is available here in a limited number of bright blue flowered booths. The prices generally are slightly higher than mainland prices.

MAUI FUDGE & ICE CREAM KITCHEN ★
2439 S. Kihei Rd. HOURS: Daily. TYPE OF FOOD: Treats! SAMPLING: Cones $1.73, fudge $8.95/lb. COMMENTS: While this might not be appropriately considered a restaurant for some, you could easily fill up on their decadent delights. This is the only spot we know of that makes it's own 20 plus flavors of ice cream on location with fresh Maui cream, seasonal fresh fruit and local eggs. Their sugar cones & fudge are made here too. Their sherbet is non-dairy. Thirty kinds of fudge that can be shipped home.

PARADISE FRUIT ★
1913 South Kihei Rd. next to Kihei Town Center (879-1723). HOURS: 24 hours. TYPE OF FOOD: "Healthy oriented" sandwiches, salads, and smoothies. SAMPLING: Veggie sandwich runs $2.60, turkey sandwich $3.10, salads priced $3-$4. Smoothies and yogurt shakes are $1.50-$2.00. COMMENTS: This is an open air fruit and vegetable market that also sells some sundry items. Tucked in the back is their walk-up snack bar. It is primarily take out, although they do have a few tables in the rear. The pizzas in their deli case for take-home baking look great. Their yogurt shakes and smoothies are delicious!

POLLI'S
101 S. Kihei Rd., Kealia Village (879-5275). HOURS: Lunch 11:30 –2:30 and dinner 5-10 p.m., happy hour 2:30-5:30, has burgers, free chips and a pupu menu. TYPE OF FOOD: Mexican. SAMPLING: Dinner combinations run $8-$12. Fresh fish prices are quoted daily. COMMENTS: A deck over the beach offers outdoor dining and cocktails. Major credit cards accepted.

THE SANDWITCH
145 North Kihei Rd., by Sugar Beach Condos (879-3262). HOURS: Mon.-Sat. 11-11, Sunday noon to 11. TYPE OF FOOD: Sandwiches, burgers, salads. SAMPLING: Large variety of sandwiches priced $4-$7 and available to go or to eat there.

SIR GECKOS
Rainbow Mall, 2439 S. Kihei Rd. (879-0080). HOURS: Breakfast 6:30-12, dinner until 10 p.m. TYPE OF FOOD: Mexican. SAMPLING: Fajitas, tacos, enchiladas, burgers, and pizza priced $5.95 –12.95. Cocktails.

SUDA SNACK SHOP
By the gas station along N. Kihei Rd. TYPE OF FOOD: Sandwiches, burgers, hot dogs, saimin, plate lunches. SAMPLING: All items very reasonably priced, burgers are only $1.15. This is a fast food outlet Maui style!

MODERATE

BUZZ'S WHARF ★
Maalaea Wharf area (244-5426 or 661-0964). HOURS: Dinner only. TYPE OF FOOD: Seafood specialty. SAMPLING: Pacific oysters $9.95, shrimp tempura $12.95, fresh fish $15.95. COMMENTS: This may be an old timer and a little out of the way, but we like the atmosphere and the quality meals.

CANTON CHEF
At the Kamaole Shopping Center (879-1988). HOURS: Lunch 11-4 p.m. and dinner 5-9:30 p.m. TYPE OF FOOD: Cantonese, Szechuan. SAMPLING: Vegetable, chicken, beef, duck, seafood and pork dishes priced $5.50-$11. COMMENTS: Owned in conjunction with the Hong Kong Restaurant. Orders to go.

CHUCK'S ★
Kihei Town Center (879-4488 or 879-4489). HOURS: Lunch 11:30 -2:30 p.m., dinner 5:30-10:00 p.m. TYPE OF FOOD: Beef and seafood. SAMPLING: Lunch items include cold beef, ham, turkey, hot BLT, cheeseburger, or French dip sandwiches. Early bird dinners are 5:30-6:30 p.m. and for $8.95 feature a choice of mahi or chicken thighs. A good salad bar is available a la carte or included with dinners such as teriyaki steak, prime rib, chicken or fish $10.95-$14.95. Fresh fish is quoted daily. COMMENTS: No reservations. Call ahead to find out what the wait will be. Children's menu has dinners $5-$8. Happy hour 11:30 -5 p.m. The salad bar is served 11:30-10 p.m.

ERIK'S SEAFOOD BROILER
2463 S. Kihei Rd., Kamaole Shopping Center (879-8400). HOURS: Lunch 12-4 p.m., dinner 5-10 p.m. TYPE OF FOOD: Seafood. SAMPLING: In addition to fresh island fish try halibut steak, Louisiana catfish, roast duck a la Grand Marnier, veal oscar, scampi. Dinners include soup or salad, bread, potatoes or rice. COMMENTS: If the menu seems familiar, it may be because this is the fourth and newest restaurant operated by Erik Jakobsen. Early bird dinner specials are offered.

HONG KONG
61 South Kihei Rd. (879-2883). HOURS: Lunch 12:30-4 and dinner 5-9. TYPE OF FOOD: Seafood, Oriental. SAMPLING: Individual dishes from $5 include Szechuan-style cooking.

IDINI'S OCEANFRONT RISTORANTE ★
760 South Kihei Rd. in the Menehune Shores Condominiums (879-1356). HOURS: Lunch 11-2:30, dinner from 5:30, seafood bar open all day. Sunday brunch 10-2, Sunday dinner buffet 6-10.. TYPE OF FOOD: French, Italian. SAMPLING: Lunches include sandwiches, lox and bagels, or entrees such as lasagna from $4.25-$8.95. Dinner includes soup or salad with entree selections ranging from beef to seafood, chicken or veal, from $15.95. Pasta dishes from $7.50. COMMENTS: Formerly the site of the Hong Kong Restaurant, the interior has been dramatically transformed to an airy, oceanview setting. Check to see if they are still offering their wonderful early-bird dinner specials! Evening entertainment.

ISLAND FISH HOUSE ★
1945 South Kihei Rd. (879-7771). HOURS: Dinner from 5:30 p.m. TYPE OF FOOD: Seafood. SAMPLING: Complete dinners include chowder or salad, au gratin potatoes or island rice, fresh vegetables and home-made bread. Chicken teriyaki $12.95, scallops $15.95, shrimp polynesian $17.95, or their daily fresh fish which is offered cooked six different ways. COMMENTS: The fish is consistently excellent, and we are very partial to the way they prepare their carrots! The service is very good and the wine list offers numerous choices. Reservations are a must here unless you plan on arriving by 6:30. You may want to try their Kahului location. Check to see if they are offering their great early bird dinner specials.

KIHEI PRIME RIB AND SEAFOOD HOUSE ★

2511 South Kihei Rd., in the Nani Kai Village (879-1954). HOURS: Dinner from 5-10 p.m. TYPE OF FOOD: Beef is their specialty. Also seafood and chicken. SAMPLING: Ribs $13.95, polynesian chicken $12.95, prime rib in varied cuts from $14.95-$18.95. Salad bar a la carte $8.95. Early bird dinner special of chicken, prime rib or fish. COMMENTS: Dinners include a salad bar, Caesar salad, or red snapper chowder, and is served either with fettucini noodles or rice. Homemade bread also accompanies your meal. The salad bar was very good, and the choices included sweet Kula onions. Our beef was good, however, our lobster was a little flavorless. The high-beamed ceilings with the hanging plants compliment the gorgeous wood carvings done by Bruce Turnbull and paintings by a German artist named Sigrid. They offer piano entertainment nightly.

KIHEI SEAS

2439 S. Kihei Rd., upstairs at the Rainbow Mall (879-5600). HOURS: Dinner 5-10 p.m. TYPE OF FOOD: Seafood, beef, chicken. SAMPLING: Early bird specials from 5-7 p.m. The regular menu includes a seafood assortment $8.95-$16.95, prime rib cuts $12.95-15.95, and two chicken selections $9.95.

LA FAMILIA

2511 South Kihei Rd., at Kai Nani Village (879-8824). HOURS: Cocktails begin at 4 p.m. TYPE OF FOOD: Mexican. SAMPLING: Tostado $7.95, and the usual Mexican entrees priced $4-$8 a la carte. Combination plate $8.95. Also available are fish, burgers, and quiche for the non-Mexican palates. COMMENTS: They no longer have their Kaanapali location, but are planning to reopen their Wailuku restaurant sometime in 1988.

LUIGI'S PASTA PIZZERIA

Azeka's Shopping Center on S. Kihei Rd. (879-4446). HOURS: Daily 11:30 a.m. until midnight, bar until 2 a.m. TYPE OF FOOD: Italian. SAMPLING: Lunch selections include pasta or pizza as well as sandwiches such as submarines, French dip or club. Dinner selections $8-$17 include pizza, calzone, spaghetti, fettucini, shrimp scampi and steak. COMMENTS: Entertainment nightly in their lounge.

MAUI LU LONGHOUSE

Maui Lu Resort, 575 South Kihei Rd. (879-5858). HOURS: Breakfast 7-10 a.m., closed for lunch, dinner 6-9 p.m. Sunday thru Friday. Saturday luau at 8 p.m. TYPE OF FOOD: Polynesian, beef, and seafood.

MAUI OUTRIGGER

2980 South Kihei Rd. (879-1581). HOURS: Breakfast, lunch and dinner. TYPE OF FOOD: Seafood, chicken, beef, and pasta. SAMPLING: Linguini marinara $10.95, NY steak $14.95, prime rib $13.95, or honey-dipped chicken at $10.95. Some menu items are available in children's portions. Dinners include salad bar and rice. COMMENTS: This restaurant is ON the beach. We would recommend it for cocktails at sunset. Visa and Mastercard.

OCEAN TERRACE
2960 South Kihei Rd., Mana Kai Hotel (879-2607). HOURS: Breakfast, lunch and dinner served between 7 a.m. and 10 p.m. TYPE OF FOOD: Polynesian, fish and steak. SAMPLING: Breakfasts include specialty pancakes, i.e. coconut or macadamia. Lunches offer salads, sandwiches and hot entrees. Dinners include seafood, beef, chicken. COMMENTS: Under new operation by the owners of Island Fish House, this restaurant has an all new contemporary look enhanced by its ocean front location. A wonderful spot to enjoy cocktails and the sunset. Pupu items range from local dishes to Chinese and Polynesian foods.

WATERFRONT
At the Milowai Condo, Maalaea (244-9028). HOURS: Lunch 11–2 weekdays, dinner 5:30–10 p.m. 7 days a week. Cocktails from 5 p.m. TYPE OF FOOD: Seafood specialty. SAMPLING: Seafood crepes, NY pepper steak, fresh fish of the day. COMMENTS: Their fresh mahi was nicely prepared. Advance reservations are requested.

EXPENSIVE

TIKI BOB'S
At the rear of Island Fish House, 1945 S. Kihei Rd., (879-7771). TYPE OF FOOD: Polynesian in the style of Trader Vic's. SAMPLING: Fresh fish, lamb, duck, and chicken prepared in an Oriental and Polynesian style. COMMENTS: This is the newest in the family of restaurants owned by Robert Glavor. They anticipate opening in 1988.

WAILEA/MAKENA

LOUNGES

MOLOKINI LOUNGE ★
Maui Prince Hotel, Makena. A wonderful opportunity for a sunset view. Entertainment and complimentary pupus served 4:00–6:30 daily.

SUNSET TERRACE ★
Stouffer Wailea Beach Resort, on the lobby level. Pleasant Hawaiian music and cocktails can be combined with a magnificent Hawaiian sunset.

INEXPENSIVE

CAFE KIOWAI
Maui Prince Hotel (874-1111). HOURS: Breakfast, lunch and dinner are served daily with snacks available between regular meal service 6:30 a.m.–10 p.m. SAMPLING: Salads and sandwiches $6 –$9. Kiowai pronounced "Key-oh-wy" means "fresh flowing water."

ED & DON'S
Wailea Shopping Center. TYPE OF FOOD: Sandwiches and ice cream.

MAKENA GOLF COURSE RESTAURANT
At the Golf Course, just beyond Wailea (879-1154). HOURS: Continental breakfast 9–11 a.m., lunch 11–3 p.m. Cocktails with pupus from 9 a.m.–7 p.m. May be opening for dinner soon. TYPE OF FOOD: Salads and sandwiches. SAMPLING: Salads (seafood, fruit, and greens $4–$7), sandwiches from $4.50. COMMENTS: Furnished in a tan and green theme, this open-air restaurant features a golf and ocean view. Visa, Mastercard and American Express.

MAUI ONION
Stouffer Wailea Beach Resort, poolside (879-4900). HOURS: 11 a.m.–6 p.m. daily. Bar service. TYPE OF FOOD: Sandwiches. SAMPLING: The menu is a limited one. Maui onion rings are scrumptiously priced at $3.75, jumbo hot dogs $5.50, cheeseburgers $7.00, grilled chicken breast sandwich $8, or shrimp and mahi brochette at $9.75.

PIZZA FRESH
2395 S. Kihei Rd at the Dolphin Shopping Plaza (879-1525). HOURS: Daily 3 p.m.–9 p.m. SAMPLING: Pizza prepared for baking at your home or condo. Choice of 20 different toppings, white or whole wheat crust. They grind their own cheese and make their own dough. Also available are mini-pupu pizzas.

SET POINT CAFE
Atop the pro shop at the Wailea Tennis Center (879-3244). HOURS: Breakfast 7–10 a.m., lunch 11–2:30. SAMPLING: Breakfast items include fresh fruit waffles or French toast made with homemade cinnamon bread. Daily breakfast

specials might include Eggs Florentine at $6.95. Sunday brunch is served 7 a.m.–2:30 p.m. and is ordered off the menu. Examples include Eggs Benedict, Eggs Louie or Eggs Blackstone, priced $7.50–$9.95. Served with your choice of a glass of champagne, screwdriver or a mimosa, plus tea or coffee. Salads, soups and lunch entrees $5.50–$7.50. Appetizers 7–7 daily.

WET SPOT
Maui Inter-Continental Wailea, by the central pool (879-1922). HOURS: Lunch and early dinner. TYPE OF FOOD: American. SAMPLING: A limited number of entrees, salads and sandwiches are priced $5–10. COMMENTS: Casual poolside dining.

WIKI WIKI PIZZA
2411 S. Kihei Rd. (874-9454). HOURS: 11 a.m.–10 p.m. TYPE OF FOOD: Pizza SAMPLING: Limited table seating outside. Pizzas are baked and available to go.

MODERATE

LANAI TERRACE ★
Maui Inter-Continental Wailea (879-1922). HOURS: 6 a.m.–11 p.m. TYPE OF FOOD: Varied. SAMPLING: The daily luncheon buffet includes an array of soups, salads, cold cuts and hot entrees served 11:30–2:30 for $12.50. Lunch selections available from the menu include hamburgers, salads or entrees priced $5.25 –$9.25. Dinners for the light appetite include salads, sandwiches, egg or pasta dishes priced $5.25–$11.50. Entrees include honey-dipped chicken, vegetable curry, fried shrimp or N.Y. steak $5.25–$16.75. COMMENTS: Wed. night is pasta night from 5–9:30 p.m. with a buffet of pastas in a variety of sauces, a salad bar and garlic bread for $12.75. An early bird prime rib dinner is available.

SAKURA JAPANESE RESTAURANT
100 Wailea Ike Drive, adjacent to the Wailea Steak House. HOURS: Dinner from 5 p.m., may be serving lunch at a later date. TYPE OF FOOD: Japanese. SAMPLING: Their menu is much improved over the Hibachi Restaurant which was here previously. The new selections include sashimi and sushi as well as teriyaki steak, sukiyai and Bento meals. Dinners run $12–$16.50.

SANDCASTLE
Wailea Shopping Center (879-0606). HOURS: Lunch and dinner daily. TYPE OF FOOD: Everything. SAMPLING: Lunch selections include soup, salads, and sandwiches $4.95-9.95. Dinner choices of fresh fish, shellfish, meat and fowl $13.95-21.95, and includes soup or salad, rice or potato, vegetable and roll.

WAILEA STEAK HOUSE
100 Wailea Ike Drive, Wailea (879-2875). Easy to find sign near the Maui Inter-Continental Wailea indicates turn-off. HOURS: Dinner from 5:30 p.m. TYPE OF FOOD: Fish and beef. SAMPLING: Top sirloin steak $25, breast of chicken $12.50, and scampi $17. COMMENTS: Located on the 15th fairway of Wailea's Blue Golf Course. Some outdoor seating available. The wine list is limited. A nice salad bar is featured. No reservations for a group of less than six.

EXPENSIVE

FAIRWAY ★

Wailea Golf Course Clubhouse (879-4060 or 879-3861). Look for the sign near Stouffer Wailea Beach Resort. HOURS: Breakfast 7:00 –11 a.m., lunch 11–3:30 p.m., and dinner 5:30–9:30 p.m. TYPE OF FOOD: Varied. SAMPLING: Breakfast selections include pancakes $3.95 and eggs benedict $6.95. Lunch offers burgers $4.95, turkey clubhouse $5.95, or chef salad at $6.95. Dinners are priced $14.95–$25.75 and include a salad bar. Entrees selections include beef, seafood, and chicken. COMMENTS: This restaurant is open-air with outdoor seating available. It offers a nice view of the golf course. Cocktails are available from the adjoining bar, the Waterhole. Their ice cream drinks are richly refreshing anytime of day. Here is a sampling to tempt your palate: Fairway Grasshopper – Creme de menthe, creme de cocoa, and ice cream all blended together, and topped with chocolate mint liqueur and chocolate sprinkles. Wailea Almond Joy – Amaretto, Kahlua, ice cream, blended and topped with whipped cream and almond slices. Brandy Alexander – Brandy, ice cream, and creme de cocoa blended and sprinkled with nutmeg. These wonderful concoctions run $5-ish. Dinner reservations are suggested and major credit cards honored.

HAKONE ★

Maui Prince Resort, Makena (874-1111). HOURS: Dinner only, 6–10 p.m. TYPE OF FOOD: Japanese. COMMENTS: Authenticity is the key to this wonderful Japanese restaurant, from its construction (the wood, furnishings and even small nails were imported from Japan) to its food (the rice is flown in as well). We selected a sukiyaki meal which was wonderful and well priced at $36 for two. Cooked at our table by a charming hostess, it included tea, soup, rice and green tea ice cream, all in very ample portions. A sushi bar is also available. Reservations recommended.

KIAWE BROILER ★

Maui Inter-Continental Wailea (879-1922). HOURS: Dinner 6–10 p.m. TYPE OF FOOD: Emphasis on seafood. SAMPLING: Dinners are served with salad bar. Among the options are deep fried calamari, breast of chicken with shrimp, sauteed scallops with wilted watercress, or broiled tiger prawns priced $13–$29 (for lobster). Beef lovers can choose from several steak cuts $19.50 –$21.50.

LA PEROUSE ★

Maui Inter-Continental Wailea (879-1922). HOURS: 6:30–10 p.m. TYPE OF FOOD: Classic international and seafood cuisine. SAMPLING: This Travel/Holiday award-winning fine-dining restaurant is a good choice for that special evening out. The specialty of the house is Callaloo Crabmeat Soup and the a la carte menu features a wide variety of continental and island dishes. COMMENTS: The decor here has an Oriental theme and is rich with koa wood. Pianist Frank Withalm entertains nightly. The service is very good and we found the Callaloo soup richly wonderful. The house green salad was more an edible picture, being artisttically arranged to include sprouts, Maui onions, cherry tomato, red cabbage, lettuce, cucumber, and mushrooms. A complimentary appetizer of fried brie arrived while we selected from their extensive wine list. Reservations are recommended and guests are asked to dress in the spirit of elegant evening dining.

MAKANI ROOM ★

Maui Inter-Continental Wailea (879-1922). HOURS: Sunday brunch only, 9 a.m.–1:30 p.m. TYPE OF FOOD: Varied. COMMENTS: The buffet is $24 adults, $12 children. Seating is on the large lanai with a scenic view of the neighboring islands or at indoor tables. The feeling at this brunch is enjoyably casual, however, there is nothing casual about their lavishly laden tables. Omelets are cooked to order, as well as other choices which vary but may include fresh seafood, beef or lamb entrees as well as eggs benedict or crepes. Don't forget to save room for at least two trips to the dessert table. The pastry chef here has a wonderful way with the more unusual fruits – we tried a gooseberry pie. Reservations are a really good idea. Major credit cards.

PALM COURT ★

Stouffer Wailea Beach Resort (879-4900). HOURS: Nightly dinners. TYPE OF FOOD: Buffet style, and off the menu. International buffet varies nightly. SAMPLING: A daily breakfast buffet is served. Their dinner buffet features the only international buffet on the island. Sunday offers French cuisine such as shrimp and scallops provencal, Duck a l'Orange and Leg of Lamb Dijonaise. On Monday it's off to the Orient with sushi, shrimp tempura, and fresh fish of the day with a sweet and sour sauce. On Tuesday travel to Great Britain, at least in spirit, and sample prime rib with Yorkshire pudding. Wednesday features an assortment of Hawaiian delicacies. Thursday is Italian night with pasta, osso buco, and chicken cacciatore among the delights. Friday celebrates seafood with steamed clams, shrimp bisque and seafood gumbo. An All American Steak Fry is featured Saturday nights with barbecued chicken, New York strip steak, spare ribs, baked beans and corn on the cob. An assortment of salads and wonderful desserts complete the nightly buffet. The buffet is priced $20. An a la carte menu is also available. COMMENTS: This open-air dining hall is festively decorated in reds and greens and offers evening breezes and an ocean view. Reservations are accepted only for a group of 10 or more. Aloha attire acceptable. Visa, Mastercard, American Express, and Diners are all honored.

PRINCE COURT ★

Maui Prince Hotel, Makena (874-1111). HOURS: Dinner 6–10 p.m., Sunday brunch 10 a.m.–2 p.m. TYPE OF FOOD: American cuisine. SAMPLING: Appetizers and salads $7–$8, soup $5, salad $4. Entrees priced $22–$32 include sensations such as steamed fresh salmon in vermouth with fettucini and fiddle head ferns, or tenderloin of veal with Olympia oysters and watercress. Sunday brunch $25 adults/$15 children. COMMENTS: Beautifully situated to offer diners a splendid view of the ocean and hotel grounds. The Sunday champagne brunch is tops on our list for a tasteful extravaganza. Over 160 items are served and might include croissants stuffed with Portuguese sausages or ham, smoked oysters, octopus or island fish, avocados stuffed with crab, or an unusual and delicious midora bisque soup. Brunch entrees during our visit ranged from roast lamb or prime rib to veal piccata. The dessert table is beyond belief! Reservations recommended.

RAFFLES' ★
Stouffer Wailea Beach Resort (879-4900). HOURS: Sunday brunch 9 –2 p.m., dinner nightly 6:30–10:30 p.m. TYPE OF FOOD: Continental. SAMPLING: Brunch includes champagne, fresh fruits, petite lamb chops, Oriental dishes, chicken, and fish. You might try gravlaks, a salmon marinated in dill and anise with mustard sauce. Also, a salad bar, eggs benedict, omelets made to your request. Pastries and desserts to delight any sweet tooth. Currently $21.00. Dinners include Rack of Washington State Lamb at $26.50, lobster at $32, broiled tiger prawns at $28.50, mahi, ono, or opakapaka (as available) at $24.50. The wine list includes Italian, French, California, Washington State, Australian, and German choices. COMMENTS: Raffles' bears an Oriental theme, in keeping with its Singapore origin. Sir Thomas Stamford Raffles (1781 - 1826) was the British founder of the city where the Raffles' Hotel has become a legend. The buffet is a terrific splurge. The dessert bar was constantly being replenished and each new offering looked better than the last. The chocolate mousse merited a second serving and the chocolate rum cake was rich and moist. Aloha wear is acceptable – an extra large muumuu might not be a bad idea!

KAHULUI/WAILUKU

Along Lower Main Street in Wailuku are a number of local restaurants which are not often frequented by tourists and may well be one of the island's best kept secrets! Don't expect to find polished silver or extravagant decor, but do expect to find reasonable prices for large portions of food in a comfortable atmosphere. Others you may wish to explore are Kete Yama, Naokee's, Dragon Drive Inn, or Seafood Charlie's.

Papa Joe's Pizza, Dairy Queen, Pizza Hut, McDonald's, Burger King, Luigi's Pasta and Pizzeria, Jack in the Box, and Sizzler are a few of the restaurants in and around Kahului and the Maui Mall. Several restaurants are located in the hotel/motels around the Kahului Bay. These don't require elaboration.

INEXPENSIVE

ARCHIE'S
1440 Lower Main St., Wailuku (244-9401). HOURS: Mon. through Sat. 10:30-2 p.m., and 5-8 p.m. Closed Sundays. TYPE OF FOOD: Japanese. SAMPLING: Their specialty is (Hama'ko) Teishoku. Don't know what that is? You'll have to stop in and find out. Sandwiches priced $1.15-$2.75, saimin 90 cents, plate lunches run $4.20-$8. Yose nabe dinners come with soup, rice and tea. COMMENTS: The food is good and the prices are reasonable.

CHILI WILLY'S
1032 Lower Main St., Wailuku (242-4118). HOURS: Mon.-Thurs. 11 a.m.-10 p.m., Friday and Saturday open until 1:30 a.m. TYPE OF FOOD: Hamburgers, saimin, plate lunches, and chili. SAMPLING: Their chili is available in three varieties, chicken, beef or bean from $2.95. Plate lunches $3.50-$4.50 include teriyaki steak, mahi, shoyu chicken and daily specials. Burgers are affordably priced from $1.25. Turkey, fruit, vegetable, macaroni or green salads. Saimin. COMMENTS: A cozy little place, only 10 booths inside. A paradise for chili lovers. Orders available to go.

CHUM'S
1900 Main Street, Wailuku (244-1000). HOURS: 5:30 a.m.-11 p.m. Sun.-Thurs., until midnight Fri. and Sat. Serves breakfast, lunch and dinner. SAMPLING: Homemade soups, stew, Hawaiian plate lunches, and chili, priced $2.50-$5.95. COMMENTS: This new restaurant is rapidly acquiring a local clientele. Their motto is "Where good friends meet great food." Charge card minimum $10.

FUJIYA'S ★
133 Market Cafe, Wailuku (244-0206). HOURS: Lunch 11-2, dinner 2-5:30 p.m.. TYPE OF FOOD: Japanese. SAMPLING: Lunch choices include tempura $6.50, teriyaki $4.50, chicken $3.90. Dinner choices also include a combination for $6.50. Beer & sake available. COMMENTS: One of our best bets for Japanese food. Sushi lovers will appreciate their new sushi bar where a large variety of selections are available at half the price that is charged in the resort area restaurants.

175

IDINI'S BAKERY & DELI ★
Kaahumanu Shopping Center, Kahului. (877-3978). HOURS: Deli open 7 a.m.–9 p.m., restaurant until midnight. Thursday and Friday with entertainment. TYPE OF FOOD: European-style deli and bar with French bakery. SAMPLING: Picnics to go, croissant sandwiches, all you can eat salad bar, espresso and cappuccino. COMMENTS: A good place to pick up a lunch enroute to Hana or Haleakala!

KOHO GRILL AND BAR
Kaahumanu Shopping Center (877-5588). HOURS: Daily for breakfast 8–11 a.m., lunch and dinner until 9:30 p.m. on Mon.–Thurs., 11 p.m. on Fri. and Sat., and 9 p.m. on Sunday. Happy Hour daily 3–6. TYPE OF FOOD: Everything. SAMPLING: Quiche or soft tacos $3.65, burgers and sandwiches from $3.45. Fresh fish is served charbroiled for an incredible $7.95. COMMENTS: Most unusual is their "Can Do!" motto. Their menu states "Have a favorite dish not mentioned? Koho has a very talented staff – eager to serve. Just tell us what you'd like and we'll do our best to serve you." They have a keiki menu and also have evening dinner specials.

LA FAMILIA
1988 Vineyard at Church St., Wailuku. (244-3904) Scheduled to reopen in 1988.

LOPAKA'S BAR AND GRILL
161 Alambra, Kahului Industrial area (871-1135). HOURS: 11 a.m. –10 p.m. TYPE OF FOOD: Varied. SAMPLING: Lunch selections include burgers and sandwiches $2.95–$7, or plate lunches such as Korean ribs and BBQ beef priced $4.95–$7.75. Dinners are served with soup or salad, rice and bread. Hamburger steak $6.95, NY steak $10.95. COMMENTS: Full bar service, handicap ramp.

MAMA DING'S PASTELES RESTAURANT
255 E Alamaha Street, Kahului (877-5796). HOURS: Breakfast 7:30 –10:30 a.m., lunch 10:30 a.m.–3 p.m., Mon. thru Sat. TYPE OF FOOD: Puerto Rican and Island favorites. SAMPLING: Inexpensive plate lunches vary daily, but might include teriyaki beef, corned beef and cabbage, or roast pork and chili. A variety of sandwiches or pasteles. (A pastele has an exterior of grated green banana and a filling of pork, vegetables and spices that is then steamed.) COMMENTS: A cozy atmosphere tucked away in the Kahului Industrial Area. No credit cards. Food is available for catering or to go.

MAUI BOY
2102 Vineyard St., Wailuku (244-7243).
HOURS: Daily 6:30 a.m.–9 p.m. for breakfast lunch and dinner. TYPE OF FOOD: Hawaiian dishes. SAMPLING: Hawaiian favorites such as Kalua pig and poi or lau lau. Local style plate lunches available for lunch and dinner include chicken or pork teriyaki, roast beef or pork. Average price is $4.95. Dinner specials begin at 5 p.m. and include beef or curry stew $4.25, New York steak $7.75, broiled chicken $5.95, calamari steak $6.25. The prime rib is available in three different cuts; Lanai is $9.50, Molokai is $10.95, and the Maui cut is $12.95. COMMENTS: Food available "to go".

MING YUEN
162 Alamaha, Kahului (871-7787). HOURS: Lunch daily 11:30 a.m. –5 p.m., dinner 5-9 p.m. TYPE OF FOOD: Chinese. SAMPLING: Cantonese and Szechuan style foods, dishes $4.95 and up. COMMENTS: A little off the beaten track, you'll find it tucked behind Safeway off Kamehameha Avenue in the industrial area.

MOON HOE CHINESE SEAFOOD RESTAURANT
752 Lower Main St., Wailuku (242-7778). HOURS: 11 a.m.–2 p.m. for lunch Mon.–Sat., daily 5-9:30 p.m. for dinner. TYPE OF FOOD: Chinese and seafood. SAMPLING: 150 menu items including a variety of preparations for duck, pork, beef, chicken, vegetables and fish. Prices generally run $3.95–$6.95.

NAZO'S
1063 Lower Main St., Wailuku, at the Puuone Plaza #C-226 (244-0529). HOURS: 11 a.m.–9 p.m. TYPE OF FOOD: Everything. SAMPLING: Sandwiches include egg salad at $1.15, or grilled ham and cheese $2.00. Entrees include soup or salad, rice or mashed potatoes, coffee, tea or fruit punch. Selections include liver with bacon for $3.90, or shrimp tempura for $5. A tossed salad adds 65 cents. Daily specials such as luau stew on Wednesday. Oxtail soup is one of their specialties. COMMENTS: Another small family-owned restaurant which is very affordable and prides themselves on their home-style cooking.

OSAKA HOUSE SUSHI BAR AND JAPANESE RESTAURANT
1063 Lower Main St., Wailuku, at the Puuone Plaza #107 (244-3414). HOURS: Lunch Mon.–Fri. 10 a.m.–2 p.m., dinner served nightly from 5-10 p.m. Sushi Bar daily. TYPE OF FOOD: Japanese and Korean. SAMPLING: Lunch selections include teriyaki steak for $7.25 or chicken at $4.50. Dinners include sukiyaki for $12, tempura, steamed fish or Udon for $7.95. COMMENTS: Their menu is complete with color photographs, so if you don't know what you are ordering, at least you can see what it is going to look like! Orders available to go.

PINO'S
2065 Main Street, Wailuku (242-9650). HOURS: Lunch Mon.–Fri. 11–2:30, dinner Tues.–Sat. 5-9. TYPE OF FOOD: Italian specialties. SAMPLING: Lunch has salads, sandwiches, or entrees for $1.75-6.50. Dinners include pasta, vegetable, bread and butter, soup or salad. Scaloppine of Calamari $10.95. Veal Piccata $16.75. Teriyaki Beef brochette $13.95. Cocktail service.

PIZZA CIRCUS ★
333 Dairy Rd., Kahului (871-1133). HOURS: Daily for lunch or dinner. TYPE OF FOOD: Only pizza. COMMENTS: Our best bet for pizza on this side of Maui. Their new location offers a seating area or get one to go. What makes this pizza great is their unusual crust which is topped with sesame seeds.

POOR BILLY'S SANDWICH SHOP AND BAKERY
199 Dairy Rd., Kahului (877-4990). HOURS: Mon.–Fri. 1 a.m.–6 p.m., Sat. & Sun. 6 a.m.–3 p.m. TYPE OF FOOD: Sandwiches, pastries. SAMPLING: Freshly made pastries. Breakfast served until 10 a.m. includes omelettes. Sandwiches and box lunches also. COMMENTS: Call ahead for their "Hana Box."

SAM SATO'S

318 North Market St., Wailuku (244-7124). HOURS: Breakfast and lunch 8-2 p.m., pastries served until 4 p.m. Closed Thurs. & Sun. TYPE OF FOOD: Noodles are their specialty. SAMPLING: Breakfast includes eggs or pancakes. Lunch options include combination plates $2.90–$3.70 such as teriyaki beef, stew, chop steak or spare ribs. Sandwiches and burgers. Saimin and chow fun are served in small portions for $1.60/$1.70, or large portions for $3.20–$3.40. COMMENTS: The homemade pastries are wonderful. The peach, apple and coconut turn-overs were fragrant and fresh. In addition to noodles they specialize in manju, a Japanese tea cake. It may come as a big surprise when you discover that these tasty morsels are actually filled with a mashed version of lima beans!

SIAM THAI ★

125 N. Market St., Wailuku (244-3817). HOURS: Lunch Mon.-Fri. 11-2:30, dinner daily 5-9:30. TYPE OF FOOD: Thai. SAMPLING: Exotic green papaya salad $3.95, eggplant beef $4.95, Thai ginger shrimp $6.95. COMMENTS: The white table cloths give this restaurant a slightly more elegant air than most in this area. According to the waiter we dined at the same table Robert Redford used when he visited this spot!

SIR WILFRED'S ESPRESSO CAFE

Maui Mall, Kahului (877-3711). HOURS: Mon.-Thurs. 9 a.m.-6 p.m., Friday 9 a.m.-9 p.m., Saturday 9-5:30, Sunday 10-3. TYPE OF FOOD: Light dining. Sandwiches, pies, cookies. SAMPLING: Continental breakfasts with fresh pastries. Bagels or deli-style sandwiches are available for lunch as well as a variety of salads or quiche. Also a selection of gourmet teas, coffees or beer and wine.

TASTY CRUST ★

1770 Mill St., Wailuku (244-0845). HOURS: Daily for breakfast, lunch and dinner. TYPE OF FOOD: Varied. SAMPLING: Unusual and delicious crusty hotcakes are their specialty, two are a meal for $1.50, or french toast for the same price. Add an egg for 45 cents. Lunches and dinners a la carte. Spaghetti $3.25, roast beef $4.35, hamburgers and sandwiches $1.25 and up. COMMENTS: Local atmosphere and no frills, just good food at great prices.

TIN YING

1088 Lower Main St., Wailuku (242-4371). HOURS: Daily 10:30 a.m.-9 p.m. TYPE OF FOOD: Chinese. SAMPLING: Selections include Hong Kong or Szechuan style. Eat in or take out.

TIPANAN

1276 Lower Main St., Wailuku (244-9466). HOURS: 10:30-9 p.m. Mon.-Sat. TYPE OF FOOD: Filipino. SAMPLING: Entrees include bistek tagalog, daing na bangus, paksiw na pata. (These translate to filet of beef tenderloin with lemon juice and soy, milkfish fried to a savory taste, and tender pork stewed in sweet-sour sauce.) Priced $3.00–$6.50 they are served with rice. COMMENTS: This restaurant has a sister facility at the Lahaina Shopping Center.

TOKYO TEI ★
1063 E. Lower Main St., Wailuku (242-9630). HOURS: Lunch 11 –1:30 Mon.–Sat., dinner daily 5–8:30. TYPE OF FOOD: Japanese. SAMPLING: Lunch specials run $4–$5. Teishoku trays $7–$8.50 include shrimp tempura, sashimi, fried fish, teriyaki pork or steak. Dinner selections such as hakata chicken, seafood platter, and a number of others that are difficult to pronounce, run $4.25–$8 and include rice, miso soup, namasu and ko-ko. COMMENTS: Small and cozy atmosphere. Good food. Take out meals also available. Cocktails.

WAKEA CAFE
335 Hoohana Blvd., #7A (877-4088). HOURS: Mon.–Fri. 10:30 –2:30. SAMPL-ING: Daily homemade specials, salads and sandwiches. Take-out lunches available as are catering services.

WAILUKU GRILL ★
2010 Main Street, Wailuku (244-7505). HOURS: Mon.–Fri. breakfast 7:30–10:30, lunch 11–3 p.m. Brunch served Sat. & Sun. 8 a.m.–2 p.m. TYPE OF FOOD: Varied. SAMPLING: Lunch selections include ginger chicken, eggs Wailuku or quesadilla $4.95–$5.95. Pasta and sandwich selections also available. COMMENTS: Take-out orders available. All the desserts are homemade. They have been offering a once-a-month gourmet dinner night, call to verify date and time.

WING SING
1424 L. Main Street, Wailuku (244-3813). HOURS: Tues.–Sun. 11:30–2 for lunch, 4–8 p.m. for dinner. Closed Monday. TYPE OF FOOD: Chinese. SAMPLING: Chop suey, char sui, shrimp canton. Prices run $2.75–$5.50. COMMENTS: No checks or credit cards.

YORI'S ★
309 N. Market St., Wailuku. HOURS: Tues.–Sun. 11 a.m.–10:30 p.m. TYPE OF FOOD: Hawaiian. SAMPLING: Complete dinners $4.25 –$5. Kalua Pig and cabbage, rice and green salad $5. A la carte items available in small or large por-tions. Also beef stew, chicken with long rice, fresh fish when available, laula, or squid with coconut milk. COMMENTS: If you want to try out real Hawaiian food, skip the luaus and come to Yori's. The proprietor, Yorihito Uchida makes this restaurant special. He obviously enjoys his customers or why else would over 4,000 photos (of just about everyone who has ever eaten here) cover the walls from top to bottom. Even more incredible is that Yori remembers them all, or almost. At 70 years he admits to slowing down a little bit and he does now write down the names of the people when taking the snap shot. A fellow came in while we were dining that had been in the previous year and sure enough, Yori took him right to the spot where his picture hung. Yes, he took our picture, look for us high on the wall by the fourth fan!

MODERATE

CHART HOUSE ★
500 N. Puunene Ave., Kahului (877-2476). HOURS: Dinner 5:30–10 p.m. TYPE OF FOOD: Seafood, beef, and chicken. SAMPLING: Prime rib is their specialty, also fresh seafood and chicken priced $12–$20. COMMENTS: Large portions, excellent children's menu. You can be sure it will be less crowded on this side of the island. No reservations taken, but a nice ocean view is a consolation. Served with a table service salad bar.

MARK EDISON
Iao Valley outside Wailuku, right above the Heritage Gardens (242-5555). HOURS: Lunch 10–3, dinner 5–10 p.m., Sunday brunch. TYPE OF FOOD: Seafood, beef, pasta. SAMPLING: Sunday brunch offers eggs benedict $6.50, prime rib $5.95, steak & eggs $11.95. Lunch selections include kalbi ribs $4.95, honey ono chicken $5.75, burgers & hot dogs from $2.95. Evening entrees are priced $8.95–$18.95 and are served with salad bar, homemade soup, vegetables, rice or potato. COMMENTS: A cozy atmosphere with a large fireplace and cocktail area. The salad bar has a large selection, with some unusual local dishes. The snack bar located across the parking lot serves lighter fare such as chili and rice $1.95, teriyaki stick 85 cents, and tuna sandwich $2.95. Early bird dinner specials.

MICKEYS ★
Kahului Bldg., 333 Lono Ave. (877-7225). HOURS: Lunch and dinner. TYPE OF FOOD: Seafood. COMMENTS: Great fresh fish! They have a sister facility in Kihei (Island Fish House) that is very popular as well.

MR. Z'S RISTORANTE
296 Alamaha St., Kahului (871-1178). HOURS: Lunch Mon.–Fri. 11:30–2 p.m., dinner Mon.–Sat. 5–9 p.m. TYPE OF FOOD: Italian. SAMPLING: All entrees priced for a medium or regular portion. Veal dishes $10.50–$11.20 medium size, $14.90–$15.90 regular. Pastas $6.95–$11.30, seafood $6.90–$14.90. COMMENTS: We had read some good reviews and were disappointed when we visited. The medium size portions, in our opinion, would more appropriately be called "small" and while the prices looked reasonable, they seemed high for the quantity. Dinners include only linguini or Mr. Z's potatoes, no salad or vegetable. Bar service and evening entertainment.

UPCOUNTRY

INEXPENSIVE

DAIRY QUEEN
Pukalani Shopping Center

MCDONALD'S
On the Haleakala Highway, Pukalani

BULLOCK'S OF HAWAII
Just past Pukalani Shopping Center on the right side going up the mountain. HOURS: Breakfast, lunch, and dinner. TYPE OF FOOD: Fast. SAMPLING: Usual breakfast items, omelettes from $2.25, French toast $1.75. A moonburger runs $3.25 (it was lunchtime here when the first astronaut walked on the moon), a guava shake at $2.75, sandwiches from $1.75, and plate lunches around $3.50. Breakfasts include two eggs, bacon, and toast for $2.25. The lunch and dinner menus are the same. COMMENTS: They have recently enlarged their seating area.

KITADAS RESTAURANT
3617 Baldwin Avenue, Makawao. HOURS: 6 a.m.–1:30 p.m. daily except Sunday. COMMENTS: Popular local eatery.

MYRNA'S PLACE
On the Haleakala Highway, Pukalani. HOURS: Mon.–Thurs. 11 –9 p.m., Fri. & Sat. 11–10 p.m., and Sunday 11–7 p.m. TYPE OF FOOD: Sandwiches, salads, saimin, Grandma's hamburgers. COMMENTS: It's always nice to see new family operations get started. This new restaurant is operated by Mildred Madeiros and Kidd Andrade. Myrna's Place is named after her uncle and operated by herself with the help of her children, husband and niece. Skip McDonald's (located across the street) and give Myrna's a try!

MODERATE

KULA LODGE
Five miles past Pukalani on Haleakala Hwy. (878-1535). HOURS: Breakfast 7–1:30 p.m., lunch 11–3 p.m.; dinner 5:30–9 p.m. Dinner is served only on Saturday and Sunday, reservations are recommended. TYPE OF FOOD: American. SAMPLING: Breakfast selections include omelettes from $4.50 and French toast $3.50. Lunches include sandwiches, salads, and burgers from $5, also hot entrees. Dinners include rice or potato, vegetable, French bread and are priced $9.95-$15.95 for rack of lamb, sesame chicken, curry bombay, or mahi mahi almandine. COMMENTS: An added benefit here is the fireplace, a warming delight after a cold trip to the mountain top, a panoramic view, and cocktails. Children's portions available.

MAKAWAO STEAK HOUSE ★

3612 Baldwin, Makawao (575-8711). HOURS: Dinner 5-9:30, Sunday brunch 9:30-2 p.m. TYPE OF FOOD: Steaks, fresh fish, salad bar, and freshly baked breads. SAMPLING: Chicken Zoie $12.95 (breast stuffed with creamed spinach), Scampi $17.95, N.Y. steak $14.95, fresh fish varies daily. Dinners include salad bar. COMMENTS: Cocktails & wine list. We enjoyed fresh Muu, a mild white fish, and have never found or heard of it since!

PARTNERS

Makawao Town (572-6611). HOURS: Lunch 11-2, dinner from 5 p.m. TYPE OF FOOD: Charbroiled chicken, steak, ribs. SAMPLING: Hamburgers and sandwiches $3.95-$5.95. Dinner choices include pizza or charbroiled chicken $8.95, steak $11.95, ribs $10.95. Small pizza from $8.95. COMMENTS: Cocktails and evening entertainment.

POLLI'S   *new italian place across street*

1202 Makawao Ave., Makawao (572-7808). HOURS: 11:30-11:30 with Sunday brunch served 10:30-2:30. TYPE OF FOOD: Mexican and vegetarian Mexican. SAMPLING: Dinner combinations run $8-$12. Fresh fish prices are quoted daily. COMMENTS: This small Mexican restaurant is also open for Sunday brunch!

PUKALANI TERRACE COUNTRY CLUB

3600 Pukalani Rd. (572-1325). Turn right just before the shopping center at Pukalani and continue down until the road ends. HOURS: Open 10-2 for lunch, 5-9 for dinner. TYPE OF FOOD: Hawaiian is their specialty. SAMPLING: Lunch offers a Kalua pig Hawaiian plate for $7.15, or tripe stew for $6.30. Dinner menu offers similar selections at slightly higher prices. Salad bar only $6.50, salad bar with dinner $2.50. COMMENTS: They were offering an early bird dinner from 5-6:30 and nightly dinner specials priced at $7.15. We understand the golf course and restaurant have recently changed ownership, so there may be some changes in their menu. A great view of Maui from here. You might consider a stop on the way down for a drink and a nice sunset.

SILVERSWORD INN

About five miles past Pukalani and across the road from Kula Lodge (878-1232). HOURS: Daily for breakfast 7:30-11, lunch 11:30-1:30, and dinner 5:30-9. Dinners are $8.95-$16.95 and include seafood, or teriyaki chicken. Bar service.

PAIA

There are two restaurants in the Paia area that are our favorites and would be a pleasant stop on your way to Hana or Haleakala.

INEXPENSIVE to MODERATE

DILLON'S ★
Downtown Paia, 89 Hana Hwy. (579-9113). HOURS: Breakfast, lunch, and dinner. TYPE OF FOOD: Burgers, spaghetti, fish and chips. SAMPLING: Complete dinners such as pepper steak, spaghetti or fish run $11.95–$17.95 and include Dillon's house pasta. COMMENTS: We enjoyed a hearty breakfast with generous portions and some unusual items, such as Kahlua French toast. Opens early for diners desiring breakfast enroute to Hana or Haleakala. Dancing each evening 9 p.m.

KIHATA RESTAURANT
115 Hana Hwy., Paia (579-9035). TYPE OF FOOD: Japanese. HOURS: 10 a.m.–2 p.m. for lunch daily, dinner 5–9 p.m. daily except Sunday. SAMPLING: Bento lunches, seafood, Japanese-style steak. COMMENTS: This new restaurant in Paia is oriented toward family dining and food is specially prepared by the owner/chef.

EXPENSIVE

MAMA'S FISH HOUSE ★
On Hwy. 36 just 1½ miles past Paia, look for the ship's flagpole and the angel fish sign (579-9672). HOURS: Lunch served 11–2, happy hour and pupus 2:30–4:30, dinner from 5:30 p.m. TYPE OF FOOD: Seafood. COMMENTS: Mama opened her home, located on a peaceful beachfront in 1973, as Hawaii's first fresh fish house. Her mission was "to serve creative seafood dishes with that elusive taste of Maui island cooking." Mama engages her own fishermen to catch their daily fare. Samples include Ono sauteed in mango butter and Baked Opakapaka Hana. Non-seafood entrees such as Kalbi ribs or chicken in papaya are available. It is a little out of the way, but you can be assured of a quality seafood meal. Reservations suggested.

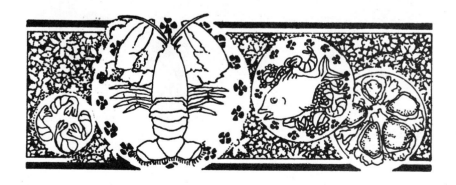

HANA

This quiet town offers a limited choice of eateries.

INEXPENSIVE

HANA RANCH STORE
Open daily with an assortment of ready-made sandwiches and hot dogs.

HASEGAWA GENERAL STORE
Open daily with food items as well as a little bit of everything else!!

TUTU'S
Hana Bay. HOURS: 8:30-4 p.m. TYPE OF FOOD: Sandwiches, plate lunches.

MODERATE

HANA RANCH RESTAURANT
Downtown Hana (248-8255). HOURS: 6:30-10 a.m. daily for breakfast (take out only), 11-4 p.m. for lunch, dinner served Fri. & Sat. 6-9 p.m. TYPE OF FOOD: Varied. SAMPLING: Entrees include fresh fish, smoked baby back ribs, grilled tiger shrimp, and T-bone steak. The lunch buffet is $7.75 which includes hot foods as well as an assortment of salads. Salad bar only is $5.75. The take-out counter serves hot and cold sandwiches as well as plate lunches. COMMENTS: The restaurant has recently had some significant improvements in its food quality. A tree shaded picnic area outside the restaurant is also provided. Attire is casual. Full bar service. Major credit cards accepted. Dinner reservations recommended.

EXPENSIVE

HOTEL HANA MAUI DINING ROOM ★
(248-8211). HOURS: Breakfast 7:30-10 a.m., a la carte or buffet lunch 11:30-2 p.m., dinner 6:30-8:30. SAMPLING: Dinners are a la carte. Wednesday and Sunday evenings is a buffet of seafood, beef, lamb, chicken, fish, or cold seafood. Lunch entrees include grilled ahi, NY steak, or sweet and sour shrimp. Dinner entrees (vary with specials offered) and might include grilled ahi, bamboo steamed mahi mahi, chicken in mango thyme butter, appetizers and dessert. COMMENTS: Wonderful food served with unusually, light, delicious sauces. Non-hotel guests need to call in advance to see if there is space available. Current prices for non-guests are $14 for breakfast, $18 for lunch, and $46 for dinner.

SUNSETS AND NIGHTLIFE

Here are a few suggestions as to what to do when and after the sun goes down on Maui. These locations usually offer entertainment, however, call to see what they are offering and which night, as it varies. Also check the Bulletin Board publication, This Week or the Holiday section of the Friday edition of the Maui News, which lists current late night happenings.

SUNSET WATCHING SUGGESTIONS

On the front lawn of the Pineapple Hill Restaurant near Kapalua
From the lobby bar of the Kapalua Bay Resort with their wonderful pupus
At the Kapalua Grill and Bar
On the promontory at the Bay Club, Kapalua
Atop Black Rock in the Sheraton's Discovery Room
At the Hyatt Regency's Lahaina Provision Company
Enroute down from Haleakala, the Pukalani Country Club
The Maui Outrigger provides your sunset view from surfside.
The Fairway at the Wailea Golf Course (try an ice cream drink)
Enjoy the lobby bar at Stouffer Wailea Beach Resort.

NIGHT SPOTS & ENTERTAINMENT

Consult the *Holiday* section of the *Maui News,* Friday edition, to see who is playing when and where. The following spots generally offer entertainment:

LAHAINA/KAANAPALI/KAPALUA AREA

Lahaina: – Moose McGillycuddy's is always hopping for the young crowd. Also check Blackie's Bar, Chris's Smokehouse, Keg Boathouse, Lahaina Broiler, Longhi's, Pioneer Inn, Westin Maui, Whaler's Pub, Whale's Tail.

Kaanapali: – Two of the most popular spot currently are the Banana Moon at the Marriott Hotel, which parties until 1:30 a.m., and Spats at the Hyatt Regency which is open until 4 a.m. El Crab Catcher, Kaanapali Beach Hotel, Nanatomi, Royal Lahaina, Sheraton, Westin Maui also offer evening entertainment.

Napili/Kahana: – Kahana Keyes, Napili Kai Beach Club

KIHEI/WAILEA/MAKENA AREA NIGHTSPOTS

The Inu Inu Lounge at the Maui Inter-Continental Wailea and the Lost Horizon at Stouffer Wailea Beach Resort are the Wailea hot spots. Entertainment may be frequently enjoyed at the Fairway, Idini's, Kihei Seas, La Familia and Maui Prince Resort.

Beaches

INTRODUCTION

If you are looking for a variety of beautiful, uncrowded tropical beaches, nearly perfect weather year round and sparkling clear waters at enjoyable temperatures, Maui will not disappoint you.

With beaches that range from small to long, white sand to black sand or rock, and from well developed to (at least for a little longer) remote and unspoiled, there is something for everyone. The lay-on-the-beach-under-a-palm-tree type, or the explorer-adventurer will not want for the appropriate beach.

Maui's beaches are publicly owned and most have right-of-way access, however, the access is sometimes tricky to find and parking may be a problem! Parking areas are provided at most developed beaches, but are generally limited to 30 cars or less, making an early arrival at the more popular beaches a good idea. In the undeveloped areas you will have to wedge along the roadside. It is vital that you leave nothing of importance in your car, as theft, especially at some of the remoter locations, is high.

At the larger developed beaches, a variety of facilities are provided. Many have convenient rinse-off showers, drinking water, restrooms, and picnic areas. A few have children's play or swim areas. The beaches near the major resorts often have rental equipment available for snorkeling, sailing, boogie boarding, and even underwater cameras. These beaches are generally clean and well maintained. Above Kapalua and below Wailea, where the beaches are undeveloped, expect to find no signs to mark the location, no facilities, and sometimes less cleanliness.

Since virtually all of Maui's good beaches are located on the leeward side of East and West Maui, you can expect sunny weather most of the time. This is because the mountains trap the moisture in the almost constant trade winds. Truly cloudy or bad weather in these areas is rare but when the weather is poor in one area, a short drive may put you back into sun again.

Swells from all directions reach Maui's shores. The three basic swell sources are the east and north-east trade winds, the North Pacific lows, and the South Pacific lows. The trades cause easterly swells of relatively low heights of 2 - 6 feet throughout most of the year. A stormy, persistent trade wind episode may cause swells of 8 - 12 feet and occasionally 10 - 15 feet on exposed eastern shores. Since the main resort areas are on leeward West and East Maui, they are protected.

North Maui and Hana are exposed to these conditions, along with strong ocean currents, therefore very few beaches in these areas are considered safe for casual swimming.

Kona winds generated by southern hemisphere storms cause southerly swells that affect leeward Maui. This usually happens in the summer and will last for several days. Surf heights over eight feet are not common, but many of the resort areas have beaches with fairly steep drop offs causing rather sharp shore breaks. Although it may appear fun to play in these waves, many minor to moderate injuries are recorded at these times. Resorts will post red warning flags along the beach during times of unsafe surf conditions. Most beaches are affected during this time causing water turbidity and poor snorkeling conditions. At a few places, such as Lahaina, Olowalu and Maalaea, these conditions create good surfing.

Northerly swells caused by winter storms northeast of the island are not common, but can cause large surf, particularly on the northern beaches, such as Baldwin, Kanaha and Hookipa Beach Parks.

Winter North Pacific storms generate high surf along the northwestern and northern shores of Maui. This is the source of the winter surf in Mokuleia Bay (Slaughterhouse), renowned for body surfing, and in Honolua Bay which is internationally known for surfing.

Land and sea breezes are local winds blowing from opposite directions at different times depending on the temperature difference between land and sea. The interaction of daytime sea breezes and trade winds, in the Wailea-Makena area particularly, produce almost daily light cloudiness in the afternoon and may bring showers. This is also somewhat true of the Honokowai to Kapalua region.

Oceanic tidal and trade wind currents are not a problem for the swimmer or snorkeler in the main resort areas from Makena to Kapalua except under unusual conditions such as Kona storms. Beaches outside of the resort areas should be treated with due caution since there are very few considered safe for casual swimming and snorkeling except by knowledgeable, experienced persons.

Maui's ocean playgrounds are probably the most benign in the world. There is no fire coral, jelly fish are rare, and sharks are well fed by the abundant marine life and rarely come into shore. However, you should always exercise good judgement and reasonable caution when at the beach.

1. "Never turn your back to the sea" is an old Hawaiian saying. Don't be caught off guard, waves come in sets with spells of calm in between.
2. Use the buddy system, never swim or snorkel alone.
3. If you are unsure of your abilities, use flotation devices attached to your body, such as a life vest or inflatable vest. Never rely or an air mattress or similar device from which you may become separated.
4. Study the ocean before you enter; look for rocks, breakers or currents.
5. Duck or dive beneath breaking waves before they reach you.
6. Never swim against a strong current, swim across it.
7. Know your limits.
8. Small children should be allowed to play near or in the surf ONLY with close supervision and should wear flotation devices.
9. When exploring tidal pools or reefs, always wear protective footwear and keep an eye on the ocean. Also, protect your hands.
10. When swimming around coral, be careful where you put your hands and feet. Urchin stings can be painful and coral cuts can be dangerous.

Surface water temperature varies little with a mean temperature of 73.0 in January and 80.2 in August. Minimum and maximum range from 68 to 84 degrees. This is an almost ideal temperature (refreshing, but not cold) for swimming and you will find most resort pools cooler than the ocean.

BEST BETS
On East Maui our favorite beaches are Makena for its unspoiled beauty, Maluaka for its deep fine sand and beautiful coral, Wailea and Ulua/Mokapu for their great beaches, good snorkeling and beautiful resorts, and Keawakapu and Kamaole II which offer gentler offshore slopes where swimming is excellent.

On West Maui, Kapalua offers a well protected bay with very good swimming and snorkeling. Hanakaoo Beach has a gentle offshore slope and the park has lots of parking, good facilities, numerous activities, and is next to the Hyatt. Olowalu has easy access and excellent snorkeling. An excellent place for small children to play in the sand and water is at Pu'unoa Beach, which is well protected by a large offshore reef.

Beaches of Maui County, by John Clark, is *THE* comprehensive guide to all the Island's beaches, and also includes much historical information.

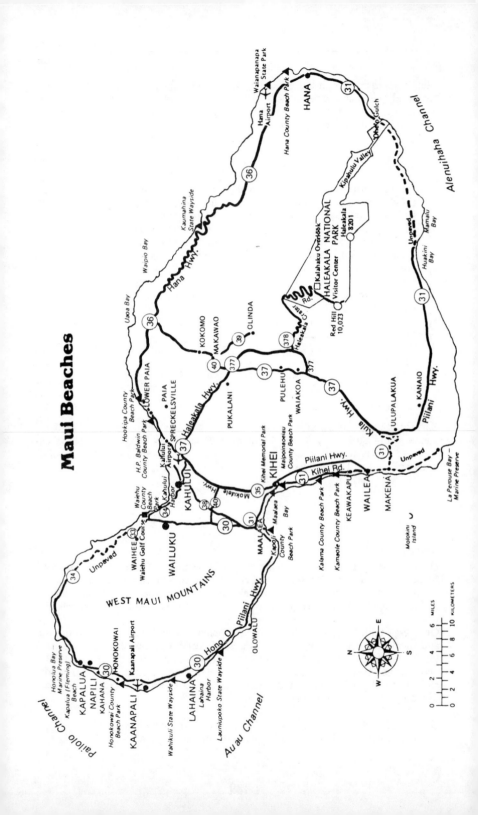

Maui Beaches

BEACH INDEX

MAALAEA TO LAHAINA

The beaches are described in order from Maalaea to Lahaina and are easy to spot from Honoapiilani Highway. They are all narrow and usually lined by Kiawe trees, however, they have gentle slopes to deeper water and the ocean is generally calmer and warmer than in other areas. The offshore coral reefs offer excellent snorkeling in calm weather, which is most of the time. These beaches are popular because of their convenient access and facilities as well as good swimming and snorkeling conditions.

PAPALAUA STATE WAYSIDE PARK

As you descend from the sea cliffs on your way from Maalaea you will see an undeveloped tropical shoreline stretch before you. At the foot of the cliffs at mile marker 11, Papalaua Park is marked by an easily seen sign. There are picnic tables, BBQ grills, and portable restrooms. The beach is long, (about 1/2 mile) and narrow and lined with Kiawe trees that almost reach the waters edge in places. The trees provide plenty of shady areas for this beautiful beach. Good swimming and fair snorkeling, popular picnicking area.

UKUMEHAME BEACH PARK

The entrance to the park is near mile marker 12, but there is no identifying sign. There is off-street paved parking for about 12 cars. Five concrete picnic tables. This is also a narrow 1/2 mile long sand beach with lots of Kiawe trees providing shade. Good swimming, fair snorkeling.

OLOWALU BEACH ★

About 2/10 miles before and after mile marker 14 you will see a large, but narrow stand of Kiawe trees between the road and the beach, followed by a few palm trees, then a few more scattered Kiawe trees. Parking is alongside the road. No facilities. This narrow sand beach slopes gently out to water four or five feet deep making it good for swimming and beach playing. There are extensive coral formations starting right off-shore and continuing out a quarter mile or more, and a fair amount of fish expecting handouts. The ocean is generally warmer and calmer than elsewhere, making it a popular snorkeling spot.

AWALUA BEACH

The beach at mile marker 16 may be cobble stone or sand depending on the time of year and the prevailing conditions. No facilities. At times when Kona storms create a good southern swell, this becomes a very popular surfing spot for a few days until the swells subside.

LAUNIUPOKO STATE WAYSIDE PARK

This well-marked beach park near mile marker 18 offers a large paved parking area, restrooms, many picnic tables, BBQ grills, rinse-off showers, drinking water, pay phone, and a large grassy area with trees, all of which makes for a good picnic spot. There is a large man-made wading pool constructed of large boulders centered in the park. (Sand has accumulated to the extent that even at high tide there is no water in the pool). To the right is a rocky beach and to the left is a 200-yard dark sand beach with fairly gentle slope. It looks nice, but signs posted warn "Sharks have been seen in the shallow water off this beach. Entry into the water is discouraged." This area is rumored to be a shark breeding ground with shark fishing done here in the past. There is also a no alcohol sign posted. For some reason the beach does not seem to be used for much besides picnicking!

PUAMANA BEACH PARK
Well marked beach park near mile marker 19, just south of the Puamana Resort complex. Parking for 20 cars in paved parking area, with additional parking along the highway. Nice grassy park with seven picnic tables and plenty of shade trees. At the park itself there is no sandy beach, only a large pebble beach. The only beach is a narrow 200 yard long white sand beach just north of the park and fronting Puamana Resort. Fairly gentle slope to shallow water.

LAHAINA AND KAANAPALI

LAHAINA BEACH
There is a large public parking lot across from the 505 Front Street shopping center with easy access to the beach through the mall. There is also on-street parking near the Lahaina Shores with public right of way to the beach at the south end of the complex. Restrooms and showers are only available at the resort. The Lahaina Sailing Center is located on the beach. This narrow sand beach fronts the Lahaina Shores and 505 Front St. and is protected by a reef 30 – 50 yards out. The beach is generally sandy offshore with a gentle slope. The water stays fairly shallow out to the reef and contains some interesting coral formations. The area offers fair snorkeling in clear water on calm days. A good place for beginning snorkelers and children, but not good for swimming due to shallow water and abundant coral.

PUUNOA BEACH ★
The beach is situated at the north end of Lahaina between Kai Pali Road and the old Mala Wharf and can be seen as you leave Lahaina on Front Street. Southern Access: Take Kai Pali Road off Front street. Parking for about 20 cars along the road which is the entrance for the Puunoa Beach Estates. Public Beach access sign with concrete sidewalk to the beach. Mid Beach Access: Take Puunoa Place off Front Street at the Public Beach access sign. Parking for about four cars at the end of the road which ends at the beach. A rinse off hose here is the only facility for the beach. North Access: Take Mala Wharf off Front Street. Parking for approximately 20 cars along the road just before the entrance to the Mala boat launching parking area.

This narrow, dense, darker sand beach is about 300 yards long and well protected by a reef approximately 100 – 150 yards offshore. The beach slopes gently to water only 3 – 4 feet deep. Unfortunately, rock and coral near the surface make swimming unadvised. There are areas of the beach clear of coral 10 – 15 feet out where children can play safely in the calm, shallow water. At high tide there are more fish to see while snorkeling.

WAHIKULI STATE WAYSIDE PARK
There are three paved off-street parking areas between Lahaina and Kaanapali. Many covered picnic tables, restrooms, showers, and BBQ grills are provided. The first and third parking areas are marked but have no beach. The second unmarked area has an excellent, darker sand beach with a gentle slope to deeper water. There is some shelf rock in places but it's rounded and smooth and not a problem. With the handy facilities, trees for shade, and the nice beach, this is a good, and popular, spot for sunning, swimming, and picnicking.

HANAKAOO BEACH PARK ★
Off Honoapiilani Highway, immediately south of the Hyatt Regency, there is a large well-marked, off-street parking area. The park has rinse-off showers, restroom, and picnic tables. Wide, darker sand beach with gentle slope to deeper water. This is a popular area because of the easy parking, facilities, good beach, shallow water and good swimming, and you are right next to the Hyatt.

HANAKAOO BEACH ★ (Kaanapali Beach)
The beach fronts the Hyatt Regency, Marriott, Kaanapali Alii, Westin Maui, Whaler's Shopping Center and condos, Kaanapali Beach Hotel, and the Sheraton, and is known as Kaanapali Beach. Access is through the Kaanapali Resort area. Turn off Honoapiilani Highway at either of the first two entrances. This area was not designed with non-guest use in mind, and parking is definitely a problem.

A) The Hyatt end of the beach is only a short walk from the large parking area of Hanakaoo Beach Park.
B) Public right-of-way with parking for 10 cars to left of the Hyatt's lower parking.
C) Public right-of-way between the Hyatt and Marriott, no parking.
D) Public right-of-way between Marriott and Kaanapali Alii with parking for 11 cars only.
E) Public right-of-way between Kaanapali Alii and Westin Maui, no parking.
F) Public right-of-way between Kaanapali Beach Resort and the Sheraton with parking for 11 cars only.
G) The Whalers Shopping Center has a three-story pay parking lot, but with beach access only through the complex.
H) There is no on-street parking anywhere in the Kaanapali Resort complex.

The Hyatt, Marriott, Westin Maui, and Sheraton all have restrooms, showers, bars, and rental equipment. There is a beautiful, long, wide, white sand beach with an abrupt drop-off to deep water. There are small areas of offshore coral from the Hyatt to the Westin Maui at times, but no true offshore reef. Great swimming and good wave playing with the exception of two or three points along the beach where the waves consistently break fairly hard. In the winter, snorkeling can be fair off the Westin Maui when the coral is exposed underwater. The best snorkeling is at Black Rock, fronting the Sheraton Hotel. The water is almost always clear and fairly calm, with many types of nearly tame fish due to the popularity of hand feeding by snorkelers. (Bread, frozen peas and packaged dry noodles seem popular). Not much colorful coral. The best entrance to the water is from the beach alongside Black Rock.

195

KAANAPALI BEACH (South End)

This beach begins at the north side of Black Rock and runs for over a mile to the north fronting the Royal Lahaina Resort and the Maui Kaanapali Villas. Turn off Honoapiilani Road at the last Kaanapali exit at the stop light by the Maui Kaanapali Villas. There are a few places to park on the side of the road near the Public Access beach sign. With the airport now closed there is more parking available. This area is being prepared for future hotel and condo developement and should eventually have much improved public access, facilities and parking. The only facilities now are those of the nearby hotels. This wide (usually) white sand beach has a steep drop-off to deep water, and is usually calm – a good place to swim. Snorkeling around Black Rock is almost always good.

KAHANA, NAPILI, KAPALUA AND BEYOND

KAANAPALI BEACH (North End)

This section of beach fronts the Mahana Resort, Maui Kai, Embassy Suites, Kaanapali Shores, Papakea, Maui Sands and Paki Maui from south to north, and ends at the Honokowai Beach Park. Access is generally only through the resorts. Most of the resorts have rinse-off showers convenient to the beach, however, no other facilities are available. This is a long narrow white sand beach which is fronted by a close in reef. All the resorts except the Kaanapali Shores and Embassy Suites have retaining walls along the beach. The Kaanapali Shores has, over the last couple of years, suffered considerable erosion of its once wide beach and has recently completed an expensive new under-the-sand retaining wall in an effort to stabilize and restore it. There is also a cleared area through the coral in front of the resort. This is the only good swimming area on the north section of the beach and is the only good access through the reef for snorkeling.

The reef comes into shore at the south end of Papakea and again at the Honokowai Beach Park. At low tide the reef fronting Papakea can be walked on like a wide sidewalk. (See GENERAL INFORMATION – Children, for night walking on the reef) The reef is generally only 10 – 20 yards offshore and the area between is very shallow with much coral and rock making it undesirable for swimming and snorkeling. The middle section of beach, fronting the old Kaanapali Airport, is slated for future development.

HONOKOWAI BEACH PARK

Turn off the Honoapiilani Hwy. on the first side street past the airport (at the Honokowai sign) and get onto Lower Honoapiilani Hwy., which parallels the ocean. The park is across the street from the Honokowai Grocery Store. There is paved off-street parking for 30 cars. There are 11 picnic tables, 5 BBQ pits, restrooms, showers, and a grassy park with shade trees. Grocery store across the street with pay phone outside. The white sand beach is lined by a wide shelf of beach rock. Between the shelf rock and reef there is a narrow, shallow pool with sandy bottom which is a good swimming area for small children. There is a break in the reef at the north end of the beach where you can get snorkeling access to the outside reef. Water sport equipment for rent at the Honokowai Store.

KAHANA BEACH

In front of the Kahana Beach Condominiums, Sands of Kahana, Royal Kahana, Valley Isle Resort and Hololani from south to north on Lower Honoapiilani Hwy. There is limited off-road parking at the south end of the beach. Other access would be through the condos. The only facilities available are at the condos, usually rinse off showers. There are several grocery stores, one at the Valley Isle Resort, the other at the Hololani condos. This white sand beach varies from narrow to wide and its offshore area is shallow with rock and sand, semi-protected by reef. Good swimming, fair snorkeling. Beach may be cool and windy in afternoons.

KEONENUI BEACH ★

The beach is in front of and surrounded by the Kahana Sunset with no convenient public access. A lovely wide crescent of white sand with a fairly gentle slope to water's edge, then fairly steep slope to deeper water. The beach is set in a small shallow cove, about 150 yards wide, which affords some protection. At times, especially in winter, rough seas come into the beach. When calm (most of the time) this is an excellent swimming and play area with fair snorkeling.

ALAELOA BEACH ("The Cove")

This miniature jewel-like cove is surrounded by low sea cliffs. The small, approximately 25 – 30 yard long, white sand beach has a gentle slope with scattered rocks leading into sparkling clear waters. Pavilion and lounge chair area for use by Alaeloa guests. Good swimming and snorkeling with very clear and calm waters except when storm-generated waves come in. Fortunately, or unforturately, depending on your point of view, this small cove is surrounded by the Alaeloa residential area which has no on or off-street public parking, therefore, no public access to this beach.

NAPILI BAY ★

There are two public accesses to this beautiful beach. There is a small, easily missed public right-of-way and Napili Beach sign just past the Napili Shores at Napili Place street. On-street parking at sign for Napili Surf Beach Resort. The public beach right-of-way sign shows the entrance to the beach. Public telephone in parking lot of Napili Surf. The second entrance is at the public beach right-of-way and Napili Sunset, Hale Napili, and Napili Bay signs on Hui street. On-street parking and pay phone at entrance to beach walk.

This is a long, wide crescent of white sand between two rocky points. The offshore slope is moderately steep. Usually very safe for swimming and snorkeling except during winter storms when large waves occasionally come into the bay. At the south end of the beach are a series of shallow sandy tide pools which make an excellent place for children, but only under close supervision. Coral formations 30 – 40 yards offshore can provide fair snorkeling on calm days especially at the northern end of the beach. No facilities other than at the hotels fronting the beach. There is a grocery store just past the second entrance at the Napili Village Hotel. Look for the Napili Grocery Store sign.

KAPALUA BEACH ★ (Fleming Beach)

Just past the Napili Kai Beach Club you will see a public beach right-of-way sign. Off-street parking area for about 30 cars. Showers and restrooms. A beautiful crescent of white sand between two rocky points. The beach has a gentle slope to deeper water, maximum about 15 feet. From the left point, a reef arcs toward the long right point creating a very sheltered bay, probably the nicest and safest swimming beach on Maui. Shade is provided by numerous palm trees lining the back shore area. Above the beach are the lovely grounds of the Kapalua Bay Resort. Swimming is almost always excellent with plenty of play area for children. Snorkeling is usually good with many different kinds of fish and interesting coral. *REMEMBER*, this popular beach has limited parking.

NAMALU BAY

Park at Kapalua Beach and take the concrete path along the beach, up through the hotel's grounds, and out to the point of land separating Kapalua Bay from Namalu Bay. This small bay has a shoreline of large lava boulders, no beaches. On calm days snorkeling is very good and entry and exit over the rocks is easy. This little known spot is definitely worth the short walk.

ONELOA BEACH

Enter at the public right-of-way sign just past the Kapalua Bay Resort. Paved off-street parking for 12 – 15 cars only, no other facilities. Long, straight white sand beach with a shallow sand bar that extends to the surfline. The beach is posted with a warning sign "No swimming at time of high surf due to dangerous currents." This area tends to get windy and cloudy in the afternoons, especially in the winter months. We have usually found this beach deserted.

D. T. FLEMING BEACH PARK

Off-street parking on both sides of the road. Restrooms, showers, picnic tables, and BBQ's on the grassy dunes above the beach. The long white sand beach is steep with an offshore sand bar which may cause dangerous water conditions when swells hit the beach. The beach is posted "Dangerous Swimming".

MOKULEIA BEACH ★ (Slaughterhouse)

On Highway 30, past D. T. Fleming Beach Park, look for cars parked along the roadside and the Mokuleia-Honolua Marine Reserve sign. Park your car and hike down one of the steep dirt and rock trails – they're not difficult. There are no facilities. The wide, white sand beach has a gentle slope to deep water and is bordered by two rocky points and is situated at the foot of steep cliffs. The left middle part of the beach is usually clear of coral and rocks even in winter when the beach is subject to erosion.

During the winter this is *THE* bodysurfing spot, especially in when the surf is heavy, however, dangerous water conditions also exist. The summer is generally much better for swimming and snorkeling. Snorkeling is fair to good, especially around the left rocky point where there is a reef. Okay in winter when the ocean is calm and visibility good. NOTE: The beach is known as Slaughterhouse because of the once existing slaughterhouse on the cliffs above the beach, not because of what the ocean can do to body surfers in the winter when the big ones are coming in! Remember this is part of the Honolua-Mokuleia Bay Marine Life Conservation District – look, but don't disturb or take.

HONOLUA BAY ★

The next bay past Slaughterhouse is Honolua Bay. As you drive down into the bay, watch for a dirt side road on the left. Park here and walk in along the road. There is no beach, just cobblestone with irregular patches of sand and an old concrete boat ramp in the middle. Excellent snorkeling in summer, spring, and fall especially in the morning, but in winter only on the calmest days. In summer on calm days the bay resembles a large glassy pond and in our opinion, this is the best snorkeling on Maui. You can enter at the boat ramp or over the rocks and follow the reefs either left or right. Remember this is a Marine Life Conservation area, so look but don't disturb.

There is an interesting phenomenon affecting the bay. As fresh water runoff percolates into the bay, a shimmering boundary layer (usually about three feet below the surface) is created between the fresh and salt waters. Depending on the amount of runoff it may be very apparent or disappear entirely. It is less prevalent on the right side of the bay. Honolua Bay is also an internationally known winter surfing spot. Storm generated waves come thundering in around the right point creating perfect waves and tubes. A good vantage point to watch the action is the cliffs at the right point of the bay, accessible by car on a short dirt road off the main highway.

KIHEI BEACHES

The Kihei beaches aren't quite as beautiful as Wailea's. They don't have the nicely landscaped parking areas, or the large, beautiful resort complexes (this is condo country). They do offer increased facilities such as BBQs, picnic tables, drinking water, and grassy play areas. The Kamaole I, II and III beaches even have lifeguards. The beaches are listed in order from Maalaea Bay to Wailea.

MAALAEA BAY BEACH

This gently curving white sand beach stretches three miles from the Maalaea boat harbor to Kihei. For the most part, the beach is backed by low sand dunes and large generally wet, sand flats. Public access is from many areas along South Kihei Road. There are no facilities. Casual beach activities are best early in the morning before the strong mid-morning prevailing winds begin to sweep across the isthmus. Due to the length of the beach and the hard-packed sand near the water, this has become popular place to jog. Windsurfing is popular in the afternoons.

A secluded section of beach offering a large swimming-pool-like area formed from rocks and reef, a narrow beach, good swimming and fair snorkeling, and some protection from the afternoon wind, lies about 2/10 mile past the condos in Maalaea. Drive down into the Maalaea condo area to the end of the paved road, then continue on the dirt road for about 2/10 mile and turn right.

MAI POINA OE IAU BEACH PARK

On South Kihei Road, fronting Maui Lu Resort. Paved parking for 8 cars at the Pavilion (numerous other areas to park are along the road). 5 picnic tables, restrooms, showers. This is actually still part of the previous beach. Inshore bottom generally sandy with patches of rock, fronted by shallow reef. Swimming and snorkeling are best in the morning before the early afternoon winds come up. Popular windsurfing area in the afternoon.

KAONOULULU BEACH PARK

Located across the street from the Kihei Bay Surf. Off-road parking for 20 cars, restrooms, drinking water, rinse-off showers, picnic tables, and four BBQ grills. Very small beach, well protected by close-in reef.

KAWILIKI POU PARK

Located at the end of Waipulani Street. Paved off-street parking for 30 cars, restrooms, large grassy area, and public tennis courts. Fronts Laule'a, Luana Kai and the Maui Sunset Hotel. Tall graceful palms line the shoreline. Narrow sandy beach generally strewn with coral rubble. (See GENERAL INFORMATION – Children, for frog hunting information)

KAWILILIPOA AND WAIMAHAIKAI AREAS

Any of the cross streets off South Kihei Road will take you down toward the beach where public right-of-ways are marked. Limited parking, usually on street. No facilities. The whole shoreline from Kalama Park to Waipulani Street (3 – 4 miles) is an area of interrupted beaches lined by residential housing and small condo complexes. Narrow sandy beaches with lots of coral rubble from the fronting reefs.

KALAMA BEACH PARK

Well-marked 36 acre park. 12 pavilions, 3 restrooms, showers, picnic tables, BBQ grills, playground apparatus, soccer field, baseball field, tennis courts, volleyball and basketball courts. Lots of grassy area. There is no beach (in winter), only a large boulder breakwater. Good view of the cinder cone in Makena, Molokini, Kahoolawe, Lanai, and West Maui.

KAMAOLE I

Well-marked beach across from the Kamaole Beach Club. Off-street parking for 30 cars. Picnic tables, restrooms, rinse-off showers, rental equipment, children's swimming area, and lifeguard. Long white sandy beach offering good swimming, poor to fair snorkeling. NOTE: The small pocket of sand between rock outcroppings at the right end of the beach is known as Young's Beach. It is also accessible from Kaiau Street with parking for about 20 cars. Public right-of-way sign at end of Kaiau Street.

KAMAOLE II

Located across from the Kai Nani shopping and restaurant complex. On-street parking, restrooms, rinse-off showers, rental equipment, and lifeguard. White sand beach between two rocky points with sharp drop-off to overhead depths. Good swimming, poor to fair snorkeling.

KAMAOLE III ★

Well-marked beach across from the Kamaole Sands Condominiums. Off-street parking, picnic tables, BBQ's, restrooms, rinse-off showers, drinking water, playground equipment, a grassy play area, and a lifeguard. 200 yard long, narrow (in winter) white sand beach with some rocky areas along beach, and a few submerged rocks. Good swimming, fair snorkeling around rocks at south end of the beach.

WAILEA BEACHES

This area generally has small, lovely, white sand beaches which have marked public access. Parking is off street and restrooms as well as rinse-off showers are provided.

KEAWAKAPU BEACH ★

There are two convenient public accesses to this very nice but generally underused beach. There is paved parking for 50 cars across the street from the beach, about 2/10 mile south of Mana Kai Resort. Look for the beach access sign on the left as you travel south. There are two small crescent shaped, white sand beaches separated by a small rocky point. Good swimming, off-shore sandy bottom, fair snorkeling around rocks at far north end. There are rinse-off showers and a restaurant at the Mana Kai which is right on the beach. Access to southern end of beach – go straight at left turn-off to Wailea, road says "Dead End." Parking for about 30 cars. Beautiful, very gently sloping white sand beach with good swimming. Snorkeling off rocks on left. Popular scuba diving spot. Four hundred yards off shore in 80 – 85 feet of water is an artificial reef of 150 car bodies.

MOKAPU BEACH ★

A public access sign (Ulua/Mokapu Beaches) is near the Stouffer Wailea Beach Resort. Small parking area, restrooms and showers. Rental equipment at nearby Wailea Resort Activities Center at Stouffer's. Beautiful white sand beach. Excellent swimming. Good snorkeling in mornings around the rocks which divide the two beaches.

ULUA BEACH ★

A public access sign (Ulua/Mokapu Beaches) is located near the Stouffer Wailea Beach Resort. Small paved parking area with a short walk to beach. Showers and rest rooms. Rental equipment is only a short walk away at the Wailea Ocean Activities Center. Beautiful white sand beach fronting the Elua Resort complex. Ulua and Mokapu Beaches are separated by a narrow point of rocks. The area around the beaches is beautifully landscaped because of the resorts. The beach is semi-protected and has a sandy offshore bottom. Good swimming, usually very good snorkeling in the mornings around the lava flow between the beaches. Come early to get a parking space!

WAILEA BEACH ★

One half mile south of the Inter-Continental Resort there is a public beach access sign and a paved road down to a landscaped parking area for about 40 cars. Restrooms and rinse-off showers. Rental sailboats and windsurfing boards are available. Beautiful wide crescent of gently sloping white sand. Gentle offshore slope. Good swimming. Snorkeling is only fair to the left (south) around the rocks (moderate currents and not much coral or many fish). This area is slated for development of several new luxury resorts.

POLO BEACH

Turn right at the Wailea Golf Club-Fairway Restaurant sign and head down to the Polo Beach Resort condominiums. The public access sign is easy to spot. Parking for 40 cars in paved parking area. Showers and restrooms. The beaches are a short walk on a paved sidewalk and down a short flight of stairs. There are actually two beaches, 400 foot long north beach and 200 foot long south beach, separated by 150 feet of large rocks. The beaches slope steeply offshore and are not well protected, causing a rough shore break. The beach is dotted with large rocks. Fair swimming, generally poor snorkeling.

MAKENA BEACHES

This area includes the beaches south of Polo Beach, out to La Perouse Bay (past this point, you either hike or need to have a four-wheel drive). The Makena beaches are undeveloped and relatively unspoiled, for a while longer at least, and not always easy to find. There are no signs, confusing roads, and some beaches are not visible from the road. No facilities and parking where you can find it. The nearest grocery is at the Wailea Shopping Center.

This area has been changing in the last few years. The new road is now completed to the Makena Golf Club and on past the Maui Prince Hotel. Although development is progressing, much more is desired by various commercial interests. Local opposition has managed, so far, to keep this in check. We hope our directions will help you find these sometimes hard-to-find, but very lovely beaches.

PALAUEA BEACH
As you leave Wailea, there is a four-corner intersection with a sign on the left for the Wailea Golf Club, and on the right for the Polo Beach Condos. 8/10 mile past here turn onto the second right turnoff at the small "Paipu Beach" sign. At roads end (about 1/10 mile), park under the trees. Poolenalena Beach lies in front of you. Walk several hundred feet back towards Polo Beach over a small hill (Haloa Point) and you will see Palauea Beach stretching out before you.

If you drive down to the Polo Beach Condos instead, you can continue on Old Makena Road which will loop back to Makena Alanui Road after about a mile. Palauea Beach lays along this road, but is not visible through the trees. .35 miles from Polo Beach there is a break in the fence with a well worn path to the beach. Although this is all private and posted land the path and the number of cars parked along side the the road seems to indicate that this beautiful white sand beach is getting much more public use than in the past. Good swimming. No facilities.

POOLENALENA BEACH PARK
See directions for Palauea Beach. This is a lovely wide, white sand beach with gentle slope offering good swimming. This used to be a popular local camping spot, however no camping signs are now posted. It still seems to be a popular local beach though.

UPCOUNTRY ROAD
1.4 miles from Polo Beach. Currently closed in dispute over maintenance.

CHANG'S BEACH
Continue another 2/10 to 3/10 miles on Makena Alanui Rd., past Poolenalena and you will come to the Makena Surf Town Houses (about 1.2 miles from the Wailea Golf Club sign). This development surrounds Chang's Beach, however, there is a public beach access sign and paved parking for about 20 cars. It's a short walk down a concrete path to the beach. A rinse-off shower is provided. This small but sandy beach is used mostly by guests of the Makena Surf.

ULUPIKUNUI BEACH

Turn right just past the Makena Surf and immediately park off the road. Walk down to the beach at the left end of the complex. The beach is 75 to 100 feet of rock strewn sand and is not too attractive, but is well protected.

FIVE GRAVES

From the Makena Surf, continue down Old Makena Road another 2/10 mile to the entrance of Five Graves. There is ample parking. The 19th century graves are visible from Makena Rd. just a couple hundred feet past the entrance. There is no beach, but this is a good scuba and snorkeling site. Follow the trail down the shore where you'll see a good entrance to the water.

MAKENA LANDING - PAPIPI BEACH

Continue another 2/10 mile on Old Makena Rd. to Makena Landing on the right. There is off-street parking for 22 cars. The beach is located at the entrance and is about 75 - 100 feet with gentle slope, sometimes rockstrewn. Not very attractive and is used mostly for fishing, but snorkeling can be good if you enter at the beach and follow the shore to the right.

NOTE: Instead of turning right onto Old Makena Road at the Makena Surf, you can continue straight to the Makena Golf Course, just follow signs. About 9/10 mile past the Makena Surf there is another turnoff onto Old Makena Rd. At the stop sign at the bottom of the hill, you can turn right and end up back at Makena Landing or turn left for Maluaka Beach, where the road ends. To continue on, you must go back and around the Maui Prince Resort.

KEAWALAI CHURCH U.C.C.

2/10 mile past the stop sign you will see the old church and cemetery. Sunday services continue to be held here. Along the road is a pay phone.

MALUAKA BEACH ★ (Naupaka)

3/10 mile past the stop sign there is a public entrance to this beach on the right. Parking is alongside the road at this time although, as the Maui Prince is developed, there will most likely be improved public parking and facilities. This gorgeous 200-yard beach is set between a couple of rock promontories. The very fine white sand beach is wide with a gentle slope to deeper water. Snorkeling can be good in the morning until about noon when the wind picks up. There are interesting coral formations at the south end with unusual abstract shapes, and large coral heads of different sizes. Coral in shades of pink, blue, green, purple and lavender can be spotted. There are enough fish to make it interesting, but not an abundance. In the afternoon when the wind comes up, so do the swells, providing good boogieboarding and wave playing.

NOTE: The Makena Alanui Rd. is now completed past the Maui Prince and intersects the Old Makena Hwy. near the entrance to Black Sand and Makena beaches. Directions to the following beaches are from this intersection.

ONEULI BEACH (Black Sand Beach)

On Old Makena Hwy. just past the intersection of the new road is a dirt road turnoff. A 4-wheel drive is good idea for the very rutted 3/10 mile to the beach. The beach is coarse black sand and the entire length of the beach is lined by an exposed reef. No facilities.

ONELOA BEACH ★ (Makena Beach)

The entrance for the north end of the beach is at the second dirt road to the right off Old Makena Hwy. after the intersection of the new road. It is 3/10 mile from the turnoff to the beach and parking area, with room for about 20 cars. It is another 6/10 mile on Old Makena Hwy. to the parking area at the southern end of the beach, which is visible from the road. There are two mid-beach dirt entrance roads from the main road.

This very lovely white sand beach is long (3/5 mile) and wide and is the last major undeveloped beach on the leeward side of the island. Work continues to make this a park to prevent further development. The 360-foot cinder cone (Pu'u Olai) at the north end of the beach separates Oneloa from Puuolai Beach. The beach has a quick, sharp drop-off and rough shore break particularly in the afternoon. Body surfing is sometimes good. Snorkeling around the rocky point at the cinder cone is only poor to fair with not much to see, and not for beginners due to the usually strong north to south current.

PUUOLAI BEACH (Little Makena)

Take the first Oneloa Beach entrance, and park at Oneloa Beach. From there, you hike over the cinder cone. There is a flat, white sand beach, with a shallow sandy bottom which is semi-protected by a shallow cove. The shore break is usually gentle and swimming is good. Bodysurfing sometimes. Snorkeling is only poor to fair around the point on left. Watch for strong currents. Although definitely illegal, beach activities here tend to be au naturel.

AHIHI-KINAU ★ (NATURAL RESERVE AREA)

About 1.3 miles from the intersection of the new road, a sign indicates the reserve. There is a small, 6-foot wide sandy beach alongside the remnants of an old concrete boat ramp. Although it's located in a small cove and is well protected, the beach and cove are very shallow with many urchins. There is also very limited parking here. Up around the curve in the road is a large parking area. It's a short walk to the shore on a crushed lava rock trail. Another couple hundred feet to a very small (3 foot) and partially hidden sand and pebble beach that makes a better entrance to the water than over the rocks. Right off shore there is excellent snorkeling to the right and left. Remember, this is a marine reserve – look, but don't disturb. No facilities.

LA PEROUSE BAY

2 miles past Ahihi-Kinau over a fairly rough road carved through Maui's most recent lava flow is the end of the road unless you have a 4-wheel drive. The "road" is extremely rough and we would recommend a hike rather than a ride. It's about 3 or 4 miles from roads end at La Perouse Bay to the Kanaio beaches. If you hike, wear good hiking shoes as you'll be walking over stretches of sharp lava rock. There are a series of small beaches, actually only pockets of sand of various compositions, with fairly deep offshore waters and strong currents.

WAILUKU – KAHULUI BEACHES

Beaches along this whole side of the island are usually poor for swimming and snorkeling. The weather is generally windy or cloudy in winter and very hot in summer. Due to the weather, type of beaches, and distance from the major tourist areas on the other side of the island, these beaches don't attract many tourists (except Hookipa, which is internationally known for wind surfing).

WAIHEE BEACH PARK
From Wailuku take Kahekili Highway about three miles to Waihee and turn right onto Halewaiu Road, then proceed about one-half mile to the Waihee Municipal Golf Course. From there, a park access road takes you into the park. Paved off-street parking, restrooms, showers, and picnic tables. This is a long, narrow, brown sand beach strewn with coral rubble from Waihee Reef. This is one of the longest and widest reefs on Maui and is about one thousand feet wide. The area between the beach and reef is moderately shallow with good areas for swimming and snorkeling when the ocean is calm. Winter surf or storm conditions can produce strong alongshore currents. Do not swim or snorkel at the left end of the beach as there is a large channel through the reef which usually produces a very strong rip current. Area is generally windy.

KANAHA BEACH PARK
Just before reaching the Kahului Airport, turn left, then right on reaching Ahahao Street. The far south area of the park has been landscaped and includes BBQs, picnic tables, restrooms, and showers. Paved off-street parking is provided. The beach is long (about one mile) and wide with a shallow offshore bottom composed of sand and rock. Plenty of thorny Kiawe trees in the area make footwear essential. The main attraction of the park is its peaceful setting and view, so picnicking and sunbathing are the primary activities. Swimming would appeal mainly to children. Surfing can be good here.

H. A. BALDWIN PARK
The park is located about 1.5 miles past Spreckelville on the Hana Highway. There is a large off-street parking area, a large pavilion with kitchen facilities, picnic tables, BBQs, and a tent camping area. There are also restrooms, showers, a baseball and a soccer fields. The beach is long and wide with a steep slope to overhead depths. This is a very popular park because of the facilities. The very consistent, although usually smallish, shorebreak, which is good for bodysurfing. Swimming is poor. There are two areas where exposed beach rock provides a relatively calm place for children to play.

HOOKIPA BEACH PARK
Located about two miles past Lower Paia on the Hana Highway. Restrooms, showers, four pavilions with BBQ's and picnic tables, paved off-street parking, and a tent camping area is provided. Small, white sand beach fronted by a wide shelf of beach rock. The offshore bottom is a mixture of reef and patches of sand. Swimming is not advised. (The area is popular for the generally good and at times (during winter) very good surfing). Hookipa is internationally known for its excellent wind surfing conditions. This is also a good place to come and watch both of these water sports.

HANA

WAIANAPANAPA STATE PARK
About four miles before you reach Hana on the Hana Highway is Waianapanapa State Park. There is a trail from the parking lot down to the ocean. The beach is not of sand, but of millions of small, smooth, black volcanic stones. Ocean activities are generally unsafe. There is a lava tunnel at the end of the beach that runs about 50 feet and opens into the ocean. Other well marked paths in the park lead to more caves and fresh water pools. An abundance of mosquitos breed in the grotto area and bug repellent is strongly advised.

HANA BEACH PARK
If you make it to Hana, you will have no difficulty finding this beach on the shoreline of Hana Bay. Facilities include a pavilion with picnic tables, restrooms and showers, and also Tutu's snack bar. About a 200-yard beach lies between old concrete pilings on the left and the wharf on the right. Gentle offshore slope and gentle shore break even during heavy outer surf. This is the safest swimming beach on this end of the island. Snorkeling is fair to good on calm days between the pier and the lighthouse. Staying inshore is a must, as beyond the lighthouse the currents are very strong and flow seaward.

KAIHALULU BEACH (Red Sand Beach)
This reddish sand beach is located in a small cove on the other side of Kauiki Hill from Hana Bay and is accessible by trail. At the Hana Bay intersection follow the road up to the school. A dirt path leads past the school and disappears into the jungle. The trail almost vanishes as it goes through an old cemetery, then continues out onto a scenic promontory. The ground here is covered with marble-sized pine cones which make for slippery footing. As the trail leads to the left and over the edge of the cliff, it changes to a very crumbly rock/dirt mixture that is unstable at best.

You may wonder why you're doing this as the trail becomes two feet wide and slopes to the edge of a 60 foot cliff in one place. The trail down to the beach can be quite hazardous. Visitors and Hana residents alike have been injured seriously. It is definitely not for the squeamish, those with less than good agility or youngsters. And when carrying beach paraphernlia, extra caution is needed. The effort is rewarded as you descend into a lovely cove bordered by high cliffs and almost enclosed by a natural lava barrier seaward. The beach is formed primarily from red volcanic cinder, hence its name. Good swimming, but stay away from the opening at the left end because of rip currents. Although definitely illegal, beach activities here may be au naturel at times. The Hotel Hana Maui has plans to improve the access to this beach sometime in the future.

KOKI BEACH PARK
This beach is reached by traveling 1.5 miles past the Hasegawa Store toward Ohe'o Gulch. Look for Haneoo Road where the sign will read "Koki Park – Hamoa Beach – Hamoa Village". This beach is unsafe for swimming and the signs posted warn "Dangerous Current."

HAMOA BEACH ★
This gorgeous beach has been very attractively landscaped and developed by the Hotel Hana Maui in a way that adds to the surrounding lushness. The long white sand beach is in a very tropical setting and surrounded by a low sea cliff. To reach it travel toward Ohe'o Gulch after passing through Hana. Look for the sign 1.5 miles past Hasegawa store that says "Koki Park – Hamoa Beach – Hamoa Village." There are two entrances down steps from the road. Parking is limited to along the roadside. The left side of the beach is calmer, and offers the best snorkeling. Because it is unprotected from the open ocean, there is good surfing and bodysurfing, but also strong alongshore and rip currents are created at times of heavy seas. The Hana Hotel maintains the grounds and offers restrooms, changing area, and beach paraphernalia for the guests. There is an outdoor rinse-off shower for non-hotel guests. Hay wagons bring the guests to the beach for the hotel's weekly luau.

Recreation and Tours

INTRODUCTION

Maui's ideal climate, diverse land environments, and benign leeward ocean has led to an astounding range of land, sea and air activities. With such a variety of things to do during your limited vacation time, we suggest browsing through this chapter and choosing those activities that sound most enjoyable. The following suggestions should get you started.

BEST BETS:

To see and experience the real Maui, take a hike with guide Ken Schmitt.

For spectacular scenery and lots of fresh air try the 38-mile coast down the world's largest dormant volcano on a bicycle.

For great snorkeling try Honolua Bay, Ahihi Kinau, or Olowalu.

Take a helicopter tour and get a super spectacular view of Maui.

Golf at one of Maui's four premier resort courses.

Sail to Lanai and snorkel Hulopoe Beach with the Trilogy Cruise.

If the whales are in residence, take a whale-watching cruise with the Pacific Whale Foundation.

For an underwater thrill consider an introductory scuba adventure, no experience necessary.

For a wet and wild tour of Lanai or Molokini, with snorkeling, try a Zodiac raft trip.

If you're really adventurous consider parasailing, or sea kayaking.

OCEAN ACTIVITIES

SNORKELING

Maui offers exceptionally clear waters, warm ocean temperatures and abundant sea life with safe areas (no sharks or adverse water conditions) for snorkeling. If you are a complete novice, most of the resorts and excursion boats offer snorkeling lessons. Older folks can enjoy this sport that needs little experience and there is no need to dive to see all the splendors of the sea. If you are unsure of your abilities, the use of a floatation device may be of assistance. Be forewarned that the combination of tropical sun and the refreshing coolness of the ocean can deceive those paddling blissfully on the surface, and result in a badly burned backside. Water resistant sunscreens are available locally and are recommended.

Equipment is readily available at resorts and dive shops, and as you can see, much less expensive at the dive shops (even better are the weekly rates). For a listing of dive shops see Scuba Diving.

TYPICAL RENTAL PRICES –
MASK/FINS/SNORKEL FOR 24 HOURS:

Maui Dive Shop in Kihei – $7.25
Fun Rentals in Lahaina – $5.00
Kihei Sea Sports in Kihei – $6.00
Hyatt Regency Resort at Kaanapali – $20.00

Good snorkeling spots, if not right in front of your hotel or condo, are only a few minutes drive away. The following are our favorites, each for a special reason.

WEST MAUI

Black Rock – At the Sheraton in the Kaanapali Resort. Park at the Whaler's Shopping Center and walk down the beach. Clear water and a variety of tame fish – these fish expect handouts!
Kapalua Bay – Public park with off street parking, restrooms and showers. A well protected bay and beautiful beach amid the grounds of the Kapalua Resort. Limited coral and some large coral heads, fair for fish watching.
Namalu Bay – At the Kapalua Resort, walk over from Kapalua Bay. Very good on calm days.
Honolua Bay – No facilities, parking alongside the road and a 1/4 mile walk to the bay, but the best snorkeling on Maui, anytime but winter.
Olowalu – At mile marker 14, about 5 miles south of Lahaina. Generally calm and warmer waters with ample parking along the roadside. Very good snorkeling. If you find a pearl earring, let us know.

EAST MAUI

Ulua/Mokapu Beach - Well-marked public beach park in Wailea with restrooms and showers. Ocean Activities Center amid grounds of Stouffer Wailea Beach Resort offers rental equipment. Fair to good snorkeling around the rocky point separating these two picturesque and beautiful beaches.

Maluaka Beach - Located in Makena, no facilities and along the road parking. Good coral formations and a fair amount of fish at the left end of the beach.

Ahihi Kinau Natural Reserve - Approximately five miles past Wailea. No facilities. This is not a very crowded spot and you may feel a little alone here, but the snorkeling is great with lots of coral and a good variety of fish.

Generally at all locations the best snorkeling is in the morning until about 1 p.m., when the wind picks up. For more information on each area and other locations, refer to the BEACHES chapter.

A good way to become acquainted with Maui's sea life is a guided snorkeling adventure with Ann Fielding, marine biologist and author of *Hawaiian Reefs and Tidepools*. She takes small groups to Honolua Bay in summer and Ahihi Kinau in winter. These morning excursions begin with a practical seminar on reef systems and marine life followed by snorkeling. Floatation devices, snorkel gear and refreshments are provided for the $30 fee. Phone 244-7572 for information.

You may feel the urge to rent an underwater camera to photograph some of the unusual and beautiful fish you've seen, and by all means try it, but remember, underwater fish photography is a real art. There are two new video tapes of Maui's marine life available at the island bookstores if you want a permanent record of the fish you've seen.

There are two other great places to snorkel, however, you need a boat to reach them. Fortunately, a large variety of charter services will be happy to assist.

Molokini Crater - This small semicircular island is the remnant of a volcano. Located about 8 miles off Maalaea Harbor, it affords good snorkeling in the crater area. These waters are a marine reserve and the island is a bird sanctuary. Molokini is usually a 1/2 day excursion with a continental breakfast and lunch provided. Costs are $40 - $50 for adults, $25 - $35 for children under 12. (You may find rates even lower with current price wars among the heavy competition.)

Hulopoe Beach, Lanai - This is our favorite. Located on the island of Lanai, it's worth the trip for the beautiful beach and the abundance of coral and fish. We saw a school of fish here that was so large that from the shore it appeared to be a huge moving reef. After swimming through the school and returning to shore we were informed that large predatory fish like to hang out around these schools! Lanai is usually a full-day excursion with continental breakfast, BBQ lunch and a possible tour of the island. Costs run $90 - $110 for adults. Some half-day trips are available.

A variety of snorkel/sail/tour options are available for snorkeling along East and West Maui's coastline, Molokini, Molokai or Lanai. Your first decision is choosing between a large or small group tour. Large groups go out in substantial monohull or catamaran motor yachts of 60 - 90 feet in length. They get you there comfortably and fast, but without the intimate sailing experience of a smaller, less crowded boat. There are also many sleek sailboats (monohull, catamaran or trimaran) that you can share with 4 to 8 people or privately charter. A fairly new addition to the Maui sea excursions are the Zodiac type rafts that use 20 - 23 foot inflatable rafts powered by two large outboards. These rides can be rough, wet and wild. All tours provide snorkel gear with floatation devices if needed, and instruction. Food and refreshments are provided to varying degrees. For a list of outings, see the section on Sea Excursions.

A TRIP TO MOLOKINI
Molokini is a 10,000 year old dormant volcano with only one crescent shaped portion of the crater rim now providing a sanctuary for marine and bird life. The crater on the inside of the island offers a water depth of 10 - 50 feet, a 76 degree temperature and visibility sometimes as much as 150 feet on the outer perimeter.

In past editions we have elaborated on our pleasant experiences while boating to Molokini for a morning of snorkeling. In recent years things have changed dramatically. Someone in government determined that the unexploded bombs, which remained from the years when this site was used as a target, should be destroyed. Not a bad idea, but they detonated them where they lay on the crater floor. This resulted in the destruction of a good portion of the marine life, including a great deal of coral. After the first group of bombs were destroyed, a group of excursion operators made a night time raid and using ropes towed the bombs out of the crater and into deep water.

Another explosion has also recently effected the crater, the explosion in charter boat tours. During our first trip, there were no more than a half dozen boats that brought visitors out to explore this interesting reef. During our last trip we counted no fewer than 30 boats which ranged in size from rafts to 100 plus passenger vessels. It appeared that Molokini Crater was a parking lot for boats and a sea of floating snorkelers. (Perhaps more snorkelers than fish?) More boats also means more anchors tearing up the remaining coral. Fortunately, semi-permanent concrete mooring anchors are being installed. What they do about limiting the number of boats remains to be seen. In any case, we were disappointed with the changes and don't feel that a Molokini trip can currently be rated as a best bet. Considering the beauty of the crater in the "pre-bomb years", the current state of the crater is not only deplorable, but an embarrassment. Despite the problems, it remains a pleasant boat ride, the snorkeling is fun, and the prices are good. If you wish to get the maximum snorkeling try **Blue Water Rafting**. They arrive at the crater first and snorkel the best spot before the big boats come in. Then it's a stop at the far crater wall for a second snorkeling opportunity. A third stop takes you to a spot over the underwater crater rim where the water on the crater side is shallow, but drops off out of sight dramatically on the other side.

215

SCUBA DIVING

Maui, with nearby Molokini, Kahoolawe, Lanai and Molokai, offers many excellent diving locations. A large variety of dive operations offer scuba excursions, instruction, certification and rental equipment. If you are a novice, a great way to get hooked is an introductory dive. No experience is necessary. Instruction, equipment and dive, all for $40 - $50. This is one of the best buys around. For those who are certified but rusty, refresher dives are around $40.

The mainstay of Maui diving is the two-tank dive, two dive sites with one tank each. Prices depend on location: Maui coast $40 - $55, Lanai or Molokini $70 - $80, which includes all equipment. If the bug bites and you wish to get certified, the typical course is four days of six hours each, at an average cost of $250 - $300. Classes are generally no more than 6 persons, or if you prefer private lessons, they run slightly more. Advanced open water courses are available in deep diving, search and recovery, underwater navigation and night diving (at a few shops). If you wish to rent equipment only, a complete scuba package including wet suit runs about $25 per day.

The larger resorts also offer instruction and some offer certification courses and arrange for excursions. Many of the dive operators utilize boats specifically designed for diving. Information, equipment, instruction and excursions can be obtained at the following dive shops and charter operators. As you can see by the number of listings, diving is very popular around Maui.

WEST MAUI

Aquatic Charters
879-0976

American Dive Maui
628 Front Street
Lahaina, 661-4885

Beach Activities
Kaanapali, 661-5500
Kapalua, 669-4664

Blue Chip Charters
Kaanapali, 661-3226

Captain Nemo's
700 Front St.
Lahaina, 661-555
1-800-367-8088

Central Pacific
Divers ★
Lahaina, 661-8718
1-800-551-6767

Dive Maui, Inc.
Lahaina, 667-2080

Extended Horizons
P.O. Box 10785
Lahaina, 667-0611

Hawaiian Reef Divers
129 Lahainaluna
Lahaina, 667-7647

Lahaina Divers
710 Front St.
Lahaina, 667-7496

Lahaina Shores
Watersports
Lahaina, 667-4363

Maui Dive Shops
Lahaina Cannery
661-5388

Maui Sun and Surf
Maui Marriott
667-9302

Scuba Schools of Maui
1000 Limahana Place #A
Lahaina, 661-8036

Sundance
Lahaina, 661-4126

Tropical Dive and Sail
711 Mill St.
Lahaina, 661-5488

Underwater Adventures
Lahaina, 661-8957

EAST MAUI

Hawaiian Watercolors
P.O. Box 616
Kihei, 879-3584

Kihei Sea Sports
Kihei Town Center
Kihei, 879-1919

Makena Coast Charters
P.O. Box 330764
Kahului, 874-1243

Maui Dive Shops
Azeka's Shopping Center
879-3388

Maui School of Diving
PO Box 330684
Kahului, 879-7681

Maui Sun Divers
Kihei, 879-7011
or 879-3631

Mike Severns
P.O. Box 627
Kihei, 879-6596

Ocean Activities Center
Wailea Shopping Center
Wailea, 879-4485

Ocean Safaris
101 N. Kihei Rd.
Kihei, 879-7242

Skin Dive Maui
2411 South Kihei Rd.
Kihei, 879-1502

Steve's Diving
Adventures of Maui
1993 S. Kihei Rd
879-0055

The Dive Shop
1975 South Kihei Rd.
Kihei, 879-5172

Tropical Hydro
871-2686

Valley Isle Divers
Kihei, 879-3483

Books of interest available at dive shops or area bookstores:
Comprehensive Guide to Scuba Diving in Hawaii by Phil Hoffman. $6.95.
Diver's Guide to Hawaii by Chuck Thorne and Lou Zitnik. 248 pages, $9.95.
Skin Diver's Guide to Hawaii by Gordon Feund. 72 pages, $2.50.
Hawaii Diver's Manual, 162 pages, $3.00.

SEA EXCURSIONS

Maui offers a bountiful choice for those desiring to spend some time in and on the ocean. Boats available for sea expeditions range from a three-masted schooner, to spacious trimarans and large motor yachts, to the zodiac type rafts for the more adventurous. Your choice is a large group trip or a more pampered small group excursion with a maximum of six people. Two of the most popular snorkeling excursions are to Molokini and Lanai. Most sailboats motor their way to these islands and, depending on wind conditions, sail at least part of the return trip. All provide snorkel equipment. Food and beverage service varies and is reflected in the price.

Many sailboats are available for hourly, full day or longer private charters.

Excursion boats seem to have a way of sailing off into the sunset. The number of new ones is as startling as the number of operations that have disappeared since our last edition. As mentioned previously, competition to Molokini has become fierce. Twenty to thirty boats a day now arrive to snorkel in this area. Many more boats now take trips to Lanai as well. Currently there is only one company offering Molokai excursions.

RECREATION AND TOURS_____
Sea Excursions

In the following list, phone numbers of the excursion companies are included in case personal booking is desired, however, most activity desks can also book your reservation. The best deal is with *Tom's Cashback Tours* who can book most boats and offers a 10% refund. They are located in Lahaina and can be reached at 661-8889.

PRICES PER PERSON WILL RUN YOU ACCORDINGLY:

1/2 day trip to Lanai $40 – $60
Full day trip to Lanai $90 – $110
1/2 day trip to Molokini $35 – $60
1/2 day Maui coastline (3-4hrs.) $40 – $65
Full day Maui coastline $70 – $85
Sunset sails (1 1/2 – 2 hrs.) $30 – $35
Whale watching (3 hrs./seasonal) $30
Private charters $75 per hour and up
Private charters $400 per day and up

EXCURSION – CHARTER LISTING

ALIHILANI YACHT CHARTERS
Aikane, 46' catamaran, Lanai snorkel, afternoon or sunset sail
Makani Wiki, 36' trimaran
1/2 and full day trips to Lanai
Maui coastline sail/snorkel
Sunset sail, private charters also
Departs offshore near Lahaina or Lahaina Harbor, 661-3047

ALOHA VOYAGES *Machias*, 80'
full rigged schooner
Its name means "Little bird on big water", Snorkel or scuba to Molokai
Departs from beach near Lahaina
667-6284

Between the Sheets, Morgan 42 MKII
3 & 5 hr. snorkel/sail
Sunset sail, whale watching
Max. 6 persons, 661-4095
Departs from Lahaina Harbor

★ BLUE WATER RAFTING
3½ hr. Molokini snorkel,
(3 different sites in the crater)
2 hr. economy Molokini, snorkel one site for $29

Departs Kihei launch ramp
4 hr. plus, north shore tour from Hookipa to Keanae, see dozens of waterfalls, jungle and impressive seacliffs, also lunch and snorkeling, cost – about $100
Departs Maliki launch ramp
Enjoy your ride on the latest concept in inflatable boats, the Novurania, a sleek Italian hybrid that features a ridged fiberglass deep V hull, for a smooth ride, and inflatable pontoons for stability, and easy entry and exit for snorkeling.
Max. 6 people, 879-7238

CAPT. KIRK'S ENTERPRISE
Zodiac-type boats, snorkel wherever the conditions are best
Lahaina, 661-5333 or 667-9740

CAPT. NEMO'S
Seasmoke, 58' catamaran
Morning snorkel, sunset sail
Introductory or certified dive
Seasonal whalewatch, 661-5555
Departs Kaanapali Beach

CAPTAIN JACK'S
Foxy Lady, Cal 27' sloop
Molokini, max. 6 people
Departs Maalaea, 879-4673

CAPTAIN ROLLY'S CHARTER
Phantom, Lancer 36
1/2 day, full day snorkel/sail
Maui coast or Lanai, sunset cruise
Departs Lahaina, 661-5888

CAPTAIN ZODIAC RAFT
Snorkeling, whalewatching
Depart Mala Wharf near Lahaina
Maximum 15
667-5351 or 667-5862

CINDERELLA YACHT
CHARTERS
Cinderella, 50' Columbia Sloop
3/4 day sail/snorkel, max. 6 people
Kealia Beach Plaza, 879-0634

CLASSIC VENTURES *Alihilani*,
40' wood cutter
Snorkel cruise, whalewatching
Private charters,
Departs Kihei Cove, 879-7986

CLUB LANAI
Kaulana, large power catamaran
Departs Lahaina Harbor daily for
private beach on Lanai. Snorkeling,
kayaking, swimming, biking, picnic
Also dinner cruise. 871-1144

Coral Sea, 65' glass bottom boat
1/2 day Molokini snorkel/cruise
Departs Lahaina, 661-8600

DESTINATION PACIFIC
26' diesel, Marine biologist, skipper
and owner, Ted Mickowski offers
sportfishing, snorkeling and scuba
for beginners or advanced, professional photography, underwater
video. 6 people max., can launch
from Kihei or Lahaina. 242-5004 or
874-0305

FRIENDLY CHARTERS
Maalaea Kai, 45' catamaran
Molokini snorkel/cruise and
2-4 hr snorkel/sail, max. 26
Private charters available
Maalaea Harbor, 871-0985

★ GENESIS YACHT CHARTERS
Genesis, 48' ketch
1/2 day snorkel/sail to offshore
Lanai
Sunset dinner cruise
Private charters available
Departs Lahaina, 669-5667

IDLEWILD CHARTERS
34' Hawaiian sailing cat
Max. 24 persons, snorkel/sail, whale
watching, private charter also
Departs Maalaea, 572-8964

Kahili, Cal 33'
1/2 & all day snorkel
Private charters, max. 6
Lahaina, 669-4729

Kai Kanani, 46' catamaran
Departs beach at Maui Prince Resort
for Molokini, 879-7218

KAMEHAMEHA SAILS, INC.
Kamehameha, 40' catamaran
Snorkel/sail, sunset sail, whale
watching, private charter, max. 15
Departs Lahaina harbor, 661-4522

KIHEI SEA SPORTS
Kihei Sea Sport, 55' motor yacht
1/2 day snorkel Molokini
Lg. groups, Maalaea, 879-1919

Kiele V, 55' Catamaran
4 hr. snorkel/sail, 1 1/2 hr.
cocktail cruise, max. 49
Departs Hyatt Regency, 667-7474

Lin Wa, 65' glassbottom boat
resembling a Chinese junk
1 1/4 hour coastline cruise
Sunset dinner cruise
Lahaina, 661-3392

MAUI ADVENTURES
Michelle II, 38' power cat.
Snorkel/introductory scuba
Lahaina, 661-3400

★ MAUI BEACH CENTER
Located at Whaler's Shopping
Village in Kaanapali. Discover the
adventure of a time long past aboard
the 45' *E'ala*, a replica of an authentic double hulled Hawaiian (built of
Koa wood) voyaging vessel. The
outing provides a cultural exchange
with an all Hawaiian crew who share
background on island traditions and
culture. They are currently offering a
picnic snorkel/sail off the Maui
coastline complete with Hawaiian
music for $40. 667-4355

MAUI CLASSIC CHARTERS
Lavengro, 60' gast rigged
Schooner, built 1926, 27 passengers
Snorkeling, sunset and whale
watching
Four Winds 53'x30' double deck,
glass bottom catamaran, with BBQ
grills and a waterslide, daily learning
snorkel, afternoon whale watch
Departs Maalaea, 879-2307

MOLOKINI CRUISES
Maika'i makani II 50' catamaran
BBQ sunset dinner sail, Molokini
snorkel, whale watch. Departs
Maalaea
667-9739 or 1-800-356-8989

MOWEE WINDS CHARTERS
42' trimaran. Sail/snorkel to
Molokini/Lanai. Sunset sail
Private charter, max. 22 people
Departs Kaanapali, 669-6445

OCEAN ACTIVITIES
No Ka Oi IV, 37' polycraft
Scuba trips, 12 max.
No Ka Oi III, 37' polycraft
Deep sea fishing, 6 max.
Wailea Kai, 65' catamaran
Snorkel, whale watch, dinner cruise

Maka Kai, 65' catamaran
Lanai trip, whale watching,
snorkeling, party boat fishing
Manute'a, 50' catamaran, Lanai
trip, cocktail sails, whale watching
All boats depart Maalaea except
Manute'a which departs Lahaina
879-4485 or 1-800-367-8047 ext. 448

PACIFIC WHALE
FOUNDATION CRUISES
Whale One, 53' accommodates 49
Whale watching, snorkeling
Departs Maalaea, 879-8811

Pardner, 46' ketch
Ranger 36' Lancer
1/2 or full-day snorkel/sail
Whale watching, max. 6
Departs Lahaina, 661-5516

MAUI-MOLOKAI SEA CRUISES
Prince Kuhio, 92' motor yacht
Whale watching, private charters
1/2 day Molokini, departs Maalaea
242-8777 or 1-800-468-1287

SAIL HAWAII
37' or 40' sailing yachts, max. 6
Trip destinations flexible
Departs Kihei Cove Park, 879-2201

SEA ESCAPE
You-Drive zodiac boat rentals
879-3721

SEABIRD CRUISES, INC.
Aikane III, lg. power cat.
Full-day snorkel/picnic to Lanai
Seasonal whale watching
Sunset dinner sail, Hula show, dance
band, open bar, accommodates 110
Lahaina, 661-3643

Scotch Mist, 36' sloop, max.6
Scotch Mist II,
Santa Cruz 50', max 19
West Maui 1/2 & full-day
snorkel/sail
Champagne sunset sail, max. 6
Lahaina, 661-0386

Spirit of Windjammer
65' 3-masted schooner
Full-day trip to Lanai, 2-hour Maui
coastline dinner cruise, lg. groups
Lahaina, 667-6834, 1-800-843-8113

Suntan, 50' Santa Cruz
Molokini snorkel, sunset sail
Kealia Beach Center, max. 25,
874-0332

Tri-Max, 46' trimaran
1/2 or full-day sails, max. 6
Lahaina, 667-7511

★ TRILOGY EXCURSIONS
Trilogy, 50' trimaran
Kailana, 40' trimaran
Manele Kai, 40' catamaran
Full-day snorkel/picnic/sightseeing
to Lanai, a definite best bet
1/2-day sail/snorkel
Departs Lahaina Harbor
661-4743 or 1-800-874-2666

White Wings, 35' trimaran
6-hr. sail/snorkel/fishing
Available for overnight and
inter-island excursions, max. 6
Maalaea Harbor, 572-8457

A TRIP TO LANAI

A trip to the island of Lanai for an all-day snorkel excursion begins early in the morning (bring your camera). For our trip we went on the Trilogy, crewed by three members of the Coon family. Although no whales were seen, the school of nearly 300 dolphins sighted was an awesome experience. After a two-hour motoring trip, we anchored at Manele Harbor and walked the three block distance to the beautiful and spacious white sand Hulopoe Beach, which also offers restrooms and a rinse-off shower. The snorkeling was superior. We swam out to what appeared to be a moving black reef and were overwhelmed to see a mass of silvery-white fish swimming in a school of what looked like a million. We learned later that barracuda and shark sometimes lurk around the edges of these schools. The beginning snorkelers were carefully instructed in a tide pool before entering the ocean. Although many on our cruise were senior citizens, they all did splendidly and commented that they only wish they had started snorkeling years before!

After an hour or more of snorkeling, we walked back to the harbor where a table, beautifully set (no paper plates here!) was awaiting us. A green salad tossed with Mrs. Coon's secret dressing began the meal, followed by teriyaki chicken (cooked by the crew), Saimin noodles, peas, and fresh pineapple for dessert.

While dishes were being done, we hopped a tour van for a trip to Lanai City, the only "city" on the island. When the island was owned by Castle and Cook, it was one huge pineapple plantation, and almost all the island's population were employed in the pineapple industry. Now the tourism industry is moving onto Lanai. Development began in late 1987 on a 250-room resort on Manele Bay. A hunting lodge and a golf course are planned for central Lanai.

Back in the boat for the trip home, we sailed up the scenic south side of Maui. We would recommend the Trilogy trip to anyone considering a day trip to Lanai. They were extremely personable and made the outing a very special one.

DINNER CRUISES

Dinner cruises are quite popular on Maui with their free flowing Mai Tai's, congenial passengers, tropical nights, and Hawaiian music which entertains while the boat cruises along the coastline. Dinner is definitely not haute cuisine, but usually quite satisfactory, especially after a few Mai Tai's. The live Hawaiian entertainment varies from amateur to very good. Cruises typically last about two hours and prices run $50 – $60. Samples of dinners listed may vary. Most dinner cruises accommodate 50 – 100 people.

Genesis – Enjoy a gourmet sunset dinner cruise aboard this 44′ ketch, entertained by a guitarist/vocalist. Entrees are either fresh island fish or N.Y. steak served on special lap trays. A maximum of 18 people ensures a more intimate and romantic experience. Departs Lahaina six nights a week, 669-7557.

Kaulana – The Stardust Dinner Cruise departs from Lahaina Harbor 5 nights a week. Soft jazz accompanies a dinner of filet mignon, seafood newburg, or baked mahi and rice. Dancing follows dinner. Table seating. 871-1144.

Lin Wa – Sunset Polynesian dinner cruise. Depart Lahaina in this glass bottom boat. Table seating. 661-8397.

Prince Kuhio – Departs from Maalaea Harbor. This 92′ cruise boat features a dinner of fresh Mahi, beef ribs and an open bar. Hawaiian entertainment accompanies your cruise. Table seating. 242-4575.

Seabird Cruises – Departs from Lahaina Harbor. This 65′ catamaran offers a two-hour sail featuring a prime rib dinner. Table seating. 661-3643.

Wailea Kai – Departs Maalaea Harbor. Enjoy the sunset on this 65′ catamaran. Dinner is Mahi or chicken. Open bar and live entertainment. Free bus transportation is available. Table seating. 879-4485.

Windjammer – An open bar, live entertainment and a dinner of scampi and steak are served on this 75′ three-masted schooner. Table seating. Sails nightly. 667-6834.

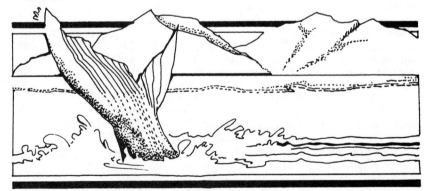

WHALE WATCHING

Every year beginning in November and continuing until April, the humpback whales arrive in the warm waters off the Hawaiian Islands for breeding, and their own sort of vacation! The sighting of a whale can be an awesome and memorable experience with the humpbacks, small as whales go, measuring some 40 – 50 feet and weighing in at 30 tons. While viewing from the shoreline is possible, you may want to join a cruise to get a closer view. Although most everyone does whale-watching tours in season, you may want to check into the one sponsored by Pacific Whale Foundation at Azeka's Place, Suite 303, Kihei, phone 879-6530 or 879-4253. As they are a research group, they are very well informed and knowledgeable about the whales. The Carthaginian at the Lahaina Harbor has a chart showing the points where whales have been sighted. You can report your sightings by calling Whale Watch Hotline at 879-6530.

DEEP SEA FISHING

Deep sea fishing off Maui is among the finest in the world and no licenses are required for either trolling or bottom fishing. All gear is provided. Fish that might be lured to your bait include the Pacific Blue, Black or Striped Marlin (Au) weighing up to 2,000 lbs., Yellow Fin Tuna (Ahi) up to 300 lbs., Jack Crevalle (Ulua) to 100 lbs., Shark to ??! lbs., Bonita-Skipjack (Aku) to 40 lbs., Dolphin Fish (Mahi) to 90 lbs., Waho (Ono) to 90 lbs., Mackerel (Opelu), Amerjack (Kahala), Grey Snapper (Uku), Red Snapper (Onaga), and Pink Snapper (Opakapaka).

Boats generally offer half or full-day fishing trips on a share or private basis with prices running from $60 – $65 shared or $300 – $350 private for a half day (4 hr.), and $100 –$110 shared or $450 –$550 private for a full day (8 hr) Some are willing to take non-fishing passengers along at half price. Most boats take 4 – 6 on a shared basis, however several, such as Excel and Sport Diver can handle larger groups.

To find a charter: Your local activity center may be able to direct you to a particular boat that they favor, or you could go down to the docks at the Lahaina or Maalaea Harbor in the afternoon and browse around. There are also a number of activity booths at both harbors that can be consulted. When reserving a spot, be aware that some boats will give full refunds only if 48-hour notice is given for cancellation. If you want to take children fishing, many have restrictions for those under age 12. If you are a serious fisherman, you might consider entering one of the numerous tournaments. Some charters offer tournament packages.

LAHAINA HARBOR

AERIAL SPORTSFISHING CHARTERS
PO Box 12, Lahaina, 667-9089

BALI HA'I CHARTERS
Lahaina, 667-6672

FINEST KIND, INC.
Exact, 31' Bertram
Finest Kind, 37' Merritt
P.O. Box 10481, Lahaina
Maximum 6 people, 661-0338

Hinatea, 41' Hatteras
PO Box 1238 Lahaina, 667-7548

ISLANDER II SPORTSFISHING
36' Uniflite, 667-6625

LAHAINA CHARTERS
PO Box 12, Lahaina
Broadbill, 36' Hardcraft
Escape, 26' Bertrum
maximum 6 people, 667-6672

LUCKEY STRIKE CHARTERS
PO Box 1502, Lahaina
Luckey Strike, 45' custom
Kanoa, 31' Uniflite, max. 6
Luckey Strike has a large cockpit
with full sunshade that can
accommodate up to 22 people
242-9277 or 661-4606

MAALAEA HARBOR

CAROL ANN CHARTERS
33' Bertram, max. 6
877-2181 or 242-4575

EXCEL FISHING CHARTERS
Excel 48' Delta
Excite 35' Bertram
max. 6 – 12 persons
PO Box 146, Makawao, 96768
877-3333

MARINE CHARTERS INC.
P.O. Box 817, Puuene
Departs Maalaea, 572-6438

OCEAN ACTIVITIES CENTER
Departs Maalaea, 879-4485

RASCAL SPORTSFISHING CHARTERS
Rascal 31', 661-0692

SMALL BOAT SAILING

Small boat sailing is available at a number of locations with rentals, usually the 14', sometimes 16' and 18', Hobie Cat. Lasers are also available. Typical rental prices are $25 - $35 per hour, and lessons are available. The Maui Inter-Continental, Stouffer Wailea Beach Resort, Hyatt Regency Maui, Marriott and Kaanapali Alii also offer free sailing clinics for their guests.

FOR MORE INFORMATION ON RENTALS CONTACT:

Sea Sails - (661-0927) Located at the Sheraton, Royal Lahaina and Kaanapali Beach Hotel, Westin, Sands of Kahana, Kaanapali Shores
Maui Sailing Center - Sugar Beach Resort (879-6260), Kealia Beach Plaza (879-5935)
Lahaina Beach Center - (661-5762) Near the Lahaina Shores Hotel
Ocean Activities Center - Stouffer Wailea Beach Resort (879-0181), Maui Inter-Continental (879-8022)
Kaanapali Boating Center - (661-5424) Kaanapali Villas
Sailing Schools of Maui - (669-4985)

WINDSURFING

Windsurfing is a sport that is increasing in popularity astronomically. Hookipa Beach Park on Maui is one of the best windsurfing sites in the world. This is due to the consistently ideal wind and surf conditions, however, this is definitely NOT the spot for beginners.

For the novice, lessons are available for $15-$20 an hour, which generally involves instruction on a dry land simulator before you get wet with easy to use beginners equipment. Equipment is available from the following:

Ocean Activities Center - At Stouffer Wailea Beach Resort (879-0818), Maui Inter-Continental (879-8022), Central office 1-800-367-8047 ext. 448 or 879-4485
Kaanapali Boating Center - At Kaanapali Villas (661-5424)
Kaanapali Windsurfing School - Hanakaoo Beach by Hyatt Regency, (667-1964)
Maui Magic Windsurfing School - Group & private lessons for all levels. Rentals & retail (877-4816)
Maui Sailing Center - Kealia Beach Center (879-5935), or Kai Nani Village (879-6440)
Sea Sails - (661-0927) Located at the Sheraton, Royal Lahaina, Westin, Sands of Kahana, Kaanapali Shores and Kaanapali Beach Hotel

Some resorts offer their guests free clinics. Rental by the hour at the above can get expensive at $15 - $20 per hour and $40 - $65 per four hours. A better rate is $35 for all day. If you are interested in renting equipment for longer periods or desire more advanced equipment try:

The Duck and Jibe - (667-2104) West Maui's only complete windsurfing shop, located in the Lahaina Industrial area — sales only

Fun Rentals - (Also known as Indian Summer Surf Shop) (661-3053), Lahaina, rents equipment ($40 for 24 hrs.) and can recommend an instructor

Freedom Maui - (871-2662) 55 Kaahumanu Avenue, Kahului

Hawaiian Island Windsurfing - (871-4981), 460 Dairy Road, Kahului

Sailboards Maui - (871-7954) 210 Dairy Road, Kahului

Typical costs are $40 for a full day, $200 for seven days. Deposit may be required. Rental includes board, universal, mast, boom, sail and soft car rack. There are no reservations and no refunds unless returned within one hour. You also pay for broken, lost or stolen equipment.

Books of interest: *How to Windsurf Hawaiian Style* by Thomas J. Cunningham, 18 pages, softcover $2.50.

SURFING

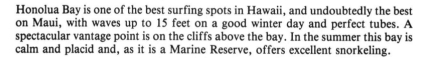

Honolua Bay is one of the best surfing spots in Hawaii, and undoubtedly the best on Maui, with waves up to 15 feet on a good winter day and perfect tubes. A spectacular vantage point is on the cliffs above the bay. In the summer this bay is calm and placid and, as it is a Marine Reserve, offers excellent snorkeling.

Also in this area is Punalau Beach (just past Honolua) and Honokeana Bay off Ka'eleki'i Point (just north of the Alaeloa Residential area). In the Lahaina area there are breaks north and south of the harbor and periodically good waves at Awalua Beach (mile marker 16). On the north shore of Hookipa Beach Park, Kanaha Beach, and Baldwin all have good surfing at times. In the Hana area there is Hamoa Beach. There are a couple of good spots in Maalaea Bay and at Kalama Beach Park.

Conditions change daily, and even from morning to afternoon around the island. Check with local board rental outlets for current daily conditions.

BODY SURFING: Mokuleia (Slaughterhouse) Beach has the best body surfing especially in the winter. This is not a place for weak swimmers or the inexperienced when the surf is up. The high surf after a Kona storm brings fair body surfing conditions, better boogieboarding, to some beaches on leeward Maui.

Books of interest available at local bookstores:
Surfing Hawaii by Bank Wright, 96 pages softcover $3.95.
How to Body Surf by Nelson Dewey, 10 pages softcover $1.00.
Hawaii Surfing Map, descriptions of 97 surfing spots

JET SKIIS

The areas off Sugar Beach in Kihei and Hanakaoo Beach Park in Kaanapali offer excellent jet skiing conditions, usually calm but with enough waves to make it interesting. Prices are usually $50 for one hour and $35 for a half hour.

Kaanapali Jet Ski – (667-7851) On the beach in front of Whaler's Village. They also have two passenger wave runners. Call for reservations.

Pacific Jet Ski Rental – (667-2066) South end of Kaanapali Beach at Hanakaoo Beach Park.

Maui Island Wave Runners Inc. – (667-5358, 661-8512 or 877-4601) Locations in Kaanapali and Kihei. Two seat addictor outboards, new Yamaha two seat waverunners.

Maui Sailing Center – (879-5935) Located in Kihei. Kawasaki 440 and 550's.

PARASAILING

Some flights start at the offshore floating platform off Lahaina. You are helped into a life jacket and special harness-like seat and instructed in takeoffs and landings. Then you are hooked up to the tow line and in four or five steps you're off and soon at 200 feet enjoying the ride and view. The flight lasts 8 to 10 minutes which seems neither too long nor too short. The landing is really no more traumatic than stepping off a high curb, unless a last second wind gust sends you off the platform's edge and into the drink (the reason you wear swimming suits). Prices range from $35 to $45 for a 8 to 10 minute ride. Some charge for an "observer" (friend) to go along, others allow them free.

UFO Paracruiser and Wailea Para Sail use a new wrinkle. You get started standing on the boat and as your parachute fills, you are simply reeled out 200 – 400 feet. When it comes time to descend, you're simply reeled back in.

Kaanapali Parasailing – (661-5988) Look for the blue and white umbrella at Hanakaoo Beach Park.

Parasailing Hawaii – (661-5322) Lahaina, reservations required. Boat trip one hour. $10 charge for observer.

Wailea Para Sail – (879-1999) Kihei, $10 observer charge, early morning discount.

West Maui Para-Sail – (661-4060) Lahaina Harbor, booth #4. Honeymoon shute for two. Dry landing. Boat departs every 30 minutes with six passengers. Call for reservations.

UFO Paracruiser – (669-7836) Observers can go free. Departs in front of the Westin Maui.

WATERSKIING

Lahaina Water Skiing Inc. – (661-5988) Hanakaoo Beach Park in front of Hyatt Regency. $35 for 15 minutes. Charters available.
Kaanapali Water Ski – (661-3325) Departs Mala Wharf. $25 one person for 15 minutes. Hourly rate for one to three skiers.

KAYAKS

Rental Kayaks available from Sea Sails (661-0927) with locations at the Maui Westin, Sands of Kahana, Kaanapali Shores, Sheraton, Royal Lahaina and Kaanapali Beach Hotel.

LAND ACTIVITIES

LAND TOURS

Land excursions on Maui are centered upon two major attractions, Hana and the Seven Pools, and Haleakala Crater. Lesser attractions are trips to the Iao Valley or around West Maui. You can do all of this by car (refer to the WHERE TO STAY – WHAT TO SEE chapter), however, with a tour you can sit back and enjoy the scenery while a professional guide discourses on the history, flora, fauna and geography of the area. The single most important item on any tour is a good guide/driver and, unfortunately, the luck of the draw prevails here.

Another option is a personalized custom tour. A local resident will join you in your car for a tour of whatever or wherever you choose. You can do the driving or sign on your guide with your rental car company to do the driving. This may allow you the opportunity to linger at those places you enjoy the most, without following the pace of a group. Your guide may also be able to take you to locations the tour vans don't include.

Driving to Hana and back requires a full day and can be very grueling, so this is one trip we recommend you consider taking a tour. A Haleakala Crater tour spans 5-6 hours and can be enjoyed at sunrise (3 a.m. departure), mid day or sunset. The West Maui and Iao Valley trips are half-day ventures. Only vans travel the road to Hana, however, large buses as well as vans are available for other trips. (Be aware that some vans are not air conditioned.) Prices are competitive and those listed here are correct at time of publication. Some trips include the cost of meals, others do not.

Also available are one day tours to the outer islands. The day begins with a early morning departure to the Big Island, Oahu or Kauai. Some excursions provide a guided ground tour, others offer a rental car to explore the island on your own.

Akami – (871-9551, 1-800-922-6485) Trips include Haleakala ($32) Hana ($48).

Aloha Nui Loa Tours – (879-7044) Haleakala ($36), Hana ($50). They also provide a special horseback tour. A drive to Hana is followed by a ride over the ranchlands of the Hotel Hana, then a lunch at a quiet beachfront.

Arthur's Limo Service – (661-5466) They provide tours to Haleakala and Hana in their luxury limousine.

Ekahi Tours – 572-9775) Herbie Watson and his crew provide tours of Hana ($55), the Keanae Peninsula ($40), or Haleakala ($35).

Grayline – (877-5507) Provides a variety of large bus and small van tours to Halekala and Hana.

★ *Historic Lahaina* – This one is a FREE 30 to 40 minute tour provided courtesy of the Lahaina area merchants. Pickups are on Papalaua St. behind the Post Office, or at the intersection of Lahainaluna Road and Front Street at the seawall. They provide an open sided tram and a narrated tour of this picturesque and historic sea port.

Guides of Maui – (877-4042) Discover Maui from the comfort of your own car with an island resident as your guide. Explore the destinations of your choice. $135 for two people.

Hana Tropical Excursions – (579-8422) Van trips to Hana.

Island Guide Service – (661-5256) They provide a personalized tour guide to the destinations of your choosing. Translators available.

Jesse's Maui Adventures – (879-1329) Pick up from the Kihei and Wailea area. Hana ($52), Haleakala sunset ($42).

No Ka Oi Scenic Tours – 871-9008) Takes you to Hana ($40), Iao Valley and Haleakala ($33–$37) or transfer service to Lahaina ($15).

One Day Tours/Kihelei Maui Tours – (871-2555) Trips from Maui to Molokai, Hawaii, Kauai or Oahu for a one day flightseeing-sightseeing, $99 – $149.

Polynesian Adventure – (877-4242) Haleakala ($33), Hana ($48), as well as one day trips to the other islands (from $115).

Roberts–Hawaii Tours – (871-6226) Offers land tours in their big air conditioned buses or vans. They depart to all scenic areas from Kahului, Kihei, Wailea, and the West Maui Hotels.

Sugar Cane Train – (661-0089) The Sugar Cane Train makes 5 round trips daily with one way fares for adults $4.50, two way is $7.50. Children 2-12 years are $2.25 one way, $3.75 round trip. Their main depot is located just outside of Lahaina, turn at the Pizza Hut sign. The Kaanapali Station is located across the highway from the resort area. The free Kaanapali trolley picks up at the Whaler's Shopping Center and drops off at this station. The Puukolii boarding platform and parking lot is located on the Kapalua side of Kaanapali. They also have several package options which include the "Orient Express", a round trip train ride plus scenic voyage on the Lin Wa II at $17 for adults, $8.50 for children. A "Historic Lahaina" excursion includes a train ride and a self-guided tour of historic landmarks and admission into the Baldwin House and the Carthaginian II for $12 adults and $3.75 children. If you plan on a full day round trip excursion, buy your return tickets early as they often sell out quickly.

Trans Hawaiian – (871-1180) A day trip to Hana ($45) departs 7 a.m. and returns about 5:30, lunch is not included. Haleakala sunrise or morning tour ($28-$32). Also available are day trips to Hawaii, Kauai, and Oahu via jet. Guided tours on the outer islands or a car can be included for self-guided exploration.

ART TOURS

Maui Art Tours offers visitors an opportunity to visit the homes and studios of Maui's finest artists, meet them and watch them work. The tour begins with a lei greeting at your hotel or condominium and an escorted tour to meet the artisans of your choice. A catered lunch may be followed by a stroll through a tropical arboretum where you can enjoy a hot tub and fresh island tea. Phone (808-472-1022) Monday thru Saturday 8 a.m. – 5 p.m. or write P.O. Box 1058, Makawao, Maui 96768.

BIKE RENTALS

Bikes and mopeds are an ambitious and fun way to get around the resort areas, although you can rent a car for less than a moped. Available by the hour, day or week, they can be rented at several convenient locations.

A & B Moped Rentals – (669-0027) 3481 Honoapiilani Hwy. at the ABC store. They have two speed, automatic mopeds available for $5/hr., $20/8 hrs., $100/week. Bikes are rented at $10/day or $50/week.

E-Z Rider Scooters – (661-3138) 161 Lahainaluna Rd., Lahaina or (879-3858) 1975 S. Kihei Rd., Kihei. Honda Aero Scooters.

Fun Rentals – (Also known as Indian Summer Surf Shop) (661-3053) 193 Lahainaluna Rd., Lahaina. In addition to bikes they have boogie boards, fishing rods, beach chairs and even baby strollers!

Go-Go Bikes – (661-3063) Located just past Kaanapali on Lower Honoapiilani Hwy. Bikes and mopeds can be rented. Choose your moped from a selection of one, two or variable 10 speed. Rates run $5/hr., $25 per day or $115 per week. (Add $5 for two speed, $10 for ten speed). Touring bikes are $15 for 9 – 5 use, $18 per day, $75 per week. Free pickup from Kaanapali area with 3-hr. minimum rental.

Let's Rent a Bike – (661-3077) 2780 Kekaa Drive at Dollar Rent a Car.

BIKE TOURS

The Hawaiian Islands offer an endless array of spectacular air, sea and land tours, but only on Maui is there an experience quite like the bicycle ride down from the 10,000 foot summit of the world's largest dormant volcano. Bob Kiger, better known as Cruiser Bob, was the originator of the Haleakala downhill, which has now expanded to a number of competitors. Cruiser Bob is reported to have made 96 individual bike runs himself to thoroughly test all aspects of the route before the first paying customers attempted the trip.

Each tour company differs slightly in its adaptation of the trip, but the principal is the same, to provide the ultimate in biking experiences. For the very early riser (3 a.m.) you can see the sunrise from the crater before biking down. Later morning and afternoon expeditions are available as well. Your day will begin with a van pickup at your hotel for a narrated trip to the Haleakala summit. The temperature at the summit can be as much as 30 degrees cooler than sea level, so appropriate wear would include a sweater or sweatshirt. For the descent, riders are equipped with windbreaker jackets, gloves, helmets and specially designed bicycles with heavy duty brakes.

A leader will escort you down the mountain curves with the van providing a rear escort. Somewhere along the way will be a meal break. Some tours provide picnics, others include a sit-down meal at the lodge in Kula, or even a champagne brunch may be featured. Actual biking time will run about 3 hours for the 38-mile downhill trip. The additional time, about 5 hours, is spent commuting to the summit, meals, and the trip from the volcano's base back to your hotel. Prices for the various tours are extremely competitive and reservations should be made well in advance.

Cruiser Bob's – (667-7717) (1-800-654-7717) This is the original Haleakala downhill trip. You can choose between an early sunrise trek (3 a.m.) for $80 with champagne brunch, or the regular excursion with picnic lunch for $75.

Maui Downhill – (871-2155) Transportation from Lahaina, Kihei, Kahului and Paia. A catered lunch is included.

Maui Mountain Cruisers – (572-0915) Pickup provided from Kaanapali, Lahaina, Kahului and Kihei.

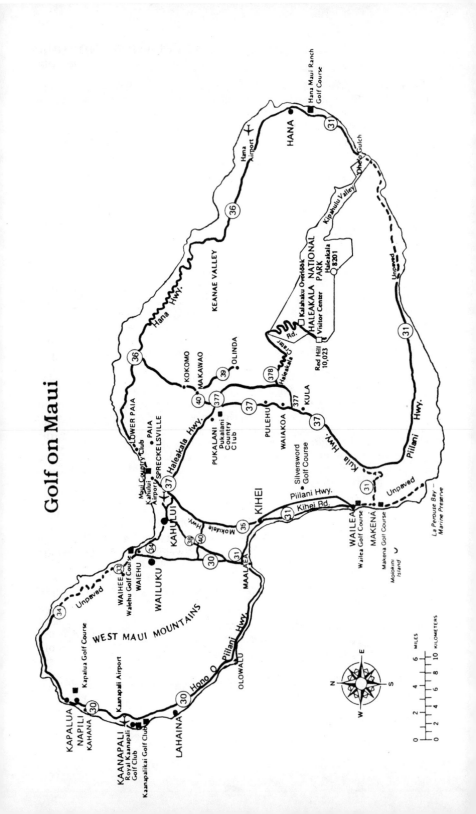

Golf on Maui

GOLF

Maui's golf courses have set for themselves a high standard of excellence. Not only do they provide some very challenging play, but they also offer distractingly beautiful scenery. Most of the major resorts offer golf packages. For the avid player, this may be an economical plan.

Sunseeker Golf Schools at Kaanapali offers golf instruction for the beginner or the advnaced. Each Wednesday and Saturday at 10 a.m. they conduct a free golf clinic. They offer private lessons ($35 for 45 minutes), playing lessons (one person $100, couple $150) and special one day ($175) or three day ($495) V.I.P. classes. Phone 667-7111.

KAANAPALI

The Kaanapali Resort offers two championship courses. Green fees are $65 for 18 holes, cart included. Phone 661-3691. Also found at the southern entrance to the Kaanapali resort area is the Royal Kaanapali driving range.

The North Course has been attracting celebrities since its inaugural when Bing Crosby played in the opening of the first nine holes. This is now home of the LPGA's Women's Kemper Open. Designed by Robert Trent Jones, this 6,305 yard course places heavy emphasis on putting skills. At par 72, it is rated 70 for men and 71.4 for women.

The South Course first opened in 1970 as an executive course and was reopened in 1977 as a regular championship course after revisions by golf architect Arthur Snyder. At 6,205 yards and par 72 it requires accuracy as opposed to distance, with narrower fairways and more small, hilly greens than the North Course. As an added distraction, the Sugar Cane Train passes by along the 4th hole.

KAPALUA

The Kapalua Resort features the Bay Course and the Village Course. Eighteen holes for hotel or villa guests is $35 plus $15 for the required cart. $60 plus $15/cart for non-guests. Guests may reserve tee-off times up to 7 days in advance. Non-guest reservations 2 days in advance. Twilight golf (2 p.m.) $25 plus cart. Phone 669-8044.

The Bay Course under the design of Arnold Palmer, opened October 13, 1975 and sprawls from sea level to the mountain's edge. This beautiful and scenic par 72, 6,850 yard course has a distinctly Hawaiian flavor and is the home of the internationally televised Kapalua International Championship of Golf. Imagine a 530-yard par four that travels downhill doglegging past the ancient stones of a pre-missionary fishing village to a green positioned on a black lava peninsula surrounded by white sand beaches. Or how about a 158-yard par 3 where the tee shot has to loop over a small bay. No wonder this course demands a controlled and knowledgeable game.

The Village Course opened in 1981 and sweeps inland along the pineapple fields and statuesque pine trees. At par 71 and 6,858 yards designer Arnold Palmer and course architect Ed Seay are reported to have given this course a European flavor. Resembling the mountainous countryside of Scotland, this course is reputed to be the most difficult and demanding in Hawaii and one of the most challenging in the world.

KIHEI

The Silversword Golf Course is the newest on Maui. This non-resort course is a 6,800 yard par 71, 18-hole course and is located off Piilani Highway near Lipoa Street. Green fees are currently $40 which includes a shared cart. Maui residents receive a discounted rate. Phone 874-0777.

MAKENA

The Maui Prince Resort features one 18-hole course at this time with plans for another 18 in the near future. Ultimately they plan to have two 36-hole courses. Their greens fees change throughout the year so it is best to call for current rates. Phone 879-3344.

The Makena Course is a Trent Jones designed 6,800 yard par 71, 18-hole course which opened in 1981. It winds among the hillsides and down along the coastline, where remnants of early Hawaiian rock boundary walls have been preserved. The large cactus which abound in this area were imported to feed the cattle which were once ranched in this area.

WAILEA

The Wailea resort offers the challenging Orange and Blue Courses. Greens fees for Wailea guests are $45 which includes cart, (May 1 – December 1 $30) non-guests $80 cart included ($50 for May 1 – December 1). Phone 879-2966.

The Orange Course is a par 72, 6,810 yard championship course designed by Arthur Jack Snyder. It opened in 1978. With more trees, ancient stone walls, narrow fairways and dog legs at half the holes, it is a considerable challenge.

The Blue Course is par 72 and 6,700 yards from the championship tees. It opened in 1972. Four lakes and 72 bunkers provide added hazards along with the exceptional scenery. The 16th hole is especially lovely with numerous people stopping to snap a picture from this magnificent vantage point.

PAIA

The Maui Country Club is a private course which invites visitors to play on Mondays. It originally opened in 1925. The front 9 holes have a par 37 as do the back nine. Greens fees are $20 for nine holes, $25 for 18 holes. The cart is optional at $10 per nine holes. Phone 877-0616.

PUKALANI

Pukalani Country Club and Golf Course is nestled along the slopes of Haleakala and affords a tremendous panoramic view of Central Maui and the ocean from every hole. Designed by Bob Baldock, the first 9 holes opened in 1980. Nine additional holes have been added making a par 72, 6,692 yard course. Greens fees are $20 for 18 holes plus $20 for the required cart. Phone 572-1314.

WAILUKU

The Waiehu Municipal Course, which is north of Wailuku, opened with nine holes in 1929 and an additional 9 holes were added later. This a par 72 course. Greens fees are $15 weekdays and $20 weekends and holidays. A cart is optional at $12, pull carts available for $1. Phone 244-5433.

TENNIS

Tennis facilities abound on Maui. Many condos and major hotels offer tennis facilities, also, there are quite a few very well kept public courts. They are, of course, most popular during early morning and early evening hours.

PUBLIC COURTS:

Hana – Hana Ball Park, one lighted court.

Kahului – Maui Community Center (Kaahumanu and Wakea Avenue) has two unlighted courts. Kahului Community Center (Onehu and Uhu St.) has two lighted courts.

Kihei – Kalama Park has two lighted courts. Six unlighted courts in park fronting Maui Sunset condos.

Lahaina – Lahaina Civic Center has two lighted courts and there are four lighted courts at Malu-ulu-olele Park.

Makawao – Eddie Tam Memorial Center has two lighted courts.

Pukalani – Pukalani Community Center has two lighted courts, located across from the Pukalani Shopping Center.

Wailuku – Maui Community College (244-9181) has four lighted courts available after school hours.

PRIVATE COURTS WITH FACILITIES OPEN TO PUBLIC:

Kapalua Bay Hotel, Kapalua, 669-5677. Offers the Tennis Garden with 10 courts. Tennis attire required at all times. FEE CHARGED.

Maui Marriott Resort, Lahaina, 667-1200. Guests and non-guests can play on five unlighted courts. FEE CHARGED.

Napili Kai Beach Club, Napili, 669-6271. Has two courts which are not lighted. FEE CHARGED.

Royal Lahaina Hotel, Kaanapali, 661-3611. Has the 2nd largest tennis facility on the island with 11 courts, 6 lighted and one is a stadium court. FEE CHARGED.

Sheraton Maui Hotel, Kaanapali, 661-0031. Has three lighted courts. FEE CHARGED.

Wailea Tennis Center, Wailea, 879-1958. Has fourteen courts, 3 lighted, 3 grass. FEE CHARGED.

HORSEBACK RIDING

Historically, the first six horses arrived on the islands in 1803 from Baja California. These wild mustangs were named "Lio" by the Hawaiians, which means "open eyes wide in terror". They roamed and multiplied along the volcanic slopes of Maui and the Big Island until they numbered 11,000. They adjusted quickly to the rough terrain and had a reputation for terrific stamina. Today these ponies, also known as Kanaka ponies or Mauna Loa ponies, are all but extinct with fewer than a dozen purebreds still in existence.

Lush waterfalls, pineapple fields stretching up to the mountain's peaks, cane fields, kukui nut forests, beaches and Haleakala's huge crater are all environments that can be enjoyed on horseback. Trips are for the beginner, intermediate or experienced rider and last as little as an hour or two or up to three days. Most stables have age restrictions.

Adventures on Horseback - (242-7445) A 5 hour waterfall ride outside Haiku is $95 per person and includes lunch and gear. Departs 10 a.m.

Aloha Nui Loa Tours - (879-7044) Drive to Hana for a tour of the town, lunch on a quiet beach, and a ride across the scenic pastureland of the Hotel Hana Ranch. Children over age 7 with experience can ride alone.

Charley's Trailride and Pack Trips - (248-8209) Features overnight trips to Haleakala with the guide arranging cabin and supplies. Rates for 4 - 6 people are $150 per person with food provided, $125 per person if you bring your own. Rates for 2 - 3 persons are $200 each with food provided. Write Charles Aki, c/o Kaupo Store, Hana, Maui, HI 96713.

Holo Lio Stables - (879-1085) Located near the Maui Prince Hotel at Makena. Shoreline, sunset or moonlight rides $20 - $35. All day trips $65.

Hotel Hana Maui - (248-8211) Offers rides around the ranch to non-guests on a space available basis. $15/hr.

Kau Lio Stables - (667-7896) Offers two hour excursions with refreshments for $41 per person. Kaanapali Resort area pick up for the half-hour drive up the slopes above Kaanapali to the stables. Pick up times 8:00 a.m., 11:00 a.m., and 2:00 p.m. A five-hour picnic excursion includes the drive, a three-hour ride and a one-hour picnic for $64. You ride up mountain sides, through cane fields, and the kukui nut forests above Kaanapali.

Makena Stables - (879-0244) Located on Makena Rd., rides are along the King's Hwy. and La Perouse Bay.

Pony Express Tours - (667-2202) Has trips into Haleakala Crater, weather permitting, Monday through Friday. The Kapalaoa Cabin Tour is 12 miles and 8 hours starting at the craters rim for $120 plus tax per person and includes lunch. Kamoa O Pele Junction Ride, 9:30 a.m.–2 p.m., is $80 and includes lunch.

The Rainbow Ranch – (669-4991) Follow Honoapiilani Hwy. 11 miles north of Lahaina, entrance near exit for Napili. They tour the mountain and beach area. Trips are available for beginning, intermediate or advanced riders in either English or Western style. 1-hour trip $20, 2-hr beach trip $45, 2-hour mountain trip $35, 2-hour sunset trip $40, 3-hour picnic ride $45, and 3-hour mountain/beach trip $60.

Thompson Riding Stables – (879-1910) Located on Thompson Rd. in Kula. Trail rides and crater tours. Day and overnight camping. Sunset and picnic rides.

HIKING

Among the most incredible adventures to be experienced on Maui is one of the fifty hikes that Ken Schmitt can guide you on. These hikes, for 2 – 6 people only, can encompass waterfalls and pools, ridges with panoramic views, rock formations, spectacular redwood forests (yes, there are!), the incomparable Haleakala Crater or ancient structures found in East Maui.

Arriving on the island some 9 years ago, he has spent much of that time living, exploring and subsisting out-of-doors and experiencing the "Natural Energy" of Maui. This soft spoken man, who looks far younger than his 45 years, offers a wealth of detailed knowledge on the legends, flora, fauna and geography of Maui's diverse areas. Ken has traversed the island nearly 400 times and established his fifty day hikes after considerable exploration. His favorites are the 8 and 12 mile crater hikes which he says offer a unique, incredible beauty and magic, unlike anywhere else in the world. The early Hawaiians considered Haleakala to be the vortex of one of the strongest natural power points on earth.

The hikes are tailored to the desires and capabilities of the individual or group and run 1/2 or full day (5 – 12 hours). They range from very easy for the inexperienced to fairly rugged. Included in the $45 – $85 fee (children are less) are waterproof day packs, picnic lunch, specially designed Japanese fishing slippers, wild fruit and, of course, the incredible knowledge of Ken. Also available are overnight or longer hikes by special arrangement. Ken can be reached at 879-5270, or by writing Ken Schmitt, PO Box 10506, Lahaina, Maui, HI 96761.

Outer Island Adventures, P.O. Box 996, Makawao, Maui, HI 96768, (808-572-6396), also offers guided hikes to Haleakala, Iao Valley and others.

Hiking off established trails without a guide is not advised, however, there are several good resources. *Hawaiian Hiking Trails* by Craig Chisholm, 128 pages, $9.95, is an excellent and accurate book with good maps and color photographs. It includes nearly 50 hiking trails throughout the islands and seven of these are on Maui. Robert Smith's book *Hiking Maui – The Valley Isle*, 132 pages, $6.95 softcover, will guide you on 29 fairly accessible trails throughout Maui. The author also has guides to Hawaii, Kauai and Oahu. A good companion book might be *Trailside Plants of Hawaii's National Parks* by Charles Lamoureux, 77 pages with great pictures for $4.95. These and other good books are available at island bookstores. Several of these books are available through Paradise Publications, see ORDERING INFORMATION.

The public is invited to joined the guided hikes of the Maui Chapter of the Sierra Club. This is a wonderful, and affordable way, to enjoy this beautiful island with a knowledgable group of people. The group has weekend outings twice a month. There is an optional donation of 50 cents. At the Sierra Club contact Carol Gentz (877-4982) or Mary Evanson (572-9724).

ARCHERY

Valley Isle Archers holds weekly meetings in Kahului at the National Guard Armory each Wednesday, visitors are welcome. An annual competitive shoot is held each year in June on Kamehameha Day.

HUNTING

Contact Hunting Adventures of Maui, Inc., 645B Kapakalua Rd., Haiku, Maui, HI 96708 (808-572-8214). They can provide assistance with licensing, packing/shipping of game, taxidermy service, four-wheel drive vehicle, complete tours. Game includes (Kao) Spanish Goat and (Pua'a) Wild Boar.

RUNNING

Maui is a scenic delight for runners. Valley Isle Road Runners can provide you with up-to-date information on island running events. They can be reached at 242-6042. For a free running map, write "Hawaii Safe Running Council", P.O. Box 23169, Honolulu, HI 96822, and tell them which islands you will be visiting. Stouffer Wailea Beach Resort also provides guests with a running guide to the Kihei/Wailea area. Also available at area bookstores is *HAWAII: A Running Guide* by Noel Murchie and Paul Ryan, softcover. $6.95.

CAMPING

County and state camping permits are required for camping in many of the parks. County permits are available at the Maui War Memorial in Wailuku (244-9018). State permits are issued 8 a.m. - noon and 1 - 4:15 p.m. Mon. through Fri. at the State Office Building, Dept. of Land and Natural Resources, 54 High St., P.O. Box 1049, Wailuku, Maui 96793 (244-4354). The maximum stay at state parks is five days.

Haleakala National Park permits are issued at the park headquarters for tent camping on a first-come basis on the day you plan to stay, beginning at 7:30 a.m. until 4 p.m. daily. The three cabins can each accommodate up to 12 people. Water, stove, wood and cooking utensils are provided. Bring your own bedding. The reservations for the Haleakala cabins are set up at a monthly lottery. Send requests to Haleakala National Park, PO BOX 369, Makawao, Maui, Hi 96768 (572-9177 or 572-9306).

Baldwin Beach Park – This county park is a grassy fenced area near the roadside. It is located near Lower Paia on the Hana Hwy. and has tent camping space, restrooms and outdoor showers.

Honomanu Bay – This county park in the Hana area has tent camping facilities.

Hookipa Beach Park – This county Park offers tent camping, restrooms and outdoor showers.

Hosmer Grove – Haleakala National Park. Tent camping. No permit required. Located at the 7,000 foot elevation on the slope of Haleakala. Three night maximum stay. Cooking area with grill, pit toliets, water, picnic tables.

Kaumahina State Wayside – Tent camping. Located in the rain forest area 28 miles from Kahului Airport on the Hana Highway. Restrooms, picnic tables, outdoor BBQ.

Ohe'o Gulch – Haleakala National Park, Hana. Tent camping. No permit required. Chemical toliets, picnic tables, BBQ grills, bring your own water. Three-day maximum stay.

Poli Springs Recreational Area – Located in Upcountry, this state park has one cabin and offers tent camping. This is a wooded two acre area at the 6,200 foot elevation on Haleakala's west slope and requires four wheel drives to reach. Extensive hiking trails offer sweeping views of Maui and the other islands in clear weather. Seasonal bird and pig hunting. Nights are cold, in winter below freezing. No showers. Toliets, picnic tables. The single cabin sleeps 10 and has bunk beds, water, cold shower, kitchenware. Sheets and towels can be picked up along with the key.

Wainapanapa State Park – Located near Hana. Tent camping, 12 cabins. More information on this location can be found under WHERE TO STAY - HANA. Restrooms, picnic tables, outdoor showers. This is a remote volcanic coastline covering 120 acres. Shore fishing, hiking, marine study, forests, caves, blow holes, black sand beach. The park covers 7.8 acres. BRING MOSQUITO REPELLENT!

Currently there are no rental companies offering camping vehicles. There have been a few companies in recent years, but they have come and gone quickly. Car rental agencies generally prohibit use of cars or vans for camping. Camping equipment is available for rent at Silversword Stoves in Makawao, phone 572-4569.

ATHLETIC AND FITNESS CENTERS

If you are interested in keeping in shape while you are on Maui and you have no fitness center at your resort, check with the following facilities which welcome drop in guests.

Nautilus Fitness Center, Dickenson Square, Lahaina 667-6100
Nautilus Fitness Center, 1325 Lower Main St., Wailuku 244-3244
Valley Isle Fitness Center, Wailuku Industrial Park, 242-6851
Lahaina Health Club, at Maui Kaanapali Beach Villas, 667-6684

HEALTH RETREATS

The Gloria Keeling Body/Mind Institute offers week-long fitness instruction at the Maui Intercontinental Resort in Wailea. In addition, you can arrange to participate in a week-long program to stop smoking with the Mierieanu Method. For rates and additional information, phone (808-575-2178) or 1-800-367-8047 ext. 217.

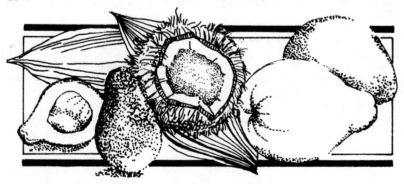

AIR TOURS

SMALL PLANE FLIGHTSEEING

Flightseeing trips are available via helicopter or small plane and include Hana and Haleakala as well as island flights to Mauna Loa on the Big Island, Oahu, Kahoolawe, Lanai or Molokai. Small plane trips are less expensive, but you won't get as close to the scenery. Prices are from $39 for half-hour flights to $125 for full-day trips combined with ground tours.

Akami Tours – (871-9551) 1-800-922-6485 Operates daily from Maui to Oahu or Hawaii for a one-day sightseeing trip. On the Big Island a 260 mile "see it all" ground tour includes a visit to a Kona fishing village, Volcanoes National Park and the Parker Ranch. On Oahu, visitors will enjoy the sites of Pearl Harbor, downtown Honolulu and Sealife Park. Hotel pickup, approximately 5:30 a.m., returning 9 p.m. Cost $119.71 plus tax.

Kihelei Maui Tours – (871-2555) Ten-passenger twin engine Beechcraft provide flightseeing to outer islands of Lanai, Kahoolawe, and the Big Island.

Maui Air Sports – (877-4253) Twin engine planes fly commuter service to Maui/Oahu.

Panorama Air Tour – (On Maui 1-800-352-3732, from mainland 1-800-367-2671) Air tour of all 8 islands with ground tour of Hawaii and Kauai (with a river boat ride on Wailua River). Transportation to and from Kahului Airport. Day trips to Oahu and the Big Island via twin engine Piper Chieftain.

Paragon Air – (878-6412) Charter service, five passenger, $325/hour.

HELICOPTER TOURS

The price of an hour helicopter excursion may make you think twice. After all it could be a week's worth of groceries at home. We had visited Maui for more than 7 years before we finally decided to see what everyone else was raving about. It proved to be the ultimate island excursion. When choosing a special activity for your Maui holiday, we'd suggest putting a helicopter flight at the top of the list. (When you get home you can eat beans for a week!)

Adjectives cannot describe the thrill of a helicopter flight above majestic Maui. The most popular tour is the Haleakala Crater/Hana trip which contrasts the desolate volcanic crater with the lush vegetation of the Hana area. Maui's innermost secrets unfold as the camera's shutter works frantically to capture the memories (one roll is simply not enough).

245

Ken Rankin (Sunshine Helicopters) loves his work so much that he even stops by on his days off to fly visitors around Maui and the neighboring islands in a Bell 206B Jet Ranger helicopter. Bearing a quick wit and a resemblance to Kris Kristopherson, pilot Ken takes you right next to waterfalls cascading down to cool mountain pools and provides an opportunity to see first-hand the unique qualities of the world's largest volcano. While scenic landmarks are narrated by the pilot, mellow music provides the perfect backdrop to this outstanding experience.

Currently the majority of helicopters depart from Kahului. One helipad between Kaanapali and Kapalua is still operating, but due to public discontent, may be shutting down.

Alexair – (871-0792) Features Tropical Adventure ($70), Hana/Haleakala ($130), Circle Island ($185). Four passenger.

Hawaii Helicopters Inc. – (877-3900) West Maui 30 min. ($70), All of Maui ($195), departs Kahului.

Kenai Helicopters – (871-6463 or 1-800-367-2603) Departs from Kahului and Kapalua Helipads. Choose from a variety of tours including the Maui No Ka Oi Deluxe (see everything) for $190/person, West Maui and North Shore of Molokai ($155), Hana/Haleakala ($135).

Lei Aloha – (877-4545) Pilot/owner operates a four passenger Bell 206 Jet Ranger. West Maui ($75), East Maui/Haleakala $130, All island tour ($195), seasonal whale watching and charters available.

Maui Helicopter – (879-1601 or 1-800-652-6550) These are the look-alike helicopters to the ones used on the Magnum PI television show. Maui unlimited tour ($200), Hana, Upcountry and Keanae ($105), Hana and Haleakala Crater ($135), or West Maui ($110).

Papillon – (669-4884 or 1-800-367-7095) Departs from the Pineapple Hill Helipad near Kapalua. Trips include Haleakala Sunrise Flight with a continental breakfast 1 1/2 hrs. ($220), Molokai ($180), West Maui ($95), West Maui/Molokai 1 hr., ($180), and Circle Island Special, 1 hr., ($180).

South Seas Helicopters – (871-8844, 667-7765 or 1-800-367-2914) Tours of Molokai, West Maui, Haleakala and Hana. Four passenger Bell 206. Caters to photographers.

★ *Sunshine Helicopters Inc.* – (661-3047) Pilot/owner Ross Scott or Ken Rankin will fly you in their four passenger Bell 206 Jet Ranger to Hana, West Maui or the top of Haleakala.

Recommended Reading

Ashdown, Inez. *Stories of Old Lahaina.* Honolulu: Hawaiian Service. 1976.

Barrow, Terence. *Incredible Hawaii.* Vermont: Charles Tuttle Co.1974.

Boom, Bob and Christensen, Chris. *Important Hawaiian Place Names.* Hawaii: Bob Boom Books. 1978.

Chisolm, Craig. *Hawaiian Hiking Trails.* Oregon: Fernglen Press. 1987.

Clark, John. *Beaches of Maui County.* Honolulu: University Press of Hawaii. 1980.

Daws, Gavan. *The Illustrated Atlas of Hawaii.* Australia: Island Heritage. 1980.

Fielding, Ann. *Hawaiian Reefs and Tidepools.* Hawaii: Oriental Pub. Co.

Haraguchi, Paul. *Weather in Hawaiian Waters.* 1983. Hazama, Dorothy. *The Ancient Hawaiians.* Honolulu: Hogarth Press.

Judd, Gerrit. *Hawaii, an Informal History.* New York: Collier Books. 1961.

Kyselka, Will and Lanterman, Ray. *Maui, How it Came to Be.* Honolulu: The University Press of Hawaii. 1980.

Lahaina Historical Guide. Tokyo: Maui Historical Society. 1971.

Lahaina Restoration Foundation, *Story of Lahaina.* Lahaina: 1980.

Nickerson, Roy. *Lahaina, Royal Capital of Hawaii.* Hawaii: Hawaiian Service. 1980.

On The Hana Coast. Hong Kong: Emphasis Int'l Ltd. and Carl Lundquist. 1987.

Randall, John. *Underwater Guide to Hawaiian Reef Fishes.* Hawaii: Treasures of Time. 1981.

Smith, Robert. *Hiking Maui.* California: The Wilderness Press. 1979.

Tabrah, Ruth. *Maui The Romantic Island.* Nevada: KC Publications. 1985.

Thorne, Chuck. *50 Locations for Scuba & Snorkeling.* 1983.

Wallin, Doug. *Exotic Fishes and Coral of Hawaii and the Pacific.* 1974.

Wisniewski, Richard A.. *The Rise and Fall of the Hawaiian Kingdom.* Honolulu: Pacific Basin Enterprises. 1979.

Index

Ordering Information

Dear Reader:

We hope you have had a pleasant visit to Maui. Since our book expresses our own opinions on accommodations, restaurants, and recreation, we would sincerely appreciate hearing of your experiences. Any updates or changes would also be welcomed. Please mail comments or suggestions to the publisher.

FREE! To keep our readers current on the most recent island changes, Paradise Publications has introduced *THE MAUI UPDATE*. A complimentary copy of this quarterly subscription newsletter is available by writing the publisher (Newsletter Dept.) and enclosing a self-addressed, stamped, #10 size envelope.

Traveling to KAUAI? Paradise Publications is pleased to announce the newest in its Paradise Guide Series, *KAUAI, A PARADISE GUIDE*, by Don and Bea Donohugh. This guide provides a fascinating and in-depth look at Hawaii's Garden Isle. In addition to information on Kauai's hotels, condominiums, restaurants and recreational options, the Donohugh's have included a unique around-the-island tour for the independent traveler. Explore the secluded beaches and ancient historical sites that most visitors never see. Personnel recommendations and travel tips are also provided. This easy to use guide has over 20 maps, is multi-indexed and illustrated.

Also available is *THE KAUAI UPDATE*, a quarterly subscription newsletter.

MAUI, A PARADISE GUIDE by Greg & Christie Stilson
        $9.95 U.S. currency plus $2 shipping
KAUAI, A PARADISE GUIDE by Don & Bea Donohugh
        $9.95 U.S. currency plus $2 shipping

THE MAUI UPDATE   —   Quarterly subscription newsletter – $5/year
THE KAUAI UPDATE   —   Quarterly subscription newsletter – $5/year

★ To order THE KAUAI UPDATE, THE MAUI UPDATE, MAUI, A PARADISE GUIDE or KAUAI, A PARADISE GUIDE send check or money order to the publisher at the following address.

      PARADISE PUBLICATIONS
      8110 S.W. Wareham
      Suite 100
      Portland, OR   97223

For other titles mentioned in this guide, see the following page.

IN RESPONSE TO NUMEROUS REQUESTS, PARADISE PUBLICATIONS IS PLEASED TO ANNOUNCE THAT WE WILL NOW BE ABLE TO PROVIDE YOU WITH OTHER POPULAR HAWAIIAN TITLES.

ON THE HANA COAST, published by Emphasis International Ltd., and Carl Lindquist. This work captures in rich color photographs and descriptive text, the history of a people who arrived in double-hulled canoes to create a new life on the wind-ward side of Maui. 6 x 9, 164 pgs., $11.95, paperback. HIGHLY RECOMMENDED.

MAUI, THE ROMANTIC ISLAND, by K.C. Publications, presents full color photographs which depict the most magnificent sights on Maui. 9 x 12, 48 pages, $4.95, paperback. Other recommended photographic books by K.C. Publications:
WHALES, DOLPHINS, PORPOISES OF THE PACIFIC, 9 x 12, paperback, $4.95
HALEAKALA, 9 x 12, paperback, $4.95
HAWAII VOLCANOES, 9 x 12, $4.95

MY TRAVELS IN HAWAII, by Steve and Paul Roth, offers 56 delightful pages for the young traveler. A unique activity book for use on vacation or at home. Recommended ages K – 6. 56 pages, 8½ x 11, paperback. $2.95.

HAWAIIAN HIKING TRAILS, by Craig Chisolm. This very attractive and accurate guide details 49 of Hawaii's best hiking trails. Includes photography, topographical maps, and detailed directions. 6 x 9, paperback, 152 pgs., $9.95.

HIKING MAUI, by Robert Smith. Discover over 30 hiking areas all around Maui. 5 x 8, paperback, 130 pages. $7.95. Also by Robert Smith and Wilderness Press: *HIKING HAWAII, THE BIG ISLAND*, 116 pgs., $7.95; *HIKING KAUAI*, 120 pgs., $7.95; *HIKING OAHU*, 124 pgs., $7.95.

For a full listing of current titles send request to Paradise Publications.

SHIPPING: Add $2 per book title, maximum of $4.00 to same address.
A gift? Just supply us with their name and address!
Orders promptly shipped first class mail.
Prices are subject to change without notice.

PARADISE PUBLICATIONS
8110 S.W. Wareham
Suite 100
Portland, OR   97223

Ordering Information

Dear Reader:

We hope you have had a pleasant visit to Maui. Since our book expresses our own opinions on accommodations, restaurants, and recreation, we would sincerely appreciate hearing of your experiences. Any updates or changes would also be welcomed. Please mail comments or suggestions to the publisher.

FREE! To keep our readers current on the most recent island changes, Paradise Publications has introduced *THE MAUI UPDATE*. A complimentary copy of this quarterly subscription newsletter is available by writing the publisher (Newsletter Dept.) and enclosing a self-addressed, stamped, #10 size envelope.

Traveling to KAUAI? Paradise Publications is pleased to announce the newest in its Paradise Guide Series, *KAUAI, A PARADISE GUIDE*, by Don and Bea Donohugh. This guide provides a fascinating and in-depth look at Hawaii's Garden Isle. In addition to information on Kauai's hotels, condominiums, restaurants and recreational options, the Donohugh's have included a unique around-the-island tour for the independent traveler. Explore the secluded beaches and ancient historical sites that most visitors never see. Personnel recommendations and travel tips are also provided. This easy to use guide has over 20 maps, is multi-indexed and illustrated.

Also available is *THE KAUAI UPDATE*, a quarterly subscription newsletter.

MAUI, A PARADISE GUIDE by Greg & Christie Stilson
$9.95 U.S. currency plus $2 shipping
KAUAI, A PARADISE GUIDE by Don & Bea Donohugh
$9.95 U.S. currency plus $2 shipping

THE MAUI UPDATE   —   Quarterly subscription newsletter - $5/year
THE KAUAI UPDATE   —   Quarterly subscription newsletter - $5/year

★ To order THE KAUAI UPDATE, THE MAUI UPDATE, MAUI, A PARADISE GUIDE or KAUAI, A PARADISE GUIDE send check or money order to the publisher at the following address.

PARADISE PUBLICATIONS
8110 S.W. Wareham
Suite 100
Portland, OR   97223

For other titles mentioned in this guide, see the following page.

IN RESPONSE TO NUMEROUS REQUESTS, PARADISE PUBLICATIONS IS PLEASED TO ANNOUNCE THAT WE WILL NOW BE ABLE TO PROVIDE YOU WITH OTHER POPULAR HAWAIIAN TITLES.

ON THE HANA COAST, published by Emphasis International Ltd., and Carl Lindquist. This work captures in rich color photographs and descriptive text, the history of a people who arrived in double-hulled canoes to create a new life on the wind-ward side of Maui. 6 x 9, 164 pgs., $11.95, paperback. HIGHLY RECOMMENDED.

MAUI, THE ROMANTIC ISLAND, by K.C. Publications, presents full color photographs which depict the most magnificent sights on Maui. 9 x 12, 48 pages, $4.95, paperback. Other recommended photographic books by K.C. Publications:
WHALES, DOLPHINS, PORPOISES OF THE PACIFIC, 9 x 12, paperback, $4.95
HALEAKALA, 9 x 12, paperback, $4.95
HAWAII VOLCANOES, 9 x 12, $4.95

MY TRAVELS IN HAWAII, by Steve and Paul Roth, offers 56 delightful pages for the young traveler. A unique activity book for use on vacation or at home. Recommended ages K – 6. 56 pages, 8½ x 11, paperback. $2.95.

HAWAIIAN HIKING TRAILS, by Craig Chisolm. This very attractive and accurate guide details 49 of Hawaii's best hiking trails. Includes photography, topographical maps, and detailed directions. 6 x 9, paperback, 152 pgs., $9.95.

HIKING MAUI, by Robert Smith. Discover over 30 hiking areas all around Maui. 5 x 8, paperback, 130 pages. $7.95. Also by Robert Smith and Wilderness Press: *HIKING HAWAII, THE BIG ISLAND*, 116 pgs., $7.95; *HIKING KAUAI*, 120 pgs., $7.95; *HIKING OAHU*, 124 pgs., $7.95.

For a full listing of current titles send request to Paradise Publications.

SHIPPING: Add $2 per book title, maximum of $4.00 to same address.
A gift? Just supply us with their name and address!
Orders promptly shipped first class mail.
Prices are subject to change without notice.

PARADISE PUBLICATIONS
8110 S.W. Wareham
Suite 100
Portland, OR   97223